P9-DNR-592

THE EFFECTS OF FEDERAL PROGRAMS
ON HIGHER EDUCATION

Paper $2.95   Library edition in cloth $5.00

HAROLD ORLANS

The Effects of Federal Programs on Higher Education

A Study of 36 Universities and Colleges

38049

THE BROOKINGS INSTITUTION
Washington, D.C.

ST. JOSEPH'S UNIVERSITY
LC173.O71e   STX
The effects of Federal programs on highe

3 9353 00039 2520

© 1962 by
THE BROOKINGS INSTITUTION

Published October 1962

Library of Congress Catalog Card Number 62-21882

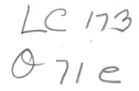

THE BROOKINGS INSTITUTION is an independent organization devoted to nonpartisan research, education, and publication
in economics, government, foreign policy, and the social sciences
generally. Its principal purposes are to aid in the development of sound
public policies and to promote public understanding of issues of national
importance.

The Institution was founded December 8, 1927, to merge the activities of
the Institute for Government Research, founded in 1916, the Institute of
Economics, founded in 1922, and the Robert Brookings Graduate School of
Economics and Government, founded in 1924.

The general administration of the Institution is the responsibility of a
self-perpetuating Board of Trustees. The Trustees are likewise charged with
maintaining the independence of the staff and fostering the most favorable
conditions for creative research and education. The immediate direction of
the policies, program, and staff of the Institution is vested in the President,
assisted by the division directors and an advisory council, chosen from the
professional staff of the Institution.

In publishing a study, the Institution presents it as a competent treatment
of a subject worthy of public consideration. The interpretations and conclusions in such publications are those of the author or authors and do not
necessarily reflect the views of other members of the Brookings staff or of
the administrative officers of the Institution.

BOARD OF TRUSTEES

MOREHEAD PATTERSON, *Chairman**
ROBERT BROOKINGS SMITH, *Vice Chairman*
WILLIAM R. BIGGS, *Chairman, Executive Committee*

Arthur Stanton Adams
Dillon Anderson
Elliott V. Bell
Louis W. Cabot
Robert D. Calkins
Leonard Carmichael
Thomas H. Carroll
Edward W. Carter
Colgate W. Darden, Jr.
Marion B. Folsom
Gordon Gray
Huntington Harris

David M. Kennedy
John E. Lockwood
H. Chapman Rose
Sydney Stein, Jr.
Donald B. Woodward

Honorary Trustees

Daniel W. Bell
Mrs. Robert S. Brookings
Huntington Gilchrist
John Lee Pratt

* Died August 5, 1962.

Foreword

THE FEDERAL GOVERNMENT has been providing increasing financial support for various programs at colleges and universities during the last decade. A review of these activities was published in 1961 by Brookings in Alice Rivlin's *The Role of the Federal Government in Financing Higher Education*. The recent expansion of federal funds to colleges and universities—for scientific research, facilities, and education; for dormitory construction; for foreign language centers; for the staffing and administration of educational missions overseas; for student aid; and for countless other purposes that draw upon the human talent and other resources of higher educational institutions—has been sufficiently great to cause concern over the effects of these expenditures on the institutions themselves. At a time when federal policies in regard to funds for scientific research and higher education are being debated, it is important to have a reliable impression of the effect which such support has had on the institutions participating.

The Congress expressed its interest in this problem in Title X of the National Defense Education Act of 1958, by requiring the Secretary of the Department of Health, Education, and Welfare to obtain comprehensive information on federal programs at institutions of higher education and to develop policies and procedures "which will strengthen the educational programs and objectives of the institutions of higher education." In response to this provision, the U.S. Office of Education undertook a study of federal programs in higher education under the direction of Dr. J. Kenneth Little. As part of that study it requested the Brookings Institution to evaluate the educational and administrative impact of federal programs on a sample of institutions of higher education.

In response to that request Brookings undertook this study designed to examine the effects of federally supported research programs upon selected departments of science, social science, and the humanities at thirty-six universities and colleges. It is hoped that the study will advance our knowledge of the effects of federal funds for research upon teaching and research, and thereby contribute to the improvement of policies affecting federal activities at colleges and universities.

An earlier draft of this report was submitted to the U. S. Commissioner of Education in March 1962. The present version has been considerably revised to take into account the suggestions made by representatives of the institutions which participated in the study and other readers of the draft. In keeping with the traditional practice of the Brookings Institution, the report was also circulated to a reading committee whose comments were particularly helpful. Members of the committee included Arthur S. Adams, Past President of the American Council on Education and at the time Professor of Education at the University of Colorado; J. Douglas Brown, Dean of the Faculty, Princeton University; Charles V. Kidd, Associate Director, National Institutes of Health; and John A. Perkins, President, University of Delaware.

J. Kenneth Little, Director, Survey of Federal Programs in Higher Education, U. S. Office of Education, George A. Graham, Director of Government Studies, the Brookings Institution, and Franklin P. Kilpatrick of the Brookings Senior Staff constituted an informal advisory committee for the conduct of the study, and Dr. Kilpatrick also contributed a great deal to the initial study design. Kathleen Sproul edited the manuscript for publication.

The opinions and conclusions presented are those of the author and do not necessarily represent the views of the institutions participating in the study, of the U. S. Office of Education, of the advisory groups, or of the staff, officers, and trustees of the Brookings Institution.

ROBERT D. CALKINS
President

October 1962

Author's Acknowledgments

THIS STUDY could not have been conducted without the cooperation of the president or other principal officer and the liaison representative appointed by him at each of the twenty-two participating universities, two institutes of technology, and twelve colleges. We regret that the promise of anonymity precludes their identification.

Some 400 administrative officials, department chairmen, and faculty gave us the benefit of their experience and judgment during interviews at 32 of the institutions. In addition, 3,500 faculty were kind enough to complete our questionnaire, frequently appending helpful comments and writing further letters of explanation. We owe them one apology. We said that the questionnaire "should take only 15 minutes to complete," which was an honest error based upon preliminary trials. Judging from many indignant remarks, exclamation marks, and time notations, the careful respondent probably averaged half an hour to do the job.

Among the many individuals at private educational and professional agencies who provided statistical information or were helpful in other ways were: Charles F. Schumacher, American Association of Medical Colleges; Garrison Cattell, *American Men of Science;* Douglas D. Dillenbeck and John M. Duggan, College Entrance Examination Board; Bernard Berelson, Eli Ginzberg, and Helmut Guttenberg, Columbia University; Arthur E. Traxler, Educational Records Bureau; Philip R. Harvey, William B. Schrader, Mrs. Marshall Smith, and Morey J. Wantman, Educational Testing Service; Arthur E. Nealy, Marquis-Who's Who, Inc.; Lindsey Harmon, Herbert Soldz, and M. H. Trytten, National Academy of Sciences; Raymond C. Maul, National Education Association; Carl Billman, United Chapters of Phi Beta Kappa; Leon Cohen, University of Maryland; William Gray and Hans Rosenhaupt, Woodrow Wilson National Fellowship Foundation; and H. E. Zabel of Deer Creek, Minnesota.

Among the staff and officers of federal agencies who supplied statistics and gave other help were: Walter E. Hughes, Atomic Energy Commission; Frank A. Andy, Willis Foster, and Jane Pugh, Department of Defense; Pere F. Seward and Sidney H. Woolner, Housing and Home Finance Agency; T. L. K. Smull, National Aeronautics and Space Administration; Thomas J. Kennedy, Jr., Charles V. Kidd, and Herbert Rosenberg, National Institutes of Health; Paul Barron, Oscar Levine, J. E. Luton, Jacob Perlman, Richard J. Petersen, Henry Riecken, Randal Robertson, and John T. Wilson, National Science Foundation; W. Robert Bokelman, Louis A. D'Amico, Justin C. Lewis, and George Lind, U.S. Office of Education; and H. D. York, Veterans Administration.

William G. Bowen of Princeton and Daniel S. Cheever, then of Harvard and now at the University of Pittsburgh, kindly supplied advance copies of reports which each had prepared on the effect of federal programs on their respective institutions.

The design of this study owes much to J. Kenneth Little of the University of Wisconsin and the U.S. Office of Education and to George A. Graham and Franklin P. Kilpatrick of the Brookings Institution, who provided helpful advice and condolence during all the vicissitudes of the work. Robert D. Calkins, President of the Institution, gave critical help at certain stages.

Denis Strong, then in the Department of History at Princeton and now at the Riverside campus of the University of California, undertook the interviews at a number of campuses and some federal agencies; Mrs. Evelyn Myers helped with the statistics and the questionnaire; Miss Marcia Marple (now Mrs. Joseph Stowers), Miss Elizabeth Jones, and particularly Mrs. Judith O'Leary did the secretarial work.

This report has benefited greatly from corrections, criticism, and comment by many well-informed readers. In addition to the members of the advisory and reading committees cited in the Foreword, the following offered helpful comments: William G. Colman, Herbert S. Conrad, William V. Consolazio, A. Hunter Dupree, Delphis C. Goldberg, John J. Honigmann, Raymond F. Howes, William A. Jaracz, Paul E. Klopsteg, Marion J. Levy, Herbert E. Longenecker, Reece McGee, Lawson McKenzie, Joseph R. Strayer, Russell I. Thackrey, Nelson A. Wahlstrom, Elmer D. West, and Raymond J. Woodrow.

As this study was conducted under contract for the U.S. Office of

Education and the direct or devious inhibition of the freedom of investigators by federal agencies is so common a theme in some quarters, it is a special pleasure to record that the Office did not influence or attempt to influence a word of this report. The only influence exercised by the officers of the Brookings Institution was to seek to improve the quality of the work.

The author alone is responsible for any errors or bias, for the opinions expressed, and for the conclusions.

HAROLD ORLANS

Contents

THE EFFECTS OF FEDERAL PROGRAMS
ON HIGHER EDUCATION

Introduction

THIS STUDY HAS BEEN CONCERNED with three questions, to each of which a separate part of the report will be devoted:

1. What have been the effects of federal programs upon the quality of higher education, particularly at the undergraduate level? (Part One.)

2. To what extent can or should fuller use be made of institutions not heavily involved in present federal programs? (Part Two.)

3. What has been the experience of institutions with the administration of federal programs? (Part Three.)

These questions, listed in order of both priority and difficulty, were posed by the U.S. Commissioner of Education in September 1960 in connection with his responsibility to study specialized federal programs involving higher education and to develop policies to strengthen the institutions affected.[1] The Brookings Institution was asked to conduct the inquiry to assure its independence and the freedom of institutions to comment frankly on any agency. The questions are admittedly large, and they certainly are not the sort to which a simple answer can be

[1] The responsibility derived from Title X, Sec. 1001 (d) of the National Defense Education Act of 1958, which provided that the Secretary of the Department of Health, Education, and Welfare (who subsequently delegated his authority to the Commissioner of Education) "shall advise and consult with the heads of departments and agencies of the Federal Government responsible for the administration of scholarship, fellowship, or other educational programs with a view to securing full information concerning all specialized scholarship, fellowship, or other educational programs administered by or under any such department or agency and to developing policies and procedures which will strengthen the educational programs and objectives of the institutions of higher education utilized for such purposes by any such department or agency."

1

given, but perhaps that is also their virtue, for it is only by raising and attempting to answer such large questions that significant progress can be made in the formulation of wise public policies for higher education.

Considering the magnitude, duration, and importance of federal programs, it is, indeed, surprising that their over-all impact on higher education has been so little studied. Studies have been undertaken of the scope of individual programs or of the involvement in federally financed research of academic personnel in certain disciplines such as physiology, psychology, mathematics, medicine, and engineering; and the National Science Foundation has issued a series of useful statistical reports on research funds and personnel. But the broad empirical view of the cumulative effect of multifarious programs upon the whole fabric of education has been noticeably lacking—presumably a reflection of the specialized interests of government agencies and the conflicting interests of private agencies that have characterized the educational domain. Fortunately, there are signs that this omission is now being corrected.[2]

The present inquiry, limited in time and resources, has been focused primarily upon thirty-six institutions: twelve universities receiving relatively large sums from the federal government, twelve others receiving decidedly smaller sums, and twelve liberal arts colleges. Interviews were conducted at all but four of these institutions with about 400 persons, including representatives of the president's office, the deans of the graduate and undergraduate schools, the business officers, other individuals on the campuses knowledgeable about federal programs, and chairmen of a number of science, social science, and humanities departments. A questionnaire was completed by some 3,500 full-time faculty in the same departments; a few points were covered in schedules

[2] Charles V. Kidd's *American Universities and Federal Research* (Harvard University Press, 1959), still the most important single work in the field, was followed in successive years by the American Assembly's *The Federal Government and Higher Education,* Douglas Knight, ed. (Prentice-Hall, 1960); Alice M. Rivlin's *The Role of the Federal Government in Financing Higher Education* (Brookings Institution, 1961); and Homer D. Babbidge, Jr., and Robert M. Rosenzweig, *The Federal Interest in Higher Education* (McGraw-Hill, 1962). Reports of additional investigations can shortly be expected from J. Kenneth Little, director of the U.S. Office of Education's Survey of Federal Programs in Higher Education; John F. Morse, director of a study of federal educational programs for the Special Subcommittee on Education of the House Education and Labor Committee; and Reuben Gross and Robert Koblitz of the Study of the Federal Government and Higher Education, Carnegie Foundation for the Advancement of Teaching.

completed by a representative appointed by the president of each institution for the purpose of this study; and a good deal of statistical information was compiled from surveys conducted by government and private
agencies and from published sources.

Further details on the survey procedures and a reproduction of the
questionnaire are given in Appendix C. What should be stressed here
is that this has been a comparative investigation of three types of institutions and three types of liberal arts disciplines, chosen for their
importance and the range of educational situations exemplified—not for
their statistical representativeness. The institutions are located in
twenty-one states, with some in each major region. Public and private
universities and institutions of greater and lesser prestige are represented.
The departments surveyed included: in the *sciences,* chemistry, mathematics, physics, and the biological fields biology, zoology, botany,
biochemistry, bacteriology, biophysics; in the *social sciences,* economics,
political science and government, psychology, sociology, and anthropology; in the *humanities,* classics, English, history, modern foreign
languages, and philosophy.

Within the broad complex of federal programs, our attention has
been focused on the educational implications of research and development expenditures which comprised 75 percent of all federal funds
received by four-year educational institutions in 1957-58.[3] The liberal
arts component of universities, on which we shall concentrate, has *not*
received as large a volume of the funds contracted or granted for research and development as have either the universities' professional
schools or research centers.[4] Nevertheless, our decision to concentrate

---

[3] Some $533.9 million of the $710.8 million which all four-year institutions
received from the federal government in the fiscal year ended June 30, 1958,
derived from research contracts or grants. See George Lind, *Statistics of Land-
Grant Colleges and Universities, Year Ended June 30, 1959* (U.S. Office of Education, 1961), p. 22.

[4] In 1957-58, federal funds for research and development were distributed as
follows among the major educational components (see National Science Foundation, *Reviews of Data on Research and Development* Nos. 17, 19, 21, 23, 25,
January 1960-January 1961):

All higher educational institutions	$537.8 million	100%
Contract research centers	285.3	53
Schools of medicine, engineering, and agriculture	148.0	28
Other components of universities and colleges	104.5	19

on this component followed from a wish to compare the effects of federal programs at universities and at colleges, from the feeling that the liberal arts represent a domain central to both academic and professional studies, and from the practical research judgment that a narrower goal is more readily reached.

A brief description of the three groups of institutions studied will be useful.

Group I: Institutions receiving large sums from the federal government. The twelve universities in this group, selected from the twenty-five reporting to the U.S. Office of Education the receipt of $4 million or more in federal funds during the academic year 1957-58, include some of international renown and some of more regional standing, some of the nation's largest and some which seem small beside them although none enrolls less than 3,500 students.

Group II: Institutions receiving smaller sums from the federal government. These twelve universities were chosen from the fifty-four receiving $0.5 to $1.9 million from the federal government in 1957-58. The $2 million gap between the populations from which Groups I and II were drawn was set to clarify factors pertinent to participation in federal programs. In an effort to learn why some statistically "strong" institutions do not, in fact, receive a greater amount of federal funds, a number of schools in Group II were also chosen which have a large body of graduate students, have awarded a large number of science doctorates, are members of the Association of American Universities, or have a school of medicine or engineering.

Group III: Good liberal arts colleges. Two types of colleges are represented here: six which have sent many graduates on to receive doctorates and which are widely accepted in educational circles as representing some of the highest standards of academic excellence to be found in private liberal arts colleges not attached to a university; and six which, while of good repute, do not have quite the same stature and have not graduated as many students who went on to receive doctorates. Other factors considered in the selection included a broad geographic distribution, the enrollment mainly of full-time coeducational or male students (for greater statistical and educational homogeneity), and membership in the College Entrance Examination Board (to facilitate comparisons of student quality).

Major summary facts about the three groups are presented in the following tabulation:[5]

Factor	Group I	Group II	Group III
Number of Institutions	12	12	12
Public	6	6	—
Private	6	6	12
Members of College Board[6]	8	8	11
Members of the Association of American Universities[7]	11	4	—
Faculty, Fall 1957 (thousands)[8]	22.1	8.3	1.2
Enrollment, Fall 1957 (thousands)	211.5	95.0	14.0
Graduate Students	48.8	12.0	0.2
Federal Income, 1957-58 (millions)[9]	$312.6	$16.7	$0.3+*
Federal R&D[10]	287.9	14.3	0.3*
Excluding Research Centers	79.5	14.3	0.3*

To the foregoing statement of what this study is about, it may be well to add—if only for the guidance of the errant reader hunting what he will not find here—what it is *not* about.

This is not a primer, and still less a history, of federal programs or of federal research programs at higher educational institutions. Those seeking such information should consult a number of other works, including, in addition to the titles cited in footnote 2, numerous reports of the National Science Foundation, Charles A. Quattlebaum, and the U.S. Office of Education.[11] The most comprehensive and current review of federal programs is J. Kenneth Little's *A Survey of Federal Programs in Higher Education, Final Report* (Office of Education, Fall 1962). Dr.

[5] Amounts followed by asterisk are estimated.

[6] Members of College Entrance Examination Board or non-member colleges participating in College Scholarship Service (see *College Board Review*, Winter 1960, No. 40, pp. 32-33).

[7] As of January 1960.

[8] Number of full and part-time faculty members with the rank of instructor or above, in the first term of the 1957-58 academic year, as reported to U.S. Office of Education.

[9] Income for educational and general purposes, fiscal year ended June 1958, as reported to U.S. Office of Education.

[10] Funds for research and development, fiscal year 1958, as reported to the National Science Foundation.

[11] The NSF reports which best serve to indicate the scope of federal research

Little was also the responsible official at the Office who initiated the discussions that led the Brookings Institution to undertake the present study. His survey and this study, therefore, were planned to complement each other, although each was conducted and has been published independently.

Our focus upon current research programs affecting liberal arts departments will lead us to ignore other important federal activities, past and present, which have had and continue to have the most profound consequences for higher education—for example, the involvement of students, faculty, and facilities in World War II; the massive postwar expenditures for veterans education; the grants and contracts for agricultural research and education; and federal tax policies, as omnipresent, vital, and, at times, hazardous to higher education as water is to fish.

Our focus upon a group of universities and better colleges will lead us to neglect the average four-year and two-year colleges which, although enrolling fewer students than do universities, comprise the majority of the nation's higher educational institutions. This point is worth stressing, for some who read the title and gloss over the subtitle may expect to find more attention given to the effects of federal programs on this large and important number of institutions. Where a consistent trend—

---

programs at higher educational institutions are *Federal Funds for Science, I: Federal Funds for Scientific Research and Development at Nonprofit Institutions 1950-1951 and 1951-1952* (1953), and subsequent reports in this series running through *Federal Funds for Science, X* (1962); *Federal Support for Science Students in Higher Education 1954* (1956); *Federal Financial Support of Physical Facilities and Major Equipment for the Conduct of Scientific Research* (1957); *Graduate Student Enrollment and Support in American Universities and Colleges 1954* (1957); *Basic Research, A National Resource* (1957); *Government-University Relationships in Federally Sponsored Scientific Research Development* (1958); *Scientific Research and Development in Colleges and Universities, Expenditures and Manpower, 1953-54* (1959); and *Reviews of Data on Research and Development,* Nos. 2, 3, 6, 7, 8, 17, 19, 21, 23, 25, 27, 28, and 32.

Quattlebaum's principal publications on federal programs in higher education are *Federal Educational Activities and Educational Issues Before Congress,* House Document 423, 82d Cong., 2d sess. (1952); *Federal Aid to Students for Higher Education,* House Committee Print, 84th Cong., 2d sess. (1956); and *Federal Educational Policies, Programs and Proposals: A Survey and Handbook,* printed for the use of the House Committee on Education and Labor, 86th Cong., 2d sess. (1960). Another useful compendium of federal programs is Clayton D. Hutchins, Albert R. Munse, and Edna D. Booher, *Federal Funds for Education 1958-59 and 1959-60* (U.S. Office of Education, 1961).

for example, of increasing classroom hours or decreasing federal research expenditures—can be charted from the universities in Group
I to those in Group II to the six best, or best-endowed, colleges in Group
III to the six other colleges in Group III, one may surmise that the trend
may be extended to the average and to the poor four- and two-year
colleges not represented in our study. But such a surmise can be mistaken and is not, at best, an adequate substitute for direct inquiry. Thus,
one reader of this manuscript remarked that "the total effects of Federal
programs on all higher education are found quite as much in the institutions not under . . . survey, especially if one is looking for negative
effects. They have affected a host of good but slightly less important
and prestigious universities and colleges whose scramble for staff and
resources *may* have been made more difficult by reason of Federal
monies going elsewhere. The significant effect that Federal programs
may have upon higher education generally, even as observed in these
thirty-six institutions, is *probably* more indirect than direct."

The two "mays" which we have italicized in the foregoing passage
make a legitimate point which surely merits further investigation, but
the "probably" moves to a conclusion in advance of the facts that such
an investigation might or might not establish. And here, we must
confess, the present study has concentrated primarily upon the direct
effects of federal programs. These are not always easy to determine,
and well-informed observers may reasonably disagree about just what
certain effects have been. But it is no easier to determine indirect effects.
Our reader alludes to one which is widely held in educational circles—
that the concentration of federal funds at a few major universities has
rendered more difficult the problem of staffing at lesser institutions.
We also believe this to be true, and some supporting evidence will be
presented in Chapter 1; but this does not make it a simple, hard fact as
clear and measurable as the Washington Monument.

Another indirect effect to which we will devote much attention is the
impoverished and downcast state of the humanities, presumably a consequence, in part, of the effusion of federal funds into the sciences. But,
because most federal funds are going into the sciences and some should,
perhaps, go into the humanities, does it follow that the difficulties of the
humanities are due primarily to government policies? While departments of Latin and philosophy may suffer, departments of business and
commerce prosper without government aid. With regard to neither

the direct nor the indirect effects of government action dare we overlook the more massive influence for good or ill of American society, which preceded the government's interest in the universities and, let us hope, still reserves for itself a great domain where the government does not enter.

"Society," to be sure, is a vast and shapeless mass like "history," which is lent as much form by its interpreters as by its actors. The "government" (and its "policy") appears more rigorously definable. But is it? Assuredly, it is a convenient focus for political action, and a convenient locus for observing the interests and disinterests of the larger society. But does that make it the decisive actor on the educational stage?

That we retain some doubts on the score may be inferred from the contradictory reactions of two professors to this manuscript. One wrote:

I began to wonder if you don't overemphasize the effect of federal funds on science, and underplay the climate of public opinion, the high respect for science, and similar factors, of which Federal support is the symptom?

And the other wrote:

. . . it seems odd that you do not seem to find federal funds to be decisive at any point in instituting or terminating social trends in academe. Do they always only either complement or complicate what is already going on there anyway?

If this suggests a degree of ambiguity about the ultimate factors causing the effects to be described in ensuing chapters, we plead guilty, for we have neither sought nor found ultimate but only proximate causes.

To absolve the government of ultimate responsibility for the effects of its programs is not, however, to absolve it of all responsibility and still less to credit it only with beneficial effects. The last is the strange position adopted by some representatives of the National Science Foundation and the National Institutes of Health which, more than other federal agencies, are responsible for strengthening basic scientific research and education at universities and colleges. The good effects of their programs they happily take credit for; the bad effects they attribute to other factors—usually to the universities, the Congress, the taxpayer, or the parlous state of the world. It is no disservice to these admirable agencies, whose over-all record of achievement is excellent, to suggest that they too must bear some responsibility for the less desirable consequences of their work. This is not the first time in history that some undesirable consequences have followed from well-intentioned acts.

If more space in this report is devoted to the problems than to the successes of government programs, it is because improvement is more likely to come from analyzing what is wrong than from applauding what is right. Lest this create a misleading general impression, however, it may be well to state firmly at the outset that in the judgment of the overwhelming majority of faculty and other institutional representatives, which we share, the over-all effect of federal programs at universities and colleges has been highly beneficial.

It is noteworthy that most institutions would prefer more harm of the sort that has come their way to less aid. No amount of criticism can gainsay the fact that every agency, even the most bureaucratic, has a long list of academic clients and consultants who are happier with than without its funds. After all, outside of the compulsory military training programs and the demands of the Internal Revenue Service, no institution, professor, or student is compelled to deal with any federal agency.

A great deal of what might be called self-compulsion does exist, and, on a national basis, neither higher education nor the government any longer retains the freedom to suddenly sever their relationships without endangering the national interest and even the nation's safety. This may be stated as either a conclusion of this study or an introduction to it, for the realization that the destinies of the nation and the nation's institutions of highest learning are now so intertwined is a sound basis for evaluating the future course that their relations should take.

PART ONE

Effects of Federal Programs on Quality of Education

¶ PREFACE · One benign administrator at an excellent small university remarked "Of course, you can't tell about quality for ten years, until you see the product you've turned out." No doubt he is right, as is the Oxford historian who contends that no history can be written of events after 1900, because we are too close for the necessary detachment and all the evidence is not yet in. Let us disclaim at the outset any pretension to having reached such final truths, which are precluded both by the nature of the question and of the information available to answer it. We can only report such pieces of fact and opinion as are currently demonstrable, and see how they may fit into an over-all picture.

We will approach this task by examining the impact of federal programs on recent trends in the quality of certain educational personnel (discussed in Chapters 1 through 5), and then on certain conditions of scholarship and perquisites of scholars (Chapters 6 through 8).

Chapters 1 and 2 seek to determine if there are any significant recent trends in the quality of faculty and students, respectively, attributable to federal programs. Pertinent trends in the number of faculty and students in the sciences, social sciences, and humanities are also discussed, because these numerical trends are of some present importance, because quantity is easier to measure than quality, and because an influence on quality becomes at least plausible if an influence on quantity can be established. The loss of contact with undergraduates and, indeed, of interest in teaching by many senior faculty engaged in research, often

11

said to be a consequence of federally sponsored research, is considered in Chapter 3. The following two chapters deal with two special groups whose present and potential impact on instruction is markedly affected by government policies—graduate assistants (Chapter 4), and full-time research associates (Chapter 5).

Thus, the first five chapters examine some of the educational consequences of federal programs upon faculty of various ranks, undergraduate and graduate students, teaching assistants, and professional research staff. The major group of educational personnel overlooked in this presentation is administrative staff, whose numbers have grown in recent years, in no small part owing to the work involved in servicing federal contracts and grants. While we did not gather enough information to warrant separate treatment of the educational influence of this important group, the position they have taken in major policy issues that have arisen in the administration of federal research programs is discussed at some length in Part Three.

The remainder of Part One is concerned with the divergent impact of federal expenditures on faculty research (Chapter 6), teaching loads (Chapter 7), and income (Chapter 8) in the sciences, social sciences, and humanities. Essentially, the subject of these chapters is the cleavage that has developed between conditions of university employment in the sciences and the humanities as a result of the government's and the nation's massive thrust in the sciences. On a narrow view of our task, it might be said that none of this need be gone into, as none of it has any direct and necessary relation to the question of educational quality. But all of it has a direct and obvious relation to the prevailing climate of higher education, to the balance and integrity of educational institutions, and, ultimately, to the viability of the faculty of liberal arts and sciences as a single community of scholars with common academic standards and goals. On a broader view, no subject is more central to this inquiry into the effect of federal programs on higher education.

CHAPTER 1

Trends in Faculty Quality

NO SUBJECT IS MORE DEBATED in the educational fraternity than the extent of the present and pending faculty "shortage" and its implications for academic standards. The widely cited National Education Association studies showing a decline from 31.4 percent in 1953-54 to 25.8 percent in 1960-61 in the proportion of new full-time teachers with doctorates have, unfortunately, several methodological weaknesses which somewhat obscure the nature of the trend.[1] However, there is no reason to dispute the major conclusions that emerge from these and other studies: the problem of maintaining staff quality is most acute (1) in institutions of lesser prestige which offer the poorest rewards and heaviest burdens for academic service, and (2) in certain fields, particularly the sciences, with attractive employment opportunities outside the academic fold.

[1] See National Educational Association, *Teacher Supply and Demand in Universities, Colleges, and Junior Colleges, 1959-60 and 1960-61* (May 1961).

The surveys do not hold constant the number of institutions canvassed, which rose from 656 in 1953-54 to 1,085 in 1960-61, and it is likely that some of the decline in the proportion of doctorates noted is attributable to the increased number of small colleges, state colleges, and teachers colleges represented in later years, as these are precisely the types of institutions employing low proportions of new faculty with doctorates. The highest values for new faculty with doctorates yielded in the NEA series are 31.4 percent for 1953-54 and 28.4 percent for 1954-55; both figures were obtained on the first go-round of the biennial survey, when 'running-in' pains are usually greatest and respondents' replies may be least reliable; the values for subsequent years—26.7, 23.5, 25.3, 23.8, 25.9, and 25.8—do not indicate a clear trend. Finally, abrupt changes that can be discerned from year to year do not enhance confidence in the reliability of the trends,

EVIDENCE OF FACULTY SHORTAGE

Earl McGrath is alarmed at this situation, Bernard Berelson is not;[2] but both are in essential agreement in their description of it, and both agree, further, that the situation is not merely impending: it is here, and that sanctum sanctorum of educational enterprise, the independent liberal arts college, is suffering. Most college presidents report difficulty in filling some staff positions, especially in mathematics and the sciences, and many educators—presidents, graduate deans, and faculty —believe that the liberal arts college is now receiving only the poorer products of graduate schools. (What we do not know is how many believed the same thing in 1950 or 1940.)

Of the 503 college presidents replying to McGrath's question "Have you had difficulty in the past several years in obtaining properly qualified teachers?" 75 percent said "Yes" or "Yes" in certain fields; of the 601 college presidents responding to Berelson's question "Have you experienced any unusual difficulties in getting qualified college teachers for your staff in the past few years?" 81 percent said "Yes." Asked by Berelson to comment on the statement, "Some people believe that under the pressure of the years ahead, the liberal arts colleges will be

at least in certain fields, as shown in the following tabulation (and see *ibid.*, p. 11).

Field	Percent of New Faculty with Ph.D.'s In Various Neighboring Years		Year A
	Year A	Year A+1	
Agriculture	23.8%	35.0%	1956–57
Business and Commerce	8.8	17.4	1956–57
Geography	40.9	21.0	1953–54
Home Economics	21.0	11.1	1953–54
Industrial and Vocational Arts	4.1	13.5	1957–58
Library Science	11.3	1.8	1959–60
Other (unspecified) Fields	9.5	24.2	1958–59

[2] See Earl J. McGrath, *The Quantity and Quality of College Teachers* (Teachers College, Columbia University, 1961), and Bernard Berelson, *Graduate Education in the United States* (McGraw-Hill, 1960).

able to attract, on the average, only the less able Ph.D.'s in competition with the universities and industry," 43 percent of the college presidents, 54 percent of the graduate deans, and 66 percent of the graduate faculty who expressed an opinion agreed that this is "already happening"; most of the remainder felt it "probably will happen."

Liberal arts colleges, however, are not the only institutions with problems; in some ways second-rank universities may be in more serious difficulty, as the following NEA data suggest:[3]

	Universities	Private Colleges
Number Reporting	203	634
Number with One or More Unfilled Teaching Positions in 1959-60 or 1960-61	149 (73%)	226 (36%)
Number of Unfilled Positions	647	345

True, a university department generally has more ways of coping with a staff shortage. On a large campus, *someone* can usually be found to teach the essential course, and there is always that work-horse of educational endeavor, the graduate student. The impoverished one- or two-man college department has only the alternatives of overwork or failure.

Examination of the NEA data on new full-time faculty hired in the academic years 1960 and 1961 by the institutions in our study shows that relatively more faculty with doctorates were acquired by Group I universities (receiving large sums from the federal government) than by Group II universities (receiving smaller sums). Too few staff were hired by the colleges in our study (Group III) to permit a reliable statement about the position in individual fields, but over-all, their quota of new faculty with doctorates was comparable to that of the universities in Group II. (See Appendix A, Table A-1.) These findings are, in general, consistent with what we would expect about the balance of trade for new Ph.D.'s favoring larger institutions, and the greater volume of federal funds available to Group I schools—both in absolute terms and per head of faculty—can only help their competitive position. (The data also suggest that the institutions in our study

[3] NEA, *Teacher Supply and Demand . . . 1959-60 and 1960-61,* p. 19. The universities reporting include 90 state, 13 municipal, and 100 private institutions; the colleges include 354 enrolling 500 or more and 280 enrolling under 500.

are superior, academically, to the run of universities and colleges.⁴)

But we dare not infer too much about the quality of a faculty from the single fact of the proportion holding a doctor's degree (and certainly not from the proportion of new teachers with doctorates, as many who lack the degree when they start teaching subsequently acquire it). Set aside the suspicion that the Ph.D. betokens pedantry rather than learning, and accept it as a mark of a certain intellectual attainment. Are the science departments at University X inferior to those at University Y because X gives graduate teaching assistants faculty status as instructors whereas Y does not? Are humanists inferior to scientists because fewer have doctorates? We cannot even say (what we know on other grounds) that they are less professionalized, without knowing the teaching and career pattern in each discipline.

For example, the proportion of doctorates among faculty in English and foreign language departments is frequently low because of the large numbers of instructors (often advanced graduate students with temporary appointments) who teach the mass of elementary composition and recitation sections that are the counterpart of the laboratories which, in the sciences, are handled by graduate students. A strictly accurate comparison should hold constant not only rank and discipline but probably also class size and content, since large lectures can be handled by a few professors, but multitudinous small, repetitive classes require a larger and fresher staff to maintain vitality. An institution which can afford, attract, and regularly replenish a flock of young instructors, hired for one to three years, may give better elementary instruction than one which has to rely on larger classes taught by a few permanent, deadened Ph.D.'s.

Recapitulating: There is evidence of a shortage of faculty and of doctorates, particularly in the sciences, which afflicts not only colleges but also many universities. Of the new faculty recruited in the academic years 1960 and 1961 by our three groups of institutions, there were fewer at Group II and Group III holding doctorates than at Group

⁴ The comparative percentages for new full-time faculty with Ph.D.'s, 1959-61 (adapted from NEA data), are as follows:

203 universities	31.9%
10 in Group I	59.7
12 in Group II	43.0
354 colleges enrolling 500 or more	20.1
12 in Group III	40.2

I. However, the gross percentage of faculty with doctorates is not the soundest basis for deductions about faculty quality. Let us see what other clues we can gather about recent trends in faculty quality at our three groups of institutions.

SOME QUALITY TRENDS AT OUR INSTITUTIONS

The possibility of obtaining data on the rank and academic degrees of staff teaching classes of various sizes in both a recent and an earlier year was explored, but the necessary information was not available at many institutions and the effort required to reduce the available information to meaningful form was not commensurate with its usefulness. Certain more readily obtainable evidence of the relative quality of faculty in recent decades can, however, be presented.

Scholarly Awards and Distinctions

No pronounced and consistent trend is apparent, over two decades, in the relative number of faculty from each of our three groups of institutions who held such scholarly distinctions as Guggenheim fellowships or membership in the National Academy of Sciences and the American Philosophical Society (see Table 1-1). At Group I universities far more professors were thus honored in the years examined than at Group II, both in absolute numbers and relative to the size of the two faculties. At Group III colleges very few received these honors, but, proportionate to the total number of eligible faculty, they probably did as well as the Group II faculty.

Leading Graduate Departments

In both 1925 and 1957, department chairmen throughout the country rated graduate departments at ten universities in Group I, but only two in Group II, as among the ten best in the nation in one or more of sixteen disciplines. On this test, the relative quality of their graduate faculties was maintained over these years in most fields at both Groups I and II; Group I improved its national standing in physics, psychology,

TABLE 1-1.   *Number of Faculty at Thirty-Six Institutions with Various Scholarly Distinctions, 1939-1961*[a]

Institutions and Ratios	Guggenheim Fellows			Members National Academy of Sciences			Members American Philosophical Society		
	1941	1951	1961	1940	1950	1960	1939	1949	1959
Group I	6	27	69	73	115	167	113	120	126
Group II	0	5	11	6	6	9	3	6	7
Group III	0	1	3	1	1	0	5	3	1
Ratio of [b]									
Group I : II	—	5.4	6.3	12.2	19.2	18.6	37.7	20.0	18.0
Group II : III	—	5.0	3.7	6.0	6.0	—	0.6	2.0	7.0

[a] To avoid repetition, the identifying term "thirty-six institutions" will be omitted from the titles of subsequent tables on the institutions in our study; "Group I, II, and III" will be designated in the stub column or in the column heading.

[b] The ratio of all faculty in Group I to all in Group II ranges from about 2:1 to 4:1, depending on the measure employed. The ratio of all faculty in Group II to those in Group III ranges more widely, from 2:1 to 6.5:1.

and German, whereas Group II did not gain markedly in any of the fields reviewed and may have declined in some social sciences. (See Appendix A, Table A-2.)

Granted, this method of estimating trends in faculty quality is not as satisfactory for lower as for upper levels of the educational hierarchy: it was possible, if unlikely, for Group II institutions to have risen from the fiftieth to the twenty-fifth rank in the over-all national lists without entering the top ten in any one discipline. In our opinion, this has not happened. From observations during campus visits, particularly on the movement of bright young faculty, we gained the impression that faculty quality is on the rise at four or five schools in both Groups I and II, declining at perhaps three schools in each group, and relatively stable at the remaining schools.

The difficulty and the expense of achieving dramatic improvements in quality at academic institutions should be stressed, particularly the difficulty of lifting a mediocre large university or an excellent small university to the topmost national rank. The relative stability of membership and even rank in that small number of institutions which represent the very best in graduate education can be judged from the following composite ranking of leading graduate schools by department chairmen in 1925 and 1957:[5]

1925	1957
1. Chicago	1. Harvard
2. Harvard	2. California (Berkeley)
3. Columbia	3. Columbia
4. Wisconsin	4. Yale
5. Yale	5. Michigan
6. Princeton	6. Chicago
7. Johns Hopkins	7. Princeton
8. Michigan	8. Wisconsin
9. California (Berkeley)	9. Cornell
10. Cornell	10. Illinois
11. Illinois	11. Pennsylvania
12. Pennsylvania	12. Minnesota
13. Minnesota	13. Stanford
14. Stanford	14. U.C.L.A.

Of these fourteen leading graduate schools, thirteen were identical in 1925 and 1957; after thirty-two years, nine universities remained within one rank of the position they held in 1925, while the rank of six altered substantially (Chicago, Wisconsin, and Johns Hopkins falling, and California, Michigan, and U.C.L.A. rising, three or more places).

Recent Improvement in Staff

Asked what has happened since 1955-56 to the quality of staff in their department, about six faculty in every ten who had been at the institution in those years observed either a "slight" or "marked" improvement, three felt quality had remained constant, and only one that it had fallen. University faculty in the social sciences were even more confident than those in the sciences that there had been an improvement, while faculty in the humanities at Group II universities were evenly divided on the question. Except for this possible hint of concern about staff quality in the humanities, most faculty gave surprisingly little indication that *their* department had been adversely affected by

[5] Derived from department chairmen's rankings of graduate departments in individual fields, institutes of technology excluded, as given in Hayward Keniston, *Graduate Study and Research in the Arts and Sciences at the University of Pennsylvania* (University of Pennsylvania Press, 1959), pp. 115-119. For the ranking by fields, see Appendix A, Table A-2.

the national faculty shortage. (See Appendix A, Table A-3.) It was also the unanimous judgment of the deans at the seventeen medical schools in Groups I and II that the quality of their faculties had improved.[6]

It may be said, therefore, that the faculty of Group I universities have consistently outranked those of Group II in recent decades, in the judgment of department chairmen and of the scholars responsible for awarding certain widely recognized honors. Nevertheless, a majority of our respondents at both Groups I and II believed that the quality of the faculty in their department had improved in the last five or six years.

THE EFFECTS OF FEDERAL PROGRAMS

Opinion on the effect of federal programs upon a department's ability to attract and hold the best faculty was directly related to the volume of federal expenditures in the field and institution. Most scientists stated that federal programs have helped their departments, but the majority affirming this was smaller at Group II than at Group I universities, and smaller again at Group III colleges; social scientists at the universities were pretty evenly split into one group which saw an effect and another which did not, but those at the colleges shared the humanists' predominant view that there had been no effect (see Table 1-2).

This, to be sure, is the faculty's judgment of direct effects. Indirect effects—the loss of present or potential talent from the academic world to industry, from the humanities to the sciences, and from institutions with little federal money to those with much—are more difficult to measure, if not to discuss.

On Academic vs. Other Employment

We can say little about the effect of federal activities on the distribution of professional personnel among educational, industrial, governmental, and other employment. Presumably the net effect of the

[6] Ten deans stated that the average quality of their teaching staff had improved "markedly," and seven, "slightly" or intermediately since 1953-54; none believed it had either declined or remained constant.

TABLE 1-2. *Effect of Federal Programs on the Quality of Faculty*

"What has been the over-all effect of federal programs on the ability of your department to attract and hold the best faculty?"[a]

Field and Institution Group	Percent of Faculty Replying That Federal Programs Have				
	"Helped Us"	"Had No Visible Effect"	"Handi-capped Us"	Total[b]	Number
Total					
Group I	54%	41%	4%	100%	1,452
Group II	53	44	3	100	884
Group III	30	68	2	100	373
Sciences					
Group I	76	20	4	100	694
Group II	70	27	3	100	395
Group III	52	46	1	100	143
Social Sciences					
Group I	49	48	3	100	407
Group II	60	36	3	100	245
Group III	24	70	7	100	92
Humanities					
Group I	18	77	5	100	351
Group II	19	78	3	100	244
Group III	10	89	1	100	138

[a] From the survey questionnaire; see Appendix C. Survey questions will be used as part of the headings, and thus indicate the source, of subsequent tables based on the questionnaire.
[b] Here and in other tables detail may not add to totals because of rounding.

government's bidding with its right hand (in research, development, and procurement contracts with industry) against its left (in research and development contracts and grants at universities) for scientific personnel is to raise their wages, perquisites, and marketability. We hear often enough about high salaries luring prospective teachers into the business world; department chairmen in the humanities observe that this competition, at least, they are spared, so that they have the pick of the best talent available in their field. On the other hand, lists of eminent scientists (such as Nobel awardees or members of the National Academy of Sciences) and statistics of scientific publications indicate that the most eminent and productive men remain concentrated at nonprofit rather than profit-making institutions (although the proportion of the productive, at any rate, who are in government or industry is probably slowly rising).[7]

The dominant, long-term fact is the emergence in the last several decades of a large, permanent, and relatively prosperous corps of doctorate holders outside the academic community.[8] The fields involved are not only the physical but also the biological sciences and certain social sciences as well, notably psychology and economics, and to a lesser extent sociology. This countervailing force of Ph.D.'s outside the ivied walls cannot fail to have important consequences for those within, and the major consequences are the same as will be observed directly in the government's on-campus programs: a strengthening of the status and rewards of science relative to those of the humanities, and of research relative to teaching. The off-campus scientist is, for the most part, paid to give his undivided attention to research—"applied" research, perhaps, more often than "basic," but research nonetheless—which is exactly what the campus scientist would like to spend more time at. This ever-present (and, for many, not unattractive) alternative to academic employment has made for an increasingly happy definition of the tasks and emoluments of the academic scientist.

On Faculty Distribution Between Sciences and Humanities

Regarding the possible drain of talent from the humanities to the sciences, two views are prevalent: that this is real and dangerous; and

[7] In a count of the institutional affiliations of authors of articles appearing in leading professional journals in 1958, Berelson (*op. cit.*, p. 83) found the following percentages at academic institutions: biology, 79; psychology, 77; chemistry, 68; physics, 64. It is a fair guess that the figures were higher twenty years ago.

[8] Over a short period, to be sure, the tides of employment will ebb and flow between industry and education; recent data show a decline in the proportion of new doctorate holders in the physical sciences seeking industrial employment and a rise in the proportion proposing to work in colleges and universities. The percentage of new doctorate holders in the physical sciences planning to work in business and industry was 52.6 in 1957, 47.4 in 1958, and 43.4 in 1959; the percentage intending to work in universities and colleges was 36.0, 40.3, and 44.3, respectively. "Within the physical science group . . . physics, chemistry, and engineering show a consistent drop through the three years in the percentage going into business and industry, and a consistent rise in college and university employment." See National Science Foundation, *The Science Doctorates of 1958 and 1959* (1960), p. 6.

that it is largely illusory. The former view is implicit in the repeated statement of admissions officers and deans that, with rare exceptions, their very best students are going into the sciences, especially into mathematics and physics. Student test scores will be examined later, but the contrary fact should here be noted that, by and large, there is no serious shortage of qualified new faculty in the humanities. Competition is keen for the small group of the brightest and most highly recommended new Ph.D.'s even in English and history, and a demand has arisen for Ph.D.'s in scarce, timely specialties like Russian, African, or Asian history and languages; but the ordinary Ph.D. in the humanities still faces a protracted period of poorly paid and often insecure academic employment unknown to his friends in the sciences.

One would think that changes in the distribution of faculty by field could be simply ascertained by counting, but the changes in departmental and even institutional structure over an extended period render meaningful statistical comparisons extremely difficult. We undertook several such analyses of faculty size in the sciences, social sciences, and humanities both nationally and for the thirty-six institutions in this study, but the data neither suggested a marked trend nor were sufficiently comprehensive and reliable to preclude one.

Looking back over the last hundred years, there can be no doubt that scientists and, in more recent decades, social scientists have made striking gains relative to the humanists. Over-all trends for the last decade are more in doubt. We know that the universities (particularly the public universities and those with a large federal research income) and state colleges are the bastions of the academic scientists, who there approximate or exceed the number of humanists, whereas the reverse is true at the independent private colleges, the American heirs (or executors!) of the traditional classical curriculum. (See Appendix A, Table A-4.) We know also that from 1954 to 1960, enrollment rose relatively less at universities than at liberal arts, junior, and teachers colleges, whose collective enrollment now exceeds that of universities.[9]

[9] From 1954 to 1960, enrollment at universities rose 33 percent; enrollment at liberal arts, junior, and teachers colleges, 62, 59, and 66 percent, respectively; by the fall of 1960, universities enrolled only 43 percent of all degree credit students in higher education compared to 51 percent at the latter three types of institutions. See U.S. Office of Education, *Progress of Public Education in the United States of America 1960-61* (1961), pp. 28, 32.

Assuming proportionate faculty increases, one might deduce a relative decline during these years in the science component of the faculty at all higher educational institutions.

Our conclusion cannot, however, be that federal funds have exerted *no* influence on the distribution of faculty among fields, because nothing is more patent than that specific federal fellowship and research programs and capital awards have been responsible for the burgeoning of specific disciplines such as nuclear physics, radio astronomy, oceanography, metallurgy, molecular biology, biophysics, clinical psychology, linguistics, and medical sociology—the list can be extended. Nor can we subscribe to Lee DuBridge's suggestion that federal programs have little influence because not money but some arcane, immutable mental capacity determines who becomes a humanist or a scientist:

> . . . I can't think of many first-class physicists who would have made very good historians—and I don't know any historians who would have made good scientists. I am inclined to think that the talents required . . . are of rather different kinds and that the chance of very much proselyting one way or the other is not great.[10]

We may note, in passing, that Isidor Rabi, Columbia University's Nobel physicist, has held a temporary appointment in history at Princeton; the bridge between contemporary mathematics or physics and philosophy is as plain in the work of Russell, Whitehead, Bridgman, and Heisenberg as is the bridge between biology and social science in the work of Darwin, Galton, Pavlov, Freud, Boas, and Kinsey. But even if DuBridge is right (and something about his observation rings true), surely it is an error to extend the truth about genius to the average member of a profession. Is the average physicist, Latinist, engineer, grocer, farmer, cowboy, and carpenter born or bred? Strange, if born, that he is born in numbers so appropriate to each time and region. Doubtless character and incentive affect the choice of available professions, but their availability is determined by the state of our economic, social, and educational polity. In short, we conclude that the federal government has had a significant but not paramount influence on the academic scene; many other powerful forces are at work in the market and in the cloister.

[10] L. A. DuBridge, "Implications for Natural Science," *Papers of the Fourth Conference on Scientific Manpower* (National Science Foundation, December 1954), p. 2.

On the Distribution of Scientists Among Institutions

To the final question about whether federal funds serve to concentrate or to preserve the existing concentration of scientific talent at a few major institutions, the only possible answer seems to be "yes," whether that question extends to all scientists or is confined to those engaged in teaching. It is fruitless to ask (because impossible to determine) if these funds have led or followed the prevailing distribution of scientific power; clearly they have not disturbed it.

We have already observed that, relative to the number of faculty in the humanities, there are proportionately more scientists at universities than at colleges, and still more at universities with a large yearly income from federal sources. This observation pertains to full-time faculty at or above the rank of instructor in fields common to universities and colleges.[11] There are many reasons for concluding that federal research funds have helped the universities far more than colleges, and a few universities more than others, to attract and hold these faculty. Several other factors also tilt the balance of scientific personnel heavily toward the universities:

1. The presence solely at graduate schools of scientific faculty in advanced and specialized fields (often in areas of keen interest to federal agencies) not taught at the undergraduate level.

2. The large number of scientists at schools of agriculture, engineering, and medicine (receiving large sums from the Departments of Agriculture; Defense; and Health, Education, and Welfare, respectively) who are available to supplement the training and research resources of university science departments.

3. The universities' reserve army of graduate science students (many

---

[11] To the national data reported in Appendix A, Table A-4, may be added the following count of faculty at the thirty-six institutions in our study. The count includes full-time faculty, instructor or above, for the academic year 1960-61 (source: catalogues and faculty lists), in *humanities:* classics, English, Germanic and Romance languages, history, philosophy; in *sciences:* biological sciences, chemistry, mathematics, physics.

	Total	Humanities	Sciences	Percent in Sciences
Group I	2,731	1,251	1,480	54.2%
Group II	1,604	826	778	48.5
Group III	586	365	221	37.7

supported by federal fellowships and research assistantships) who assist directly or indirectly in the educational process.

4. The rising force of postdoctoral research scientists supported by federal funds at on- and off-campus university installations, who, although generally lacking faculty status, may give undergraduate lectures, participate in graduate seminars, and assist student research.

The colleges' problem is, apparently, more to *attract* than to retain the necessary scientific talent. At least, our survey yielded no evidence that universities with large sums from the federal government are "buying up" scientists from college faculties—quite the contrary. Replies to our question "Have you ever taught at an independent, four-year, liberal arts college (i.e., one that is not part of a university)?" showed that relatively more university faculty in the social sciences, and particularly in the humanities, than in the sciences have previously taught at liberal arts colleges.

Field	Percent "Yes"		Total Respondents	
	Group I	Group II	Group I	Group II
Sciences	11.3%	11.9%	822	445
Social Sciences	20.3	17.3	493	294
Humanities	30.7	26.3	524	361
Total	19.2%	18.1%	1,839	1,100

Granted, this does not provide all the information we would like on inter-institutional faculty movements (particularly movements from colleges and small universities to large universities and institutes of technology more amply supplied with federal funds). But the results are not consistent with the assumption that undue numbers of university science faculty have been imported from college campuses, and suggest, instead, a substantial amount of movement from colleges to universities by faculty in the humanities. Does the stronger teaching orientation of the humanists and their greater power in the colleges relative to the scientists (as measured by numbers, salaries, teaching load, and domination of the curriculum) make for a greater similarity in the kinds of humanists than in the kinds of scientists attracted to colleges and universities, and therefore to the humanists' greater mobility between the two types of institutions? Department chairmen in the humanities will often advise a doctoral student to take his first appointment at a college, where he can more rapidly gain wide teaching experience, produce a book, and then strike out for a major university. College teaching is not so common a current mode of advancement in the sciences, where publication requires, not books that a single scholar can buy or borrow, but expensive equipment and often "teamwork," services, and time—all of which are more readily available at universities.

SUMMARY AND DISCUSSION

The widespread concern that faculty quality may be suffering as the shortage of qualified personnel leads to the hiring of less-qualified teachers finds little support in our survey, for the predominant opinion of faculty at the thirty-six institutions examined is that the quality of the staff in their department has been improving in recent years. (True, our survey did not extend to the smallest and poorest colleges likely to be experiencing the greatest difficulty recruiting personnel.)

Where extensive federal programs are operative—in the sciences and at university social science departments—they are said to have helped promote this improvement of faculty. So far as can be determined from the rather slim lines of evidence available, federal programs have not, however, substantially altered the relative standing of faculties at Group I and Group II institutions. Group I faculties have been more eminent than Group II for several decades at least, and they retain that lead today. The heavy concentration of federal expenditures at a few universities and their affiliated research installations, concentrating the numbers, raising the salaries, and improving the conditions of scientists at the same universities, must render more difficult the task of recruitment at poorer institutions. While the reduced teaching loads fostered and financed by federal research programs aid recruitment at universities, they also contribute to the faculty shortage by increasing the number of faculty required to handle a given number of classes.

THESE SUMMARY FINDINGS may usefully be supplemented by a few observations made during campus visits.

What is meant by faculty "quality" varies fantastically at different schools. The chairman of a mathematics department at a modest university is content—"We can get the people we want, if we're not looking for a Wiener"—whereas spokesmen for two institutions where men of Wiener's stature reside bemoan their lot; one says he cannot pay enough to hold his mathematicians, and the other complains bitterly that another university has just bought one of his mathematicians for $19,000 pieced together from the university's budget and federal research funds.

To a large extent, institutions do get what they want—or what they pay for. The well-endowed, nationally known college with outstanding students, a nine- or six-hour teaching load, and salaries rising to $15,000 has no difficulty getting good people at any rank; the poor college known to few people who are not alumni, whose students are more interested in "college life" than in learning, with a ceiling of $8,000 or $9,000 for twelve to fifteen hours of teaching, has great difficulty.

Certainly the price of good scientists has risen, in part because of the nature of federal programs, in larger part because of the scientific revolution, and perhaps primarily because of the variously hot and cold wars of recent years and the incandescent war which threatens. Not every institution can pay the price.

Perhaps the most direct effect of federal programs has been to change the nature of the academic scientist's job. Many colleges still want a scientist to devote his time solely to teaching, but fewer young scientists are now content to do this, and those who are content are not highly regarded by the leaders of their profession. The changed outlook can be attributed in good part to the changes in training, opportunity, and expectation fostered by the federal government. The research outlook of federal science agencies has swayed the major universities, penetrated the minor ones, and now confronts the colleges.

CHAPTER 2

Trends in Student Quality

FROM ONE STANDPOINT at least, it is easier to measure trends in student than in faculty quality: students must do as they are told, and more and more are told to take standardized tests of aptitude and ability. Of the many available tests, the Scholastic Aptitude Tests, prepared and administered by the Educational Testing Service for the College Entrance Examination Board, are employed by the largest number of institutions, and in order to make use of the SAT scores, a number of institutions which are members of the College Board were invited to participate in this study. Unfortunately, testing was not so widespread some years ago, particularly at public institutions (many of which are turning to the SAT and other devices as their mounting enrollment leads to more rigorous screening of applicants). Although twenty-seven of our thirty-six schools were able to supply SAT scores for their fall 1960 entering class, only twelve (ten of them private) could do so for the fall 1953 class, and only nine (six, private) for the fall of 1947.

THE RISE IN

SCHOLASTIC APTITUDE TEST SCORES

Accordingly, it is not feasible to compare trends at our three different groups of institutions; but the data (reported in Appendix A, Table A-5) do show a consistent pattern for all reporting institutions, universities as well as colleges:

1. A uniform and frequently sharp rise in the mean SAT verbal and mathematical scores is evident for the class entering in the fall of 1960 over the class entering in the fall of 1953. The median rise for the six colleges and six universities reporting was 74 points in the verbal scores and 72 points in the mathematical.

2. A uniform but smaller rise in the mean SAT mathematical scores appears, accompanied by slight increases or decreases in the mean verbal scores from the fall of 1947 to the fall of 1953. The median rise in the math scores at the six institutions reporting for both years was 23.5 against a median decrease of 5 points in the verbal scores.

As girls tend to score higher than boys on the verbal examination and lower on the mathematical, a small part of the decrease in verbal scores and rise in mathematical from 1947 to 1953 may be assigned to the larger proportion of male students taking the tests in the latter year at some institutions. However, the same fundamental trends obtain when the mean scores of each sex are examined separately.[1] One dean attributed the decline in verbal scores between 1947 and 1953 to "an enrollment drop in the early 1950's after the World War II veterans had finished and during the Korean War period. . . . In the fall of 1954 [the scores] . . . started up again and they have been going up ever since."

Factors Accounting for the Rise

The marked rise in recent years is undoubtedly a consequence of the booming applications for college. State universities established to educate a broad spectrum of youth are raising their standards for both residents and out-of-state students and, when the law requires their admission, discourage applications from those likely to flunk out in the freshman or sophomore year. Private institutions have been able to

[1] At the eighteen institutions supplying mean SAT scores for both male and female members of the entering class of 1960, the mean verbal score for female students exceeded that for males at seventeen schools (the median difference being 17 points); in contrast, the mean mathematical score for women was lower than that for men at sixteen schools (the median difference was 45.5 points).

Some thirty years ago the Thurstones similarly noted that men students do "conspicuously better" than women on arithmetic tests, women consistently better than men on "linguistic" tests; L. L. Thurstone and T. G. Thurstone, "The 1931 Psychological Examination," *Educational Record*, Vol. 13 (April 1932), p. 134.

reject some of the duller sons of their traditional clientele for some of the brighter sons of families they had not previously contacted, who can now pay their high fees and meet their rigorous personal standards. In an effort to broaden the geographic range and diversify the social composition of their student body, some schools have instituted extensive recruiting campaigns, in previously untouched areas, backed by generous scholarship funds. Prosperity has enabled more graduates of superior metropolitan high schools to attend institutions far from home, and the number of superior Jewish students at ivy league colleges has risen markedly.[2] In short, changed social and economic conditions are enabling many colleges to improve the quality of their students, primarily by careful selection from a larger and broader group of applicants.

The student loan program of the National Defense Education Act of 1958, by facilitating student migration and adding students who *want* an education to those who can afford one, may help to raise the average quality of many student bodies. The net effect is still uncertain. But another federal program which has certainly, if unexpectedly, had this effect is the College Housing Program administered by the Housing and Home Finance Agency under the Housing Act of 1950. The enlarged dormitory facilities financed by this program have permitted many institutions, formerly restricted to local students commuting from home, to greatly broaden their recruitment area for applicants. This has come at a time when the ratio of unsuccessful to successful applicants at some of the nation's best schools has risen to unprecedented heights. The second- and third-choice schools of rejected applicants have benefited thereby, and previously provincial student bodies have been noticeably improved and diversified. (The increased number of students housed

[2] Lawrence Bloomgarden states that "Jewish students now comprise 15 per cent of the undergraduate population at Princeton (it was 2 per cent in 1941), 14 per cent at Williams and Wesleyan (which had 4 or 5 per cent in 1941) and over 20 per cent at Amherst (where the proportion 19 years ago was also about 4 per cent). . . . The results of one analysis suggests that a Jewish applicant to an Ivy League college will be accepted only if his aptitude score is considerably higher than the general average. Thus, the average scores of the successful applicants from a special New York City high school (largely Jewish in its composition) to several Ivy League colleges was 675, as compared with the general average of 625, while very few graduates of this school at the general average figure were accepted. Of course, a number of other factors (geography, preferential treatment to the sons of alumni, and extracurricular activities) may have contributed to this difference." Bloomgarden, "Our Changing Elite Colleges," *Commentary*, Vol. 29 (February 1960), p. 153.

on campus has also promoted a sense of community on some campuses that had been deserted at night, and has facilitated the scheduling of evening classes and the fuller utilization of institutional facilities.)

The almost invariant rise in SAT scores, not only at the institutions participating in this study but at many others, poses two questions:

1. If the average scores at most institutions are getting better, where are the poorer students going? To colleges which do not use test scores? Are they not entering college? With the continued increase in the proportion of youth going to college, can the average quality of all students really be rising?

2. Are the tests strictly comparable over a span of years? In theory, SAT scores for 1954 or 1960 *are* comparable to those of the original reference group of 10,651 students upon whom the tests were standardized in April 1941, the linkage having been provided by the repetition of some questions in succeeding years.[3] However, spokesmen for the Educational Testing Service restrict their claim of strict comparability to a five- to ten-year period, suggesting that beyond ten years so many complicating factors intervene that some shift in the test scale may occur or that the tests may begin to measure different abilities.

The art of getting a good (or, at least, of not getting a bad) score on a multiple choice test may well be one of these abilities. The Trustees of the College Entrance Examination Board have been sufficiently concerned to issue a statement on the limited effect of coaching upon SAT scores—". . . the Verbal part seems totally insensitive to drill, while the Mathematical part for some groups may, with effort, be raised by . . . an average of 25 points on a 600-point scale. . . ."[4] Various Board studies, however, have shown gains of 20 to 35 points to result from taking the SAT at intervals of two to twelve months, to which must be added a gain of 3 to 3.5 points a month in the Verbal score due to maturation.[5] Such gains, coupled with the increasingly common

[3] See Henry S. Dyer and Richard G. King, *College Board Scores, No. 2* (College Entrance Examination Board, 1955), pp. 101-102.

[4] College Entrance Examination Board, *A Description of the College Board Scholastic Aptitude Test* (1960), p. 8.

[5] "According to these studies, a student who takes the SAT as a preliminary candidate in May of his junior year may be expected to receive a Verbal score 55 points higher in March of his senior year. In making this estimate, 20 points are allowed for practice effect and three and one-half points per month for growth over a ten-month period." (Dyer and King, *op. cit.*, pp. 49-50.)

practice of students taking the examination in their junior as well as senior year in high school have led the Board to distribute to college admissions officers recommended procedures for computing an adjusted average score for applicants whose report form contains two or more scores.[6]

The present status of educational testing is curious. Never have machine-graded tests been employed by more institutions and agencies, or been so important in determining the educational opportunities of so many students. And their importance is likely to grow as more institutions seek an efficient, objective, and equitable way to screen applicants. Surely, the goal of more objective, reliable, and comparable evaluation envisaged thirty years ago in the move from the written examinations then utilized by the College Entrance Examination Board toward the "new-type" multiple-choice examination has now been realized.[7] At the same time, attacks are leveled at "the tyranny" of the tests.[8] It is said that the tests do not adequately reflect the abilities

[6] "The Interpretation of Two or More Scores on the Same Test," memorandum to College Admissions Officers, College Entrance Examination Board (December 1961; multilithed). The publication by the College Board of sample SAT questions in the booklet *A Description of the College Board Scholastic Aptitude Test,* which is distributed to all SAT registrants, is evidently intended, in part, to equalize any advantage that might accrue to students from coaching or previous test experience.

[7] See, for example, the 1933 discussion by W. S. Learned of the Carnegie Foundation for the Advancement of Teaching of written vs. multiple-choice examinations. "Under the guidance of the College Entrance Examination Board the preparation of examinations has been conducted with great care and the reading of the papers has been reduced as nearly as seems humanly possible to a flawless formula. . . . It is because of this notable achievement of the Board in pushing the discursive written examination to the extreme limit of its technical possibilities that the inevitable shortcomings of this type of test have been clearly disclosed. . . . The defects are inherent. The same error of sampling in compiling the questions and the unavoidable variability in interpreting the answers are everywhere evident even under the best conditions. For some years, therefore, the Board has experimented fruitfully with the 'new-type' principle in the Scholastic Aptitude Test." Learned, "Admission to College," *Educational Record,* Vol. 14 (January 1933), pp. 31-32.

[8] "The nation . . . is placing enormous reliance on machine-graded multiple-choice tests as a measure of ability. But, unhappily, it can be shown that they have grave defects. Our confidence in them can have dangerous consequences, not only for education but for the strength and vitality of the nation." See Banesh Hoffman, "The Tyranny of Multiple-Choice Tests," *Harper's Magazine,* Vol. 222 (March 1961), pp. 37-44; also the letters in the May 1961 issue, p. 6, particularly the cogent reply of John Stalnaker, who cites the remark of "Old

of the best students, and, at some schools with long experience in test use and student bodies with exceptionally high SAT scores, there is a rebellion against excessive reliance upon the scores in admissions.[9] On top of a certain scepticism about the technical perfection of the instruments, it is suggested that the skills needed to obtain high scores on the SAT are not as significant as originality, curiosity, and other features of intellect and character not measured by the tests. In short, the triumph of objective measurement has gone hand in hand with its partial rejection by influential schools for a more subjective appraisal of college applicants.

It would take us too far afield to discuss more fully the adequacy of SAT scores for educational selection, and the social implications of this technical problem. For our present purpose, we will conclude that the recent sharp rise in test scores should be discounted to *some* extent, but not to the extent of doubting that marked improvement has occurred in the last half dozen years in the average quality of students at most schools in our study. This is also the conviction of faculty responding to our questionnaire: in all fields and types of institutions investigated, the predominant view of those who were present at their institution in 1955 or 1956 was that the average quality of undergraduate majors in their department, of other undergraduates taking courses in the department, and of graduate students had since improved.

It should, again, be borne in mind that, particularly with regard to undergraduate enrollment, this study is confined to a select group of institutions *not* representative of all higher educational institutions. And even if the general rise in SAT scores accurately reflects a rise in the average ability of all students taking these tests, the fact remains that they are taken by an increasing but still select number of all college applicants, and that scores are not available for students at most junior

---

Bill to his complaining companion in a shell hole: 'If you can find a better 'ole, 'op to it.' "

[9] Thus, a spokesman for Brown University was "most emphatic about the decreasing stress on test scores. . . . 'The faculty is delighted with this year's class, which was chosen on this less-objective basis'. . . .

"The trend, which appears to be developing rapidly, followed warnings by admissions officers last year. Dr. Arthur Howe, Jr., dean of admissions at Yale, was among those who had said then that excessive reliance on tests gave 'less and less of a break' to fine students with lower test scores." See Fred M. Hechinger, "Ivy League Mails Admission Notes," *New York Times,* April 17, 1962, p. 42.

colleges, state colleges and universities, teachers colleges, professional and graduate schools, and less well-known private liberal arts colleges.

As has been noted, factors measured by Scholastic Aptitude Tests are not the only ones significant for an evaluation of student quality. This is, of course, recognized by many college personnel officers whose selection procedures put much emphasis on letters of recommendation, interviews, and other less quantifiable methods of evaluating applicants. Educators at many institutions regard the veterans who returned to school directly after World War II as superior to the current crop of students in maturity and intellectual seriousness, and this judgment could hardly be invalidated merely by showing that the veterans' SAT scores were lower. In short, the educational importance, relative objectivity, and convenience of SAT scores should not blind us to their limitations as a measure of student ability.

THE EFFECT OF FEDERAL PROGRAMS

On Our Institutions' Retention of Good Students

Asked for their judgment on the effect of federal programs on the ability of their department to attract and hold the best students, the response of faculty may be summarized as follows.

1. More university faculty indicated that federal programs have had an impact on graduate students than noted an impact on undergraduates, in every field surveyed. In the natural and social sciences, over 70 percent of faculty agreed that federal programs have helped their departments attract good graduate students. As we might expect, only a minority of faculty in the humanities subscribed to this position. As we might not expect, that minority was significantly larger at Group II than at Group I universities; this probably reflects the emphasis on geographic dispersion of the National Defense Education Act programs which account for the bulk of federal aid to the humanities. The policy has, understandably, been attacked by many leading institutions not benefiting from it, and it is noteworthy that 14 percent of the Group I faculty in the humanities stated that federal programs have positively handicapped their department in attracting the best graduate students.

With little doubt, many of these faculty are referring to the adverse effects which they believe certain NDEA graduate fellowships assigned to "new or expanded" programs have had upon long-established programs in the humanities.

2. Most Group III college faculty (including a small majority of those in science departments) stated that federal programs have had no visible effect on attracting good students to their department. The large minority of college scientists who noted that federal programs have helped their departments have presumably benefited from federal research grants, faculty fellowships, summer institutes, student research participation awards, and other programs designed to stimulate undergraduate science.

The pattern of response to this question from faculty at all three institutional groups follows the distribution of federal funds by field and type of institution closely enough to lead to the surmise that faculty in fields with *any* federal money are so gratified they believe their students must benefit from it. Assuredly, many do, as students in fields without money cannot, but it does not follow that the former are any better students therefor, or the latter any worse. Is there any objective evidence to show that federal funds have either increased the number or improved the quality of students in the sciences relative to those in the social sciences or humanities? Let us see.

Relative Enrollment in the Three Fields

The question of relative numbers can be answered fairly reliably— if degrees are accepted as an accurate index of enrollment—and the answer is somewhat surprising. Science enrollment has, of course, increased greatly over the years, as has enrollment in most fields, but relative to the number of students in the social sciences and humanities *combined* it has remained remarkably stable, not only in the postwar years but since at least the 1920's.

Science degrees comprised about 30 percent of all bachelor's degrees in liberal arts disciplines in the 1920's and 1930's, and about the same percent in the 1940's and 1950's; they comprised about 54 percent of all liberal arts Ph.D.'s in the 1920's and 1930's, and precisely the same proportion in the 1940's and 1950's. A comparison of the immediate postwar years with earlier decades shows a marked decline in the proportion of bachelor's degrees awarded in the humanities and a corresponding rise in the proportion awarded in the social sciences, but very little trend of any sort is detectable after 1950. At the doctoral level, the relative decline in the number of degrees awarded in the humanities and rise in the social sciences has continued since at least the late 1930's.[10] (See Appendix A, Table A-6.)

In short, within the undergraduate liberal arts, the most remarkable relative growth in degrees awarded over the last forty years has occurred not in the natural sciences but in the social sciences. In doctoral studies, the hard sciences are in command—but that was true long before the stimulus of postwar federal research programs, and it is the social sciences, again, which have made the largest relative gains in the postwar period. Apparently, therefore, these federal programs have not (or not yet) radically altered the relative distribution of either undergraduate or graduate degrees in major liberal arts fields. The most that can be contended is that, indirectly, they may have contributed to the long-term attrition of the humanities.

This is not to say that there have been no significant changes in

[10] As trends so frequently appear and disappear with the change of a definition, it is important to understand what fields are and are not included in the above statistics. *Sciences* include biological sciences, chemistry, earth sciences, geography, mathematics, physics, and other physical sciences (but exclude agriculture, engineering, and medicine and other health professions); *social sciences* include anthropology, economics, political science, psychology, sociology (but exclude social work, and other fields termed "applied social sciences" by the U. S. Office of Education); *humanities* include fine arts, classics, English, foreign languages, history, and philosophy (but exclude journalism and religion—as well as business, education, and other major applied fields frequently embraced in a more motley usage). Cf. also Charles Kidd, *American Universities and Federal Research* (Harvard University Press, 1959) and *A Report to the Secretary of the Navy by the Naval Research Advisory Committee* (June 1, 1959), Vol. 2, pp. 38-39, both of which come to similar conclusions about the failure of federal funds to increase the proportion of doctorates awarded in the sciences.

It may be said that even if the proportion of liberal arts degrees awarded in the sciences remains constant, this represents a net gain for the sciences because the proportion of female students has risen, and they are less disposed than men to major in the sciences. However, the proportion of students who are female has been increasing only since 1956, and has not been as high recently as in certain earlier years. For example, women constituted 37.1 per cent of degree credit students in higher education in the fall of 1960, but 40.2 percent in the fall of 1939. See Edith M. Huddleston, *Opening (Fall) Enrollment in Higher Education, 1960: Analytic Report* (U. S. Office of Education, 1961), pp. 13-14.

enrollment or degrees awarded in specific disciplines attributable to federal programs—witness the upsurge, in the last half dozen years, of graduate enrollment in such fields as engineering, mathematics, physics, and psychology, in which graduate students receive heavy support from federal fellowships and research assistantships. In other disciplines, however, such as chemistry, geology, and many of the biological sciences, which have a similar high level of support, enrollment has risen less; and there is no assurance that the fields of most rapid current growth will maintain their pace in the years ahead.

There is, in short, no immediate and necessary correspondence between the relative magnitude of federal funds and of student enrollment in a given field. Federal appropriations can alter rapidly in response to international and domestic events, while enrollment responds not only to federal incentives but to independent market demands, fashions, and high-school counseling (not to mention demographic factors). Further militating against any consistency between undergraduate and graduate enrollment or degree trends over a short span of years in rapidly changing disciplines are both the filter-down effect upon undergraduate instruction of programs making their first impact at the graduate level, and the normal ten- to fourteen-year lag which can be expected between a rise in undergraduate enrollment and an increase in doctoral degrees awarded in a particular subject. Thus, from academic years 1954-55 to 1958-59, the number of bachelor's degrees in physics rose 91 percent while the number of doctor's degrees declined 6 percent, although graduate physics enrollment rose substantially.[11]

Relative Intelligence Scores in Various Fields

The best data we have been able to find on the relative ability of students in different fields are the intelligence scores published by Dael Wolfle for (1) students graduated from 41 universities and colleges in

[11] In 1954-55, 1,996 bachelor's degrees and 511 doctor's degrees were awarded in physics; in 1958-59, 3,809 bachelor's but only 482 doctor's degrees. Graduate enrollment in physics was 4,871 in the spring of 1954 and 8,840 in the fall of 1959. See U. S. Office of Education, *Earned Degrees Conferred 1954-1955* (1956), p. 115, and *Earned Degrees Conferred 1958-1959* (1961), p. 34; National Science Foundation, *Graduate Student Enrollment and Support in American Universities and Colleges, 1954* (1957), p. 45; U. S. Office of Education, *Enrollment for Advanced Degrees, Fall 1959* (1961), p. 21.

1949-51, (2) 4,500 graduate students enrolled at over 40 universities around 1950, and (3) 1,100 alumni of Minnesota and Ohio institutions who received science doctorates at any U. S. university from 1939 to 1945; and by Lindsey Harmon for 3,567 persons receiving doctorates in all fields in 1958.[12] Valuable information on the verbal and mathematical Scholastic Aptitude Test scores of large numbers of undergraduate and graduate students majoring in different fields ought to be obtainable from Educational Testing Service records, but their data have apparently not been worked up in this manner.[13]

Wolfle reports the following median intelligence scores of students in fields of interest to us:[14]

	College Graduates	Graduate Students
Natural Sciences	123	128
Humanities and Arts	122	125
Social Sciences	120	124

The scores in these broad fields are so close that it is instructive to examine the detail on specific disciplines. From Wolfle's data (see Appendix A, Table 7) it appears that:

1. As psychologists manufacture psychological tests, and psychology classes study them, there may well be a learning factor at work which somewhat inflates the scores of psychology students.

2. Students of physics and mathematics are among the brightest in all liberal arts fields, at both the undergraduate and graduate levels.

3. The median intelligence of students of biology and the earth sciences is the lowest in the sciences and below that of students in some major social sciences and humanities—psychology, English, and foreign

---

[12] Dael Wolfle, *America's Resources of Specialized Talent,* The Report of the Commission on Human Resources and Advanced Training (Harper, 1954), pp. 190-191, 317-322; Lindsey Harmon, "High School Backgrounds of Science Doctorates," *Science,* Vol. 133 (March 10, 1961), pp. 679-688.

[13] Records of test performance are made, of course, *before* entry to college. What we have in mind is a procedure whereby the college, major, and degree would subsequently be punched on the student's IBM card upon graduation from college and graduate or professional school. The additional information could be supplied readily enough, each June, by cooperating institutions. This would yield, at little expense, a continuing record of student ability by field and institution of a range and quality that is not at present available from any source.

[14] Wolfle, *op. cit.,* pp. 319-320.

languages at the undergraduate and graduate levels, economics at the undergraduate, and philosophy at the graduate level.

Harmon's mean intelligence test scores of Ph.D.'s in broad fields are not strictly comparable to Wolfle's medians for graduate students; nor are their field definitions identical. Nevertheless, this is how they compare:[15]

	Graduate Students (Wolfle, c.1950)	Ph.D.'s (Harmon, 1958)
	Median	Mean
Natural Sciences	128	132
Humanities and Arts	125	132
Social Sciences	124	132

Carried to one decimal place, Harmon's ranking actually reverses Wolfle's—humanities and arts, 132.1; social sciences, 132.0; natural sciences, 131.7—but a difference of four tenths of 1 percent in scores with a standard deviation of 16.4 to 17.0 points is hardly significant. (The social sciences come out better in Harmon's data partly because he classified psychology as a social science—as we do in this report—whereas Wolfle treats it separately.)

Harmon also reports the following additional detail on intelligence test scores of Ph.D.'s in individual sciences, which may be set beside comparable detail from Wolfle:[16]

Median (Wolfle)		Mean (Harmon)	
Physics and Mathematics[17]	138	Physics	140.3
		Mathematics	138.2
Chemistry	135	Geology	133.1
Geology[18]	134	Chemistry	131.5
Biological Sciences	129	Biological Sciences	126.1

The correspondence is striking, the only reversal in rank being that of the geology and chemistry Ph.D.'s, whose scores on both sets of data are closer than those of any other two fields.

[15] Wolfle, pp. 319-320; Harmon, p. 680.

[16] Ibid.

[17] "Physical sciences," in Wolfle, which also includes metallurgy.

[18] "Earth sciences," in Wolfle, which also includes astronomy, geography, and meteorology.

Finally, the mean verbal and quantitative Graduate Record Examination scores of the very select group of college applicants for first year National Science Foundation fellowships averaged over the eight years 1953-60:[19]

Composite Score	Verbal Test	Quantitative Test
676 physics	639 psychology	717 physics
665 mathematics	630 physics	713 mathematics
631 chemistry	619 mathematics	672 chemistry
617 psychology	590 chemistry	629 geology
603 geology	577 geology	596 psychology
569 biology	569 biology	569 biology

What inference can be drawn from these data about the effect of federal programs on the concentration of able students in certain fields? Our conclusion that, to date, there has been very little effect of this sort follows from the following facts:

1. The parallels in the ranked mean intelligence scores of students in different fields at the undergraduate and graduate levels are more marked than the differences, and the differences do not consistently favor fields with a large volume of federal support at the graduate level. Thus, philosophy undergraduates ranked tenth among the twelve fields examined, but philosophy graduate students, third; and the rank of physics, chemistry, and earth science students is lower at the graduate than the undergraduate level. (See Appendix A, Table A-7.)

2. Students in departments of biology, which have received much federal aid, have lower intelligence scores than those in many fields of humanities and social science which received no significant federal aid during the years reviewed.

3. Further, the social sciences and the humanities as a whole compare very favorably with the natural sciences in the mean intelligence of Ph.D. recipients.

4. The main point upon which an argument about federal funds leading the ablest students to select a particular field might hinge is the high

[19] Educational Testing Service scores, kindly provided by the National Academy of Sciences, Office of Scientific Personnel; scores represent the mean of the means for each of the eight years.

intelligence of students in the heavily supported fields of physics and mathematics. This argument is, however, vitiated by the stability in the relative ranking of mean intelligence in different fields over periods long antedating the federal government's interest in the sciences.[20]

We therefore see little general tendency for federal funds to concentrate the ablest students in the sciences. The answer to Princeton Dean Hugh Taylor's question[21]—"Have the scientists, without any intention on their part, been skimming the cream off the oncoming educational intelligence, and isn't that one of the difficulties that is confronting the social sciences and humanities?"—would be "no."

Our data do not, of course, exhaust this question. One aspect which might be examined is the degree to which the admixture of a substantial number of foreign-born and foreign-trained scholars imparts an intellectual vitality to certain scientific (and nonscientific) fields that is lacking in more purely "native" disciplines. And within the sciences, undoubtedly there is a tendency for some of the best graduate students and the best research administrators in Washington to work some of the same "hot" areas of knowledge, due to their stimulation by the same professors (or, it may be the graduate student who stimulates the professor still capable of learning).[22] But there are similar, if financially less rewarded, areas outside the sciences, and a large body of pedestrian work and workers in most fields, as Harmon's identical mean intelligence scores for Ph.D. recipients in the sciences, social sciences, and humanities suggest. (The degree to which federal programs have served to concentrate the best students in a few institutions will be considered in Part Two.)

[20] Wolfle reports that the relative intelligence of Ohio State University students in different fields "did not change materially" in the time periods 1920-26, 1928-36, and 1950-51 (op. cit., p. 198). Harmon similarly notes that the relative ability of applicants for National Science Foundation fellowships in seven different science fields varied little from year to year; see Harmon, *Ability Patterns in Seven Science Fields*, Technical Report No. 10 (mimeographed; Office of Scientific Personnel, National Academy of Sciences-National Research Council, October 1955), "Brief" and pp. 10-11.

[21] Association of Graduate Schools in the Association of American Universities, *Journal of Proceedings*, October 27-29, 1949, p. 49.

[22] "When the federal government pours money into a certain field of science or technology, that field acquires glamor as well as funds for fellowships and training. Young talented people tend to go into these fields and to desert the older, less glamorous ones." See Alvin Weinberg, "The Federal Laboratories and Science Education," *Science*, Vol. 136 (April 6, 1962), p. 28.

SUMMARY

The rise in Scholastic Aptitude Test scores during the postwar years points to a marked improvement in many student bodies, resulting primarily from increasing institutional selectivity from a larger and broader group of applicants. Except for the beneficial effect on student quality of college dormitory loans and possible benefits of NDEA student loans, present federal programs serve to aid students quite selectively. Their effects are observed principally in universities rather than colleges; at the graduate rather than undergraduate level; and in the sciences and social sciences rather than humanities.

Surprisingly, the vast sums invested in science have not yet significantly raised the proportion of either undergraduate or graduate enrollment in the sciences within the liberal arts curriculum. It is the social sciences and not the sciences which have gained most from the relative decline of enrollment in the humanities. Nor do the available data on student intelligence scores in different fields suggest any tendency for federal funds to concentrate the brightest students in the sciences; the social sciences and humanities have their fair quota of intelligence, which some heavily supported fields like the biological sciences evidently lack. The tendency of federal policies to concentrate undue numbers of the best students at a few famous private institutions will be discussed subsequently.

CHAPTER 3

Faculty-Student Contacts

CHANGES IN QUALITY—the quality of faculty, of students, of the curriculum—are difficult to evaluate and to reach agreement on. The judgment must eventually be made by one person about another, and try as one may to be objective, there is something invidious about it. The persons and institutions labeled as poorer are unlikely to agree with the judgment, or to agree that the particular quality judged was the right one. The frequency and type of student contacts with faculty of different rank is, at least, readily definable, measurable, and less value-laden.

It is our thesis that federal research programs, acting in concert with other educational forces, have reduced the time that senior university faculty devote to undergraduates and informal faculty contacts with students, and, in general, have attenuated the personal aspects of undergraduate education at the great universities. Among the other causes of these trends are the increase in both undergraduate and graduate enrollment, the reduced prestige of undergraduate education and teaching, the enhanced prestige of graduate education and research, and the growth in professorial administrative responsibilities.

THE SIZE OF CLASSES

That not only total enrollment but also the average size of classes has increased recently at many institutions appears clear. This is true at both the undergraduate and graduate levels and, within the former, in both lower- and upper-division courses; it is true of classes in the sciences, social sciences, and humanities at all three types of institutions examined.[1] However, the increase may be less widespread at colleges than at universities, and is most common at Group II universities newly embarking upon extensive graduate and upper-division offerings. Only in college social science departments did a majority of the faculty indicate that class size had *not* increased in the years from 1955 to 1961.[2]

TABLE 3-1. *Frequency of Large Classes*

"What is the size of the largest single class (lecture or section) in any undergraduate course in the department? And the largest graduate class?"

| Field and Institution Group | Percent of Chairmen Indicating That Their Department's Largest Single | |
	Undergraduate Class Enrolls 100 or More	Graduate Class Enrolls 40 or More
Total		
Group I	62%	37%
Group II	44	9
Group III	21	—
Sciences		
Group I	74	60
Group II	67	18
Group III	29	—
Social Sciences		
Group I	69	33
Group II	35	3
Group III	15	—
Humanities		
Group I	46	12
Group II	24	3
Group III	18	—

[1] Howard E. Bosley cites some studies showing a slight *reduction* in the median class size at state universities from 1928 to 1957, and in the average class size at state colleges from 1928 to 1949. See Bosley, "Class Sizes and Faculty-Student Ratios in American Colleges," *The Educational Record,* Vol. 43 (April 1962), pp. 148-149. While these do not contradict our observations, which pertain to the period 1955-61, they suggest the desirability of analyses over a longer span of years than we have been able to undertake here.

[2] A bare majority of Group I humanities department chairmen also stated that the average size of their classes had not increased. See Appendix A, Table A-8.

Large lecture sections with 100 or more undergraduates are far more common at universities than at colleges; at both types of institutions, they are more common in the sciences than the social sciences and humanities (see Table 3-1). This is consistent with the supposition that large classes are frequently introduced to economize on the time of expensive staff with small teaching loads, although that is doubtless not the only reason. The affectlessness of scientific facts may render the personal element less vital to their communication; certainly one encounters among humanists great insistence on the importance of discussion and personal interchange between student and teacher.

LOSS OF PERSONAL CONTACT

"The thorniest problem in connection with the large lecture classes," a 1957 conference of the University of California faculty observed, "is that of providing some mechanism for contact with the student, so that he can discuss with someone in authority his problems in the course. The students who come to the lecturer's office during his regular office hours may get the help they need, but they are generally a few of the very best students, who have no fear, or a few of the very worst, who are desperate. In fact, the lecturer could hardly spare the time to enter into discussion with any great fraction of his students."[3]

Office and Home Visits by Students

We asked faculty how often students came to their offices "to discuss matters of concern to them." Replies indicated two clear progressions: (1) upper classmen made office visits more often than did lower classmen, and graduate students more often than upper classmen; (2) undergraduates in liberal arts colleges visited more often than did those in universities. At the universities, faculty in the humanities were visited by undergraduates more frequently than were faculty in the sciences; at the colleges, the reverse was true. This is consistent with the heavier teaching load of humanists at universities and of scientists at colleges.

[3] *Quality of Education in Relation to Numbers,* Proceedings of the University of California Twelfth All-University Faculty Conference, University of California, April 1957, p. 31.

The modal response of university faculty was that undergraduates visited their offices "occasionally," graduate students "often"; of college faculty, that lower classmen visited "occasionally," upper classmen, "often."

Faculty answers to our query about student visits to their homes followed a comparable pattern: less than half of the university faculty— but 85 percent of the college faculty—had had lower classmen in their homes; more of both university and college faculty had been visited by upper classmen, while 90 percent of university faculty had had graduate students in their homes (see Table 3-2).

TABLE 3-2. *Student Visits to Faculty Homes*

"Do you ever have any students in your home, either in connection with their work or for a social occasion?"

Field and Institution Group	Percent of Faculty Who Never Had Visits from		
	Lower Classmen	Upper Classmen	Graduate Students
Total			
Group I	59%	41%	10%
Group II	55	38	10
Group III	15	7	—
Sciences			
Group I	63	46	8
Group II	60	45	8
Group III	16	7	—
Social Sciences			
Group I	66	44	9
Group II	62	39	6
Group III	19	7	—
Humanities			
Group I	45	31	14
Group II	43	30	16
Group III	11	8	—

Home visiting is, of course, easier if the faculty member lives near the campus, as he is more likely to do at colleges than at large universities, especially those in the heart of cities where urban decay, juvenile delinquency, and poor public schools have driven faculty with young children to the suburbs. At a liberal arts college in a small New England town, one professor observed that there had been a decline in home visiting

TABLE 3-3.   *Faculty Knowledge of Students' Names*

"How many senior majors and full-time graduate students beyond their first year in your department can you greet by name?"[a]

Field and Institution Group	Percent of Faculty Replying "Few" or "None"	
	Senior Majors	Advanced Graduate Students
Total		
Group I	56%	20%
Group II	34	11
Group III	2	—
Sciences		
Group I	58	17
Group II	29	4
Group III	1	—
Social Sciences		
Group I	63	19
Group II	41	5
Group III	1	—
Humanities		
Group I	47	28
Group II	35	27
Group III	3	—

[a]Faculty in departments with no senior majors or graduate students have been eliminated from this tabulation.

(and a rise in office contacts) due to the "absence of domestic servants and the reduced contacts between faculty wives and students as a result of the disappearance of the chaperone." However, at another college not far away, a map showing the location of faculty homes, posted in the library, testified that such visiting was still customary there. In the universities, it is the jump from undergraduate to graduate status that is likely to bring the student into significant personal contact with the faculty; in the colleges, the jump from lower to upper classman status.[4]

[4] A study at Amherst of faculty-student contacts outside of class noted that "informal chats,...and visits...show increased faculty association for the last two years. The increase is most marked between sophomore and junior years. The sophomore median implies a monthly contact while the junior and senior medians approximate a weekly contact." See Robert C. Birney, et al., *The Class of 1959 at Amherst College: A Preliminary Report* (Amherst College, 1960), p. 80.

A more modest test of personal interest—knowledge of a student's name—yielded results which differ from those above only in the significantly larger proportion of faculty at Group I than at Group II universities who failed the test not only for seniors majoring in their department but also for graduate students. Well over half of our respondents at Group I institutions could greet by name few or no senior majors in their department; one in five could greet few or no advanced graduate students. The performance of respondents at Group II universities was markedly better, but far below the standard of college faculty (see Table 3-3).

Undergraduate and Graduate Faculties

Ignorance of a student's name is, of course, due not only to the loss of the individual in a sea of faces but also to the fact that faculty who teach exclusively at one level have little opportunity to know students enrolled at a different level. Student numbers and such faculty activities as research and administration are important in keeping senior majors nameless to so many faculty; however, the confinement of some faculty to undergraduate instruction probably accounts for the lack of acquaintance with graduate students by a fifth of the faculty at Group I universities and a tenth at Group II.

Table 3-4 indicates the relative number of faculty in each major field teaching at the graduate or undergraduate level solely, or at both. In interpreting the table, the population represented should be clearly understood. Only those who spent at least part of their time teaching either undergraduates or graduate students are included; faculty or administrative officers who devoted all of their time to research and/or administration, doing *no* teaching during the academic year 1960-61, are excluded. Therefore this is a population of teaching faculty, all of whom had a full-time appointment during the academic year (which does not, of course, mean that they necessarily devoted their full time to teaching).

Several points can immediately be noted. From 12 to 18 percent of university faculty in the sciences and social sciences taught no undergraduates, the percentage being slightly higher at universities with a large volume of federal research funds and slightly smaller at Group II universities; a decidedly smaller fraction of university humanists taught only graduate students. Here again, we see signs that graduate programs

TABLE 3-4. *Percent of Faculty Teaching Undergraduate or/and Graduate Students, 1960-61*

"How did you actually spend your working time this academic year— September 1960 to date? (Enter percent of time you devoted to each activity. Rough approximations will do but totals should come to 100%)"[a]

Field and Institution Group	Faculty Teaching Only		Faculty Teaching Both Undergraduates and Graduate Students	Total	Number
	Under- graduates	Graduate Students			
Total					
Group I	23%	14%	63%	100%	1,782
Group II	22	10	69	100	1,084
Group III	94	—[b]	5	100	523
Sciences					
Group I	20	18	62	100	799
Group II	15	14	71	100	437
Group III	94	1	6	100	173
Social Sciences					
Group I	15	17	68	100	480
Group II	14	12	74	100	290
Group III	94	—	6	100	123
Humanities					
Group I	36	5	59	100	503
Group II	36	2	62	100	357
Group III	95	—	5	100	227

[a] Only faculty who devoted some time to teaching are included in the tabulation.
[b] 0.2 percent.

and research occupy fewer university humanists than scientists or social scientists.

But perhaps the most interesting point brought out in the table is the demonstration that, although university faculty may belong to the same department (indeed, even this is not always true, as several universities have established separate administrative units for under- graduate and particularly lower-division instruction), they really con- stitute three identifiable faculties:

1. A faculty which teaches only undergraduate courses.
2. A faculty which teaches only graduate courses.
3. A faculty which teaches both undergraduate and graduate courses.

To be sure, our information pertains to a single year, and it is likely that, over a longer period, fewer faculty would confine themselves to teaching solely at the undergraduate or graduate level—i.e., the size of faculties 1 and 2 would decrease, and that of faculty 3 would increase. Nevertheless, during that year, the number of faculty teaching only undergraduates and the number teaching only graduate students were roughly in balance within the sciences and social sciences, at both Groups I and II. In the humanities, there really are only two kinds of faculty: the 36 percent who teach only undergraduates—an undergraduate corps much larger than that of other liberal arts fields, and presumably composed of the many staff needed to teach compulsory and elementary English, foreign languages, and history, courses with very large enrollments—and the more versatile staff who teach both undergraduate and graduate students. In many departments the former are called the "composition" or "language" faculty; the latter, the "literature" faculty.

ATTENUATION OF RELATIONS
BETWEEN UNIVERSITY FACULTY AND UNDERGRADUATES

In the attenuation of relations between faculty and students at our great universities, it is the freshman or sophomore not yet decided on his major and the student of average ability at any level who suffer most. Once a student chooses his major, the department generally assigns someone to serve as his adviser, and a more meaningful, continuing relation is likely to develop than is usual between an incoming freshman and his initial faculty adviser. The bright student is such a pleasure to work with that some member of the faculty will usually "adopt" him; many departments have initiated honors courses for the best students and, especially in the junior and senior years, lavish on them the attention they can no longer give the ordinary student.

It is said that a senior at some of our best universities may not know any faculty member well enough to produce the references required for a fellowship or a job, so that a special man has to be assigned to provide them. The deans at one such public university denied this, noting that any student good enough to get a fellowship would know many faculty members by his senior year; however, they acknowledged that there was a problem in the freshman year, and have recently introduced a system of faculty advisers for each incoming student. At another state university, a 1959 faculty report stated frankly that students "often do not know any faculty members well enough to ask them for placement recommendations. They feel that they cannot consult any faculty member on academic or personal problems." At a large private university, "advisers" are assigned to sit behind desks, so that a student will find someone to consult at any time; but he may not find the same person at the same desk two times running. Experiments are already afoot in the use of data-processing machines to help advisers prepare a student's program each year throughout college.

Impersonalization has extended widely to the graduate level at many large institutions. At several departments of a great eastern university, it may take months for a graduate student to arrange an appointment with his thesis adviser—in one case it took half a year; at a smaller and more exclusive institution, a graduate student observed that it never took him more than two weeks. In one chemistry department, photographs of every graduate student were posted on the office bulletin board as an aid to recognition. It must be said for the chairman of this department that he could match all the faces to names, but the graduate dean of Harvard is on record that, in the science departments at Harvard "senior professors are so harassed that they can hardly even learn the names of their section men [graduate assistants]."[5] The able, overworked chairman of the mathematics department of a moderate-size state university acknowledges with despair that he does not know the names of all of his instructors.

Students' reactions to this state of affairs vary with their expectations. A recent survey of Woodrow Wilson fellows, certainly a highly select group of graduate students, found many disappointed with the size of classes and seminars and the kind of guidance they received at our best large universities.[6] And a 1950 survey reported medical students to

[5] Peter Elder, in Joseph Axelrod, ed., *Graduate Study for Future College Teachers,* Report of Conference on College Teacher Preparation Programs, Washington, D. C., 1958 (American Council on Education, 1959), pp. 11-12.

[6] To be quite specific: the four best graduate schools in the country in 1957 in terms of over-all strength and quality, as judged by the ratings of department chairmen in twenty-four different liberal arts fields, were Harvard, California (Berkeley), Columbia, and Yale (see Chapter 1, section on Leading Graduate Departments). Woodrow Wilson fellows attending these schools in 1959-60 were relatively more satisfied with their libraries, but less satisfied with class size and faculty guidance than were fellows at other institutions.

be bitterly critical of the lack of contact with faculty. "Statements such as 'I wouldn't know the dean if I saw him,' and 'We would like more contact with the senior men on the faculty' were made at almost every school. The exceptions were in a small minority."[7]

At one university, undergraduates sought to avoid sections handled by graduate assistants, and no doubt other stratagems are employed elsewhere. But, for the most part, students must accept what they cannot alter. And so, aloofness from the faculty becomes the mode and too much contact is regarded as "apple-polishing," an attitude reinforced by the perennial gap between the generations and the striving for independence that normally marks the college years. The university providing freshman advisers may find the freshmen uninterested in being advised. One of the nation's most distinguished physicists says his door is always open, but the (graduate) students do not enter (undergraduate students would probably not know where the office is). A Berkeley professor believes that "as university classes and seminars have grown larger and more formal, there has developed a countertendency of informal students' seminars and clubs where they read papers and dissertations to each other."[8]

We have described the diminution of faculty contact with undergraduates at some length without reference to the federal government to emphasize that the government is not the only villain in the piece. The enormous increase in enrollment is the principal cause. But government research programs which devalue undergraduate teaching and reduce the time faculty need devote to it are an important contributory factor.

DEVALUATION OF UNDERGRADUATE TEACHING

. That, outside of the independent liberal arts college, undergraduate teaching is devalued these days can hardly be disputed. An elder statesman at a private university, recalling the days in the 1920's when things were different, said with feeling, "There's not a university in the country—not Princeton or Harvard—where as much attention is given to undergraduate instruction as to graduate these days."

Reviewing the shift from the prewar emphasis on teaching to the

[7] John E. Deitrick and Robert C. Berson, *Medical Schools in the United States at Mid-Century* (McGraw-Hill, 1953), p. 335.

[8] Lewis S. Feuer, "Youth in the 60's," *The New Leader*, March 6, 1961, p. 19.

present emphasis on research, an English professor at the same university confirmed this observation. There had long been, he said, "a polemic opposition" between the university's graduate school and undergraduate college. Even in the heyday of teaching, there had been a cycle: the young man who started out teaching might later, in his middle thirties, want to turn to research, but often he had got out of the mainstream and ceased to be marketable. The generalist, who was so popular in the 1920's and so essential to the success of the college, somehow lost ground in the 1950's and now seemed "parochial" in the humanities as well as the social sciences (his status in the sciences was too evident to need stating). Another professor suggested that "among professional humanists this group [of good undergraduate teachers] still has tremendous prestige and is systematically courted in a political defensive alliance against the 'aggressiveness of the scientists.' "

An overwhelming majority of the faculty in both Groups I and II agreed that the man who teaches undergraduates exclusively is held in less esteem than the man who teaches graduate students, and, at some Group III colleges, it appeared that those who teach only lower-division courses are similarly relegated to a lower status. This is a result not only of the function, but also of the people who now exercise it. It appears that the teacher at the good liberal arts college is more widely respected in educational circles than the permanent teacher at the undergraduate college of a great university. The former is at least in an environment of his peers; the latter has to be judged against the standard set by the eminences in his graduate school.

The staff that teaches solely in the undergraduate college of the great universities seems to consist mainly of young men awaiting advancement, older professors surviving from days when undergraduate teaching was more esteemed, women, foreigners, able but doctorless souls, mediocrities *with* doctorates, and others who, for one reason or another, belong to the legion of the academically disenfranchised. Perhaps most useful and respected are the good teachers who enjoy associating with and influencing undergraduates, but have never quite made the grade in the merciless world of independent scholarship. The cases in which influential and productive men like David Riesman or C. Wright Mills have lodged for many years in the undergraduate college of a great university are so rare as to prove the rule (and it was not a coincidence that both are such unorthodox members of their profession).

One university dean who had conducted a valiant campaign to induce senior professors to teach undergraduates said wryly that any professor who *wanted* to do so, could, but "there is no stampede." Nevertheless, the senior man frequently enjoys lecturing to large groups, at least for a few terms; this gives him a forum, an opportunity to generalize on many years of work, and a chance to interest students in his field. It is the younger men with the research philosophy and opportunities of today who are often the most uninterested in undergraduate teaching. A college professor suggested that there was a visible tendency for the young man, engaged in hard but narrow empirical study or experimentation, to want his students to work beside him in a similar manner, and to regard lecturing as a waste of time—why recite what can be put down on paper and read more quickly? As he ages, however, will the same (no longer young) man want to sum up, recognize the importance of personal influence—*his* influence—and become more tolerant of lecturing? Careers as diverse as those of Tolstoy, Freud, and Einstein lend support to the thesis that early specific work may later give way to broader and more philosophical interests; but there is also a not incompatible tradition of the scholar dying with his spectacles on.

The denigration of undergraduate teaching has been traced back, variously, to the opening of Johns Hopkins in 1876, the organization of the Association of American Universities in 1900, and, in general, to the growth of graduate research and education. Earl J. McGrath argues vigorously that the decline of general liberal education "parallels almost exactly" the ascendancy of specialized graduate schools.[9] In the 1870's, when a chemistry professor at Harvard requested a few hundred dollars and a semester off to conduct some research, President Eliot denied the request on the ground that this would do the university no good; and in 1910, the University of Minnesota administration displayed no interest in a professor's chemistry research, which "in the eyes of the board of trustees and the president, . . . [was] his own private business, much like playing the piano or collecting etchings."[10] In 1914, a state investigation at the University of Wisconsin foreshadowed the criticism so widely voiced today:

[9] McGrath, *The Graduate School and the Decline of Liberal Education* (Teachers College, Columbia University, 1959), p. 14.

[10] W. H. Cowley, "Three Curricular Conflicts," *Liberal Education*, Vol. 46 (December 1960), p. 473.

That the members of the faculty are sacrificing instructional work to write books, to lecture and do other work for outside pay.

That, under the cloak of research, faculty members are shirking classroom work and devoting much time to other pursuits.

That students are deprived of personal contact with the strong men of the faculty, and that instruction is left to men of less experience.[11]

Let us repeat, therefore: the problem was *not* created by government research programs. It *has* been exacerbated by them.

THE EFFECT OF FEDERAL RESEARCH PROGRAMS

Before the emergence of federally financed research, there was some disparagement of undergraduate teaching: "One dean at Chicago a few decades ago is said to have remarked, 'The sight of an undergraduate makes me sick.' "[12] Now, there is more, and Warren Weaver observes that the disparagement has begun to extend to graduate instruction. "Some distinguished scientists are glad to have post-doctorate students associated with them, but are unwilling to take on even doctoral candidates."[13]

Reduced Teaching Loads

BEFORE: There were some reductions in teaching loads at the best universities to encourage research. Writing in 1938, Raymond M. Hughes observed:

University teaching schedules have been reduced to give time for research. While the regional standardizing agencies recognize 15 or 16 class hours a week as a reasonable teaching load for a professor in a college, a number of our universities regard 8 hours and many others 10 or 12 hours as the normal teaching load in view of the research they

[11] *Survey of the University of Wisconsin* (State Board of Public Affairs, 1914), pp. 6-7, cited by Herbert E. Longenecker, *University Faculty Compensation Policies and Practices in the United States* (University of Illinois Press for Association of American Universities, 1956), p. 6.

[12] John A. Perkins, *Plain Talk from a Campus* (University of Delaware Press, 1960), p. 142.

[13] Weaver, "A Great Age for Science," in *Goals for Americans,* The Report of the President's Commission on National Goals (Prentice-Hall, for the American Assembly, 1960), p. 117.

expect their professors to carry on. It is of interest that a number of the best colleges have reduced the normal teaching load to 10 or 12 hours for the same reason.[14]

Now: Teaching loads have been reduced so drastically at some institutions that they can hardly get much lower (in 1960-61, scientists at Group I universities taught an average of 6 hours a week; at three universities, their average load was down to 3.9, 4.5 and 4.9 hours respectively); the reductions are more widespread; and the government is reimbursing institutions for the time faculty members devote to federally-financed research during the academic year—in short, the government is paying scientists to teach less. "We have a leaky bucket," said one science dean discussing his teaching problems, "and more and more people are punching holes in it."

BEFORE: Scientists often had a heavier teaching load than humanists. In 1930-31 a study of fifty-seven midwest colleges and universities found:

> The lowest clock-hour load in any well-represented academic field is in theology and religion, with 13.9 clock-hours. Economics, education, English, history, political science, sociology, and speech, all fall in the 14-hour group. In contrast to these subjects, the laboratory subjects, including botany, chemistry, geography, geology, physics, and zoology, exceed an average of 19 hours, chemistry being the highest, at 23.5 hours.[15]

Now: The situation is reversed at the universities, and, although scientists still carry a heavier load at colleges, the gap between them and the humanists has probably been narrowed. The present study has found a mean teaching load of 6 classroom hours in the sciences and 8.3 in the humanities at Group I universities, compared with 12.7 hours in the sciences and 11.2 in the humanities at twelve liberal arts colleges.

Reduced Contact of Researchers with Undergraduates

The determination of the effect which research has upon the amount of time faculty devote to students was one of the prime objectives of

---

[14] Hughes, "Research in American Universities and Colleges," in *Research—A National Resource* (National Resources Committee, 1938), Vol. 1, p. 179.

[15] Melvin E. Haggerty, *The Evaluation of Higher Institutions:* Vol. 2, *The Faculty* (University of Chicago Press, 1937), p. 152.

this study. As one approach to the question, we asked faculty: "In your experience, does research and scholarly work in your field tend to reduce the time a man will put into preparing for his classes?"

About three fifths said "yes" and less than one fifth "no"; the remainder divided between a very few who checked the response "Quite the contrary—it tends to increase the time put into class preparation," and those who checked "I can't meaningfully separate research and teaching." Only minor differences were observable in the responses of faculty in each of the nine basic populations we have examined throughout this study (scientists, social scientists, and humanists at institutional Groups I, II, and III).

On this point, then, a majority of faculty agreed: research *does* reduce the time spent on class preparation. Those who were, in fact, heavily engaged in research were more likely to say that research reduces the time spent on class preparation "slightly"; those who did little research themselves, that it reduces preparation time "markedly." Are the former informed and the latter wrong, or are the former defensive and the latter right? The answer, provided by the two groups themselves (see Appendix B, Tables B-11 and B-12), is that persons heavily engaged in research *do* spend markedly less time on undergraduate teaching and class preparation.

The 16 to 18 percent who replied "I can't meaningfully separate research and teaching" included not only those engaged in graduate teaching, for they were as numerous in colleges as in universities; they may reflect either a special approach to teaching, as in honors courses, workshops, and research seminars, or an attitude of a few rather than a widely shared experience of many. The viewpoint is, of course, more common among researchers than non-researchers.

With a succeeding question, "What about contact with students (particularly the more informal kinds of contact)—does active involvement in research tend to reduce this?" we offered four rather complicated choices and got a correspondingly complex pattern of replies. The alternatives were:

1. Yes, reduces both frequency and depth of contact.
2. Yes, reduces frequency but increases depth of contact.
3. No, it does not affect frequency or depth of contact.
4. Quite the contrary—it tends to increase the frequency of contact.

While no single alternative elicited the approval of a majority of the faculty in any field, the modal response of scientists at colleges as well as universities was number 4; and of humanists, number 1; of university social scientists, number 2. In all fields, those who spent a lot of time on research were more inclined to choose 4, although their own testimony is that this is untrue for their contacts with undergraduates in the office or at home. The apparent inconsistency is attributable, in part, to the coarseness of our question. A number of respondents added a fifth alternative which is probably closest to the truth: "Research reduces frequency of contact with undergraduates, but increases contact with graduate students."

The final evidence to be reported is so voluminous it is presented in Appendix B. Tables B-6 to B-10 give the mean time which faculty of different ranks devoted, during the 1960-61 academic year, to teaching undergraduates and graduate students, and to research, administration, and other academic activities; Tables B-11 and B-12, the mean times allocated by those who spent much time on research and those who spent little; and Tables B-1 to B-5, the mean time faculty at each rank would *like* to spend on each activity. The evidence reported in these tables will be summarized in the remainder of this section.

Location of faculty heavily engaged in research. As a start, it will be useful to indicate the relative number and location of faculty heavily engaged in research, and those at the opposite extreme who do no research at all (see Table 3-5).

Clearly, most of the humanists in our study (even those at the great

TABLE 3-5. *Poles of Faculty Time Devoted to Research During the Academic Year September 1960-June 1961*

Field	Percent Devoting 25% or More of Working Time to Research in Institution Group			Percent Devoting No Time to Research in Institution Group		
	I	II	III	I	II	III
Total	55%	41%	14%	10%	15%	35%
Sciences	68	54	10	6	11	39
Social Sciences	57	43	24	7	12	25
Humanities	32	24	11	18	22	37

TABLE 3-6. *Mean Years Elapsing Between First Appointment to Lower and Present Rank*[a]

Field and Institution Group	Mean Years from Instructor to			Mean Years from Assistant Professor to[b]	
	Professor	Associate Professor	Assistant Professor	Professor	Associate Professor
Total					
Group I	14.5 (559)[c]	9.8 (289)	3.8 (315)	10.2 (164)	5.4 (90)
Group II	16.0 (285)	9.5 (215)	4.0 (203)	10.0 (63)	5.4 (81)
Group III	14.7 (138)	9.2 (104)	3.7 (110)	11.0 (25)	6.5 (25)
Sciences					
Group I	13.7 (256)	9.0 (116)	3.9 (135)	9.7 (89)	5.1 (46)
Group II	16.2 (117)	8.2 (85)	3.1 (64)	10.1 (36)	5.5 (41)
Group III	15.8 (40)	9.8 (33)	3.8 (37)	12.7 (9)	6.5 (8)
Social Sciences					
Group I	14.0 (141)	8.7 (76)	2.9 (62)	10.4 (54)	4.6 (30)
Group II	14.1 (71)	8.1 (50)	3.3 (54)	9.3 (16)	4.8 (32)
Group III	10.8 (32)	7.9 (21)	3.4 (27)	8.1 (7)	6.2 (10)
Humanities					
Group I	16.3 (162)	11.6 (97)	4.3 (118)	12.1 (21)	8.1 (14)
Group II	17.1 (97)	11.7 (80)	5.0 (85)	10.4 (11)	7.5 (8)
Group III	15.8 (66)	9.4 (50)	3.8 (46)	11.5 (9)	7.0 (7)

[a] This table reports an analysis of answers to six separate questions, indicating (1) present age, (2) present rank, (3) year in which this rank was first held at any institution, (4) the year in which the rank of instructor was first held or, for any respondent who was never an instructor, (5) the rank and (6) year of his first appointment. The averages thus represent the time it took incumbents of each rank to first reach their *present* rank; the time it took them to first reach each lower rank is *not* included in the averages for lower ranks.
[b] Only where first appointment was as assistant professor.
[c] The number of cases is indicated in parentheses.

universities) are not heavily engaged in research; most of the university —but not college—scientists are. While, at universities, the proportion of scientists heavily involved in research is larger than that of social scientists, at colleges it is markedly smaller. The surprising contrast between the small amount of time devoted to research by scientists at our colleges and the decidedly larger amount devoted by social scientists cannot be attributed to the relative amount of federal aid received by the two groups, since 38 percent of these scientists received federal research funds in 1960-61 (including the summer of 1960) compared to only 17 percent of the social scientists. But the scientists have a higher teaching load—12.7 mean classroom hours as against 10.1 for social scientists—and, finding it harder to devote a large portion of their time to research during the academic year, concentrate their research in the summer months.

This is confirmed by an analysis of our question about whether federal funds (for research, teaching, study, or consulting) had been received during the summer of 1960, the regular academic year 1960-61, or both. Out of a total of eighty-nine college faculty in the sciences and twenty-one in the social sciences reporting the receipt of federal funds during the aforesaid twelve months, the proportions receiving funds during the specified periods were as follows:

Field	Summer 1960	Academic Year 1960-61	Both	Total
Sciences	60%	4%	36%	100%
Social Sciences	19%	14%	67%	100%

A number of signs also suggest that the kinds of people now engaged in college teaching may differ significantly in the sciences and social sciences. For one, the social scientists at our Group III colleges are somewhat younger, at all ranks above instructor, than the scientists (see Chapter 8, Table 8-1); and they have advanced more rapidly to their present rank from their first appointment as instructor. Thus, college professors in the social sciences averaged 10.8 years to reach this rank from their first appointment as an instructor (at any institution) compared to 15.8 years for professors in the sciences—as well as in the humanities (see Table 3-6). Probably, colleges are establishing and expanding more departments in the social sciences—particularly in sociology, anthropology, and psychology—than in the sciences or humanities, and these are being staffed by young, research-minded persons.

Time spent on research and administration relative to that spent on undergraduate teaching. The reduced time which faculty heavily engaged in research devote to teaching undergraduates is strikingly demonstrated by comparing Tables B-11 and B-12 in Appendix B. What is more, the tables make clear that the reduction was in the time spent teaching undergraduates, *not* graduate students.

Thus, the Group I scientists who spent less than a fourth of their time on research devoted 38 percent of their working week to teaching undergraduates (including preparation), while those who put in more time on research devoted only 21 percent of their working week to undergraduates. But the time given to graduate teaching was very similar for both groups—20.9 percent for the former, 19.2 percent for the latter. Similarly, those scientists in Group II universities who did little research gave 38 percent of their time to undergraduate teaching compared to only 23 percent for their colleagues who did more research, but the time each group gave to graduate instruction differs by only 0.3 points. The same situation prevails in the social sciences and humanities.

University faculty heavily engaged in research are less likely than faculty who do little research to see undergraduates—either lower or upper classmen—in their offices and homes, but *more* likely to see graduate students. The story is the same for college faculty if we substitute "lower classmen" for "undergraduates" and "upper classmen" for "graduate students."

Examining the data on time devoted to teaching by faculty of different ranks (columns 1 and 2 of Appendix Tables B-7 to B-10), two strong and consistent trends are apparent: (1) as one moves up the academic ladder from instructor to full professor, there is a steady decline in the proportion of time devoted to teaching undergraduates and, concomitantly, (2) an increase in the time spent teaching graduate students. At Group I universities, professors devoted less than half as much time as instructors to teaching undergraduates, and thrice as much to teaching graduate students. Granted, instructors are few in number, particularly in the sciences; at the level of assistant professor, the teaching loads of different ranks are already in somewhat better balance.

However, it is not research but administration that robs undergraduates of so much of the full professor's time. In the science and social science departments of Group I universities, professors actually spent less time on research than did any other rank while instructors and assistant professors spent the most time. As the two lowest ranks manage to combine the highest loads of research and undergraduate teaching, surely these activities are not intrinsically incompatible. Doubtless these ranks are driven to it by the requirements of their situation: the teaching is dumped on them, and the research is willingly assumed as the main path of professional advancement. But full professors of science and social science at Group I schools spent as much time on administration as they did on undergraduate teaching—fully a fifth of

TABLE 3-7. *Actual and Desired Allocation of Working Time by Group I Scientists, by Rank, 1960-61*[a]

Activity	Professor	Associate Professor	Assistant Professor	Instructor
MEAN TIME SPENT				
Teaching and Preparation	43.2%	47.3%	48.9%	54.8%
Undergraduates	20.6	25.8	31.8	46.9
Graduate Students	22.6	21.5	17.1	7.9
Research	30.8	37.7	39.5	42.1
Administration	21.2	10.5	8.3	2.1
Other Academic Activities	4.8	4.5	3.3	.9
Total	100.0%	100.0%	100.0%	100.0%
Number	364	166	203	63
MEAN TIME DESIRED				
Teaching and Preparation	42.7%	43.3%	42.8%	48.1%
Undergraduates	18.2	20.1	19.7	27.0
Graduate Students	24.5	23.2	23.1	21.1
Research	49.3	51.5	54.0	48.2
Administration	6.3	3.1	1.7	2.7
Other Academic Activities	1.7	2.0	1.5	1.0
Total	100.0%	100.0%	100.0%	100.0%
Number	358	161	197	62

[a] From replies to two questions: "How did you *actually* spend your working time this academic year—September 1960 to date? (Enter percent of time you devoted to each activity. Rough approximations will do but totals should come to 100%.)" and "If you were free to choose, how would you like to spend your working time?"

their work week. In these fields, university professors devoted roughly twice as much time to administration as did associate professors, and there seems to be a sharper division in the amount of administrative duties assumed by the two top ranks than is true in the humanities. (Included in the data are not only department chairmen but deans and other administrative officers, usually of professorial rank, whose duties are primarily administrative but who like to keep their hand in the honorific pastime of teaching *a little*.)

If the wish is father to the act, the hapless undergraduate will come out still more poorly in the future, for in all three groups of institutions, including the colleges, faculty in every rank wanted to reduce still more the amount of time they spent teaching undergraduates, and to increase the time devoted to graduate students and research. The lower ranks (who are most burdened with teaching) would like the largest reductions of their time with undergraduates; those who did the least research (humanists and college faculty) would like the largest increases in their research time.

As has been noted, the data documenting the foregoing observations are reported fully in Appendix B. For purposes of illustration, however, Table 3-7 sets forth for Group I scientists the type of information to be found in Appendix B for faculty in the sciences, social sciences, and humanities at each of the three groups of institutions.

SOME REMEDIES

It is easy to rattle off a string of recommendations as to what universities and the government should do to remedy the reduction of meaningful contact between undergraduates and faculty; but it is not so easy to come up with practical recommendations. We have been at some pains to point out that the loss in contact is not due simply to government research programs; it is a long-standing trend, aggravated by increases in enrollments. For more and more youth today, a college education is serving the function of a high school education a generation ago, and, as college education becomes more common, many of the social values and professional benefits formerly attached to it are increasingly being transferred to graduate and even postdoctoral education.

There is no substitute for smallness.[16] There may be no loss of educational content as enrollment increases—very likely, the content improves, if more money becomes available to pay for better teachers and equipment, and if teachers prepare more carefully for large lectures than they do for smaller discussion sections.[17] But largeness brings with it a reduction particularly in the more informal and spontaneous exchanges between undergraduates and faculty, and probably also a certain narrowing of intellectual horizons to departmental lines.

We are, therefore, all for smallness, where it can be maintained. But it is not going to be maintained at many universities. Any widespread solution to the problem of impersonality must, therefore, be undertaken with the resources and conditions generally found at large universities. One of these resources (to be discussed more fully in Chapter 5) is the large number of full-time research personnel not presently fully utilized in educational activities.

A more fundamental resource is the time of good teachers which is misused in second-rate research, because the government and universities have made second-rate research more rewarding than first-rate teaching. Nothing is more essential to intellectual vitality, social progress, and national strength than a high level of high-quality research in all fields. Second-rate research is another matter. Were the optimal balance between research and teaching to be defined, not by the money, but by the talent available for each, there would be much more encouragement of research in the colleges, the humanities, and social sciences, and more encouragement of undergraduate teaching at the big universities.

[16] "But isn't there a possibility that really creative administration can create smallness within largeness?" asked one reader. "Isn't it possible that a large university might find ways of decentralizing itself into really small colleges—or call them what you will—and still keep the advantages of a central library, cultural attractions, etc., which distinguish the large institution?" Yes, indeed. It will not be easy or cheap, but as large universities are not going to close their doors and silently dwindle away, the difficult task of humanizing their education assumes great importance.

[17] In a 1949 study at the University of Minnesota, Kenneth E. Clark and Robert J. Keller observed "the direct relationship between class size and the extent to which the instructor seemed to be prepared for class meetings, and the inverse relationship between class size and the amount of original thinking demanded of students." See "Student Ratings of College Teaching," in Ruth E. Eckert and Robert J. Keller, eds., *A University Looks at Its Program* (University of Minnesota Press, 1954), p. 207.

This conclusion is shared by a majority of our faculty respondents, other than the scientists and social scientists at Group I universities and a bare majority of the scientists at Group II (i.e., those who are the major beneficiaries of the present federal programs). Virtually no faculty thought federal programs should concentrate on teaching rather than research. But there was a widespread conviction that federal programs should be more evenly balanced between teaching and research (see Table 3-8).

Ideally, one would like to see no financial differential between the good researcher and the good teacher, but only between good and poor faculty. In practice, this would require extensive programs of federal aid for teaching and teaching facilities, at least in the same fields as those in which the government now encourages research.

TABLE 3-8. *Faculty Opinions on the Present Concentration of Federal Funds*

1. *The present concentration on research should continue.*[a]
2. *Federal funds should be more evenly balanced between research and teaching.*
3. *Federal funds should concentrate on teaching rather than research.*

Field and Institution Group	Percent Replying				Number
	(1)	(2)	(3)	Total	
Total					
Group I	53%	47%	1%	100%	1,773
Group II	43	55	2	100	1,076
Group III	36	62	2	100	500
Sciences					
Group I	59	41	1	100	789
Group II	51	48	1	100	437
Group III	41	58	1	100	160
Social Sciences					
Group I	56	44	—[b]	100	487
Group II	45	54	1	100	287
Group III	37	62	2	100	120
Humanities					
Group I	38	59	2	100	497
Group II	31	66	3	100	352
Group III	32	65	3	100	220

[a] These three statements were the choices presented in the questionnaire as responses to: "What is your opinion about the present concentration of federal funds on research rather than teaching?"
[b] Less than 0.5 percent.

SUMMARY

Institutions have tended to increase the size of undergraduate lecture classes, in order to handle enrollment increases economically while maintaining low teaching hours. The result of these and other developments has been to diminish personal contacts particularly between senior university faculty and lower division students.

Federal programs have had a powerful but indirect influence on these trends because their emphasis on research has served to reduce teaching hours and to strengthen long-established tendencies to devalue undergraduate teaching at the great universities. It can be shown statistically that, in every major field and type of institution, a high degree of involvement in research is accompanied by a reduction in the time spent teaching undergraduates.

While no ready and certainly no cheap way to improve this situation is feasible, the general direction to be taken is clear: (1) a strengthening of those smaller institutions that still preserve meaningful personal contacts between faculty and undergraduates; (2) a greater effort to increase such contacts at larger institutions; and (3) a better balance of federal expenditures between aid to research and teaching.

CHAPTER 4

Federal Stipends and Undergraduate Science Instruction

THERE IS EVIDENCE that federal programs providing stipends to graduate science students may, indirectly, be lowering the quality of undergraduate laboratory instruction at some universities. Let us review the factors at work.

THE DEMAND FOR GRADUATE TEACHING ASSISTANTS

We may start with the enormous expansion in both undergraduate and graduate enrollment, taken together with faculty shortages in some fields and an effort at many institutions to raise salaries by increasing the number of students—particularly undergraduates—handled per faculty member. As faculty classroom hours have also been declining and graduate enrollment expanding, and as the number of graduate students per professor tends to be less elastic than the number of undergraduates, the economics of the situation can get pretty complicated; but the pressure to economize by increasing the number of undergraduates per course becomes all the greater. (At some famous public and private universities, over-all statistics for recent years and goals for 1970 show a *decline* in the number of students per faculty member, due to the more rapid expansion of graduate than undergraduate enrollment and the preservation of a low ratio of graduate students to graduate faculty, aided by the subsidization of both graduate students and faculty by federal research funds.)

Perhaps the most common method of increasing the number of undergraduates a professor can handle is to give him help with the routine chores of teaching—the distribution of materials, the grading of papers, the preparation and supervision of laboratory experiments, and so forth. As the size of lectures and the number of lecture halls increase, while an effort is still being made to allow for discussion and some form of direct personal contact beyond the distant observation of professorial gesticulations, introductory courses with a large enrollment are often conducted through a combination of large lectures handled by the professor and smaller discussion sections meeting under the tutelage of graduate students. These and other uses have increased the demand for graduate students until it sometimes exceeds the demand for faculty, and one is not always sure if the boom in graduate education is intended to serve the needs of society for highly educated personnel or the needs of universities for cheap teachers.

So the first major factor in the situation is the demand for graduate students to serve as teaching assistants in undergraduate courses (particularly introductory and lower-division courses). The use of teaching assistants in science courses is especially great, because, as has been shown, science faculty have relatively low teaching loads, need assistance to keep them low, are affluent enough to pay for it, and have much routine laboratory work that can readily be delegated.

Virtually all science departments at Group I and II universities and even a majority of those at Group III colleges employ teaching assistants. In the social sciences and humanities, however, a sharp contrast prevails between departments at universities, most of which employ assistants, and those at colleges, most of which do not.[1] In the judgment of most university respondents, the use of teaching assistants relative to the number of faculty in their department has increased since 1955 or 1956. If this type of judgment can be taken as a clue, the increase has been even greater in the humanities than in the sciences.[2]

[1] All told, at the universities, 96 percent of scientists, 85 percent of social scientists, and 78 percent of humanists reported that their department utilized teaching assistants; at the colleges, 63 percent of scientists but only 20 percent of both social scientists and humanists.

[2] Although a statistical study of this matter would clearly be preferable to the marshaled observations of faculty, these observations are substantially the same when confined to faculty present at the institution since the years in question, and are also the same in the better-informed judgment of the department chair-

ABSTENTION OF THE BEST
GRADUATE SCIENCE STUDENTS FROM TEACHING

The second major factor is the effective removal by government programs of a large number of the best graduate students from the potential supply of teaching assistants. The number involved is worked out in some detail in Appendix A, Table A-9, although the most important item in the calculation—the number supported as research assistants on federally financed projects—is, unfortunately, also the most unreliable. (It would be a useful service for the Office of Education or National Science Foundation to work up reliable current figures.) Our estimate comes to a total of 37,000 graduate students, some 18,000 of whom are in the biological and physical sciences, supported by federal fellowships, traineeships, and research projects.[3]

The consequent impact upon the supply of teaching assistants can be judged from the fact that, in the fall of 1959, there were only 25,600 full-time graduate students in the biological and physical sciences (their number may have risen to about 28,000 the following year). Indeed, the figures make one wonder where teaching assistants in the sciences come from, and they make readily credible the tales of first-year graduate students with pedestrian records being offered generous assistant-

---

men involved. The percent of university respondents (in departments utilizing student teaching assistants) stating that the number of student teaching assistants in their department had increased markedly since 1955 or 1956, relative to the number of faculty, was as follows:

Respondents	Sciences	Humanities
All respondents	20%	40%
Respondents at university in 1955 or 1956	19	41
Department chairmen	17	41

This increase is presumably attributable to the greater use of graduate students in the humanities for lecturing in undergraduate courses (this is their most frequent use at Group II institutions) and the greater desire of humanists to retain small discussion sections (often delegated to graduate students).

[3] This estimate does not include graduate students who are regular employees of the Department of Defense, Veterans Administration, or other government agencies; medical residents and interns in VA hospitals; nor about 19,000 students in graduate and professional schools receiving veterans benefits and over 12,000 receiving NDEA loans in 1960-61.

ships over thousands of miles, no questions asked. They also explain why stipends for teaching assistants today are competitive with those of research assistants, whereas in 1954 they were far lower.

Before continuing, let us try to answer the question: Where *do* teaching assistants in university science departments come from?

1. Many must be part-time graduate students, of whom there were 20,000 in the sciences in the fall of 1959.

2. Many are undergraduates. It is a pity that there is no earlier line against which to chart a trend, but university science departments are now apparently using relatively more undergraduates as teaching assistants than are university social science and humanity departments, and the tendency is particularly pronounced at Group II universities, which have fewer graduate students to draw on.[4]

3. At certain universities, a good many are foreign graduate students (ineligible for federal fellowships and for some research assistantships), despite the handicaps of poor English and ignorance of American higher education. In the spring of 1958, 3,700 or 9 percent of graduate students in the sciences were foreign citizens.

4. Many graduate students are simply (and unwillingly) forced to serve. As the chairman of one of the nation's great chemistry departments put it, "We've come to the point where we're just brutal about it—we tell the students 'You've *got* to teach.' " The obligation is usually for one term, but sometimes one year.

Altogether, the picture is not a happy one, and the chairmen of major science departments were widely agreed that, at present, it is the poorer and not the best graduate students who are likely to be teaching assistants. The best students prefer work-free fellowships or research assistantships which, while requiring work, contribute directly to their dissertation or at least some sort of publication; the others are left to teach. Teaching is third choice partly (1) because of lower stipends (these have generally been raised to match or occasionally exceed other awards, but government fellowships are generally more advantageous financially because of their tax-free nature, dependency allow-

---

[4] The percent of respondents in Groups I and II, respectively, who stated that their department used undergraduates as teaching assistants was as follows: sciences, 14 and 20 percent; social sciences, 5 and 14 percent; humanities, 7 and 9 percent.

ances, and free tuition); (2) because research is the "going thing" and more in line with the future employment of Ph.D.'s in many sciences; and (3) because teaching delays the completion of the doctorate. In all scientific fields and in psychology the refrain is the same, but the problem is most acute at universities with the largest number of federal fellowships and research assistantships.[5]

The contrast with the humanities is striking. There, teaching assistantships are at a premium and awarded to the best graduate students, and the problem experienced by university science departments does not arise. And the reasons are clear: teaching is more esteemed and will be the future career of more humanists than scientists; the graduate assistants are more likely to *teach,* whereas in the experimental sciences they are often merely glorified laboratory helpers; and there are few fellowships and no research assistantships to lure students away.

In the humanities, assistantships tend to go to advanced graduate students and serve as true teaching apprenticeships. In the sciences, they tend to be thrust upon hapless graduate students in their first or second year. The new science student who does not bring a fellowship with him can hardly refuse a teaching assistantship; he has not yet made the contacts for work on a research project, and many departments do not permit him to accept a research assistantship during his first year. Since a graduate student in his first year is little more knowledgeable or mature than an undergraduate and in his second year is heavily burdened preparing for his prelims, the undergraduate is, again, more poorly served by teaching assistants in the sciences than in the humanities.

CONSEQUENCES FOR LABORATORY INSTRUCTION

As to the consequences for the quality of undergraduate laboratory instruction, it is difficult to see how they can be beneficial. A committee which looked into the matter at Harvard in 1960 reported that

[5] A majority of science faculty at Group I universities, compared to a minority of those at Group II, replied "Yes" to our question: "Particularly in their first year, the best graduate students are said to be on fellowships, and therefore, the graduate students who serve as teaching assistants are not on the whole the best in the department. Is this true in your department?"

. . . departmental chairmen in the sciences are legitimately concerned that the best students are not being channeled into the teaching profession, that undergraduates are in a sense being cheated by having mediocre rather than superior younger teachers set over them, and that in the long run the sciences are inevitably bound to suffer.[6]

In the course of our campus interviews, department chairmen freely conceded that there was a problem; indeed, they conceded it so readily that the discussion rapidly turned to suggestions for remedial measures, which will shortly be summarized. Yet most of these same chairmen and most science faculty, responding to our questionnaire, denied that there has been any decline in the quality of laboratory instruction in their department resulting from the use of student assistants (see Table 4-1).

TABLE 4-1. *Student Assistants and the Quality of Laboratory Instruction*

"It is said that the use of student assistants to monitor laboratory work has led to a decline in the quality of laboratory instruction. Has this happened in your department?"[a]

Respondents	Percent Replying				
	"Yes"	"No"	"Don't Know"	Total	Number
Science Faculty					
Group I	25%	49%	26%	100%	608
Group II	26	52	23	100	351
Science Department Chairmen					
Group I	20%	67%	13%	100%	46
Group II	13	75	13	100	40

[a] The question was confined to those in departments using student teaching assistants in laboratory sections, and followed a question about the quality of the department's graduate student assistants.

Now, our question may not really have got at the exact point about *low quality* assistants—it must have missed it, because the results (as shown in Table 4-1) are so puzzling! And what is to be made of all those "don't knows": are they really reluctant "yeses"? But these are

[6] *Teaching Fellowships in Harvard College*, A Survey by the Committee on Teaching as a Career, Harvard University (October 1960), p. 49.

the findings, and they are awkward. Had they been different, they would have strengthened the supposition that undergraduate laboratory instruction has suffered; as they stand, they give us pause. We are left with the following contradictions:

1. University science departments are having trouble getting enough good teaching assistants.

2. Many science department chairmen have expressed their concern that, as a consequence, the quality of undergraduate laboratory instruction is suffering.

3. But most science department chairmen and science faculty, responding to our (improvable) question, see no decline in the quality of laboratory instruction in their department.

These facts can be reconciled by accepting 1 and 2, and discounting 3, as we are inclined to do, or by accepting all three and saying: there *is* a problem, but science departments are grappling with it and do not believe that serious damage has yet resulted. Another resolution is suggested by the bacteriologist who, after stating that the "really sharp" graduate students "get impatient" in the lab, remarked, "Deep down in our thinking, perhaps, is the feeling that, for the ordinary student, the ordinary graduate student *is* the best teacher." And perhaps the most likely explanation is that offered by personnel officers at a Group II private university who observed that, while graduate assistants in the sciences tended to be the poorer students, it did not necessarily follow that they were poorer than the students who served as assistants some years ago, because the quality of all graduate students has risen noticeably. If this is the general situation, then we would have to conclude, not that the quality of graduate assistants has declined, but that it has not risen as much as one might have expected.

SOME WAYS OF COPING WITH THE PROBLEM

Science departments have been trying to deal with the problem in various ways, such as by:

1. Requiring all students to teach part time in their first or second year.

2. Refusing permission for first-year students to work on research projects.

3. Employing full-time laboratory assistants, if they can be found. Sometimes they are faculty wives, foreigners, or other qualified personnel who for personal reasons are prepared to work at low pay; the alternative of employing postdoctoral personnel has been considered, but they are in short supply and expensive, and good ones will hardly engage in such routine work for an extended time.

4. Assigning a professor special responsibility to interest good graduate students in becoming assistants.

5. Providing assistants with continuing faculty supervision and encouragement, and genuine responsibility.

Good faculty supervision is certainly the key to the successful use of graduate laboratory assistants, and it is also the point at which too many science departments fall down. As a chemistry chairman writes: "Graduate assistants, if properly trained and supervised and properly stimulated, do a very good job. However, I have to admit there is a tendency to not put in the proper safeguards and, thus, the graduate assistants may do an inferior job."

National Science Foundation and National Institutes of Health fellowship programs are criticized by some department chairmen as contributing to the shortage of teaching assistants. The chairmen resent the independence and uncooperativeness of graduate students with their own federal fellowship money. "They are floating satellites. . . . We've no needle to stick them with," one chemist complained.

The relative abundance of federal fellowships during the first year of study, when many departments would like to use students as teaching assistants, and the shortage of second-year awards is often criticized. (However, it is also said that most graduate students should not teach in their first year, as they are simply not ready for it; some schools hold to this position so firmly as to forbid first-year graduate students to teach, preferring to offer them research assistantships.) The second year is the critical period for many students, when they must make the grade for the doctorate or settle for a master's; if they pass their exams and remain in the department, they will have no difficulty, subsequently, getting research work to complete their studies. Therefore the second year is the period when fellowships would be particularly useful, enabling students to study full time.

NSF's refusal to permit fellows to earn additional money by part-time teaching was also condemned; NIH, it was said, is more lenient on the point. (Apparently NSF has recently changed its policy, and now permits its fellows to earn up to $600 teaching.) One financial aid officer was strongly critical of all government fellowship programs on the grounds that they continually raise the size of stipends and bid up the price universities must pay for good graduate students, regardless of individual need.

On the constructive side, department chairmen would like to see:

1. More second-year fellowships.

2. Permission for federal fellows and research assistants to teach part time; some would even like teaching made compulsory, which might have the additional advantage of rendering teaching assistantships tax exempt.

3. The initiation of a program of teaching fellowships.

4. More summer research stipends for teaching assistants. These make academic year assistantships more attractive—and not only financially. By summer work on a thesis problem, a student can recoup some of the time he loses during the academic year through part-time teaching. The NSF program of summer stipends for teaching assistants was enthusiastically praised; it is popular with graduate students as well, and chairmen would like to see it greatly expanded.

Basic research grants and contracts in mathematics, probably the major science with the severest shortage of Ph.D.'s, are widely used to finance graduate teaching assistantships, with the full knowledge and approval of several federal agencies. And assistantships in mathematics are akin to those in the humanities, in that the student actually teaches an undergraduate course. This is a commendable practice. But it appears to be a case in which a serious personnel problem has led quietly to the implementation of policies warranted and at times permitted, but not openly and explicitly sanctioned, in other fields. Need, logic, and equity indicate that the aid given to teaching assistants in mathematics should be extended to graduate students in the other sciences.

Three interesting suggestions were offered at one private university:

1. A common application form could be devised for major government and private fellowship programs, to facilitate multiple applications, comparable information, and better allocation of fellowships among fields and institutions.

2. Graduate schools could agree on the stipend to be offered to each applicant, thereby eliminating competitive bidding as a factor in student choice. This would set up at the graduate level a system like the one governing scholarship offers by certain cooperating private colleges. This system also implies a means test by which cooperating institutions would examine a student's financial needs and agree on a reasonable offer, thereby spreading available funds to a larger number of students.

3. A lump award could be made by the government to each institution of a sum for graduate student stipends approximating the amount now going into fellowships, traineeships, and research assistantships. Such an award would enable the institution to work out an integrated plan for student support throughout graduate school. However, both this and the preceding suggestion are opposed by many department chairmen, who must compete for the best students with rival departments at other institutions and want to control the stipends offered.

Without evaluating the reasonableness and practicality of these suggestions, several conclusions are evident. Programs of aid for graduate teaching assistants are indicated, of which teaching fellowships and a larger number of summer research stipends appear most promising. There is also a marked need for the development of more comprehensive federal policies for the aid of graduate science students. As has been indicated, fellowships support only a minority of the graduate students aided by federal funds. The largest number of those so aided are research assistants (whose support is a by-product of the multi-hundred-million dollars of federal expenditures for research and development at educational institutions); substantial numbers of others receive veterans benefits and NDEA loans. But little has been done to integrate the major and minor programs. Present policy is about as rational as a stew made of one part lamb, tenderly cooked, and three or four parts raw beef.

Finally, there is need for periodic, reliable information on the number of graduate students presently receiving various kinds of stipends, and their distribution by field and institution. The last such study was issued in 1954 and is now entirely out of date, although providing a useful bench mark for charting trends. We do not know with any exactitude how many research assistants are now being aided by federal funds, and anyone who devotes two hours to the subject can improve the quality of official data on the point. Considering the mass of indifferent statistics published by science and education agencies, is it too much to ask for some better information on this matter?

SUMMARY

Since many of the best graduate students prefer federal fellowships and research assistantships to university teaching assistantships, it is the less able graduate students who tend to handle undergraduate science sections and laboratories. The effect has been to handicap undergraduate science instruction. In addition to measures dealing with this specific situation, the broader need is for more comprehensive federal policies embracing the many disparate programs presently aiding graduate students in the sciences.

CHAPTER 5

The Educational Use of
Research Associates

FEDERAL RESEARCH PROGRAMS have introduced into the academic community a sizable group of professional personnel who offer one way to improve the quality of education and also alleviate the reduced personal contact between students and faculty at large universities. Although they go by different names on different campuses, we will call them "research associates." Their distinctive characteristics are a Ph.D. degree and full-time research employment, generally on a federally financed project. The institution's contractual commitment to the research associate seldom extends beyond the duration of the project, although, if his performance is satisfactory, efforts will be made to continue his employment on another project. Many associates do in fact remain at the same institution for an extended period.

J. Howard McMillen has distinguished two types of associates: those who are necessary to man major facilities such as accelerators; and those whom he calls "amplifiers" of the principal investigator's talents, since their function is primarily "to increase the speed at which the principal investigator's research is being carried out."[1] It is the latter type we mainly have in mind in this discussion.[2] Organizationally, the

[1] McMillen, "Our Universities' Research-Associate Positions in Physics," *Physics Today,* Vol. 11 (August 1958), p. 15.
[2] Alvin Weinberg, director of the Oak Ridge National Laboratory, has discussed the present and potential educational role of scientists at the great national laboratories, going so far as to advocate the gradual conversion of these laboratories into "M.I.T.-type institutions . . . educating Ph.D.'s in the sciences." See "The Federal Laboratories and Science Education," *Science,* Vol. 136 (April 6, 1962), p. 29.

use of full-time research staff is often associated with the formation of a separate research institute under the guidance of a senior professor, with a permanent staff head, and divorced, to a greater or lesser degree, from normal departmental educational purposes and controls. (At one university pressed for space, the decision was taken to divorce research institutes physically, as well, to the periphery of the campus.) The recurring conflict between institutes and departments is merely another phase of the continuing battle for perquisites and power between the research and teaching sectors in higher education.

Some science professors with a large and continuing volume of research appear to be turning to research associates where they would formerly have used graduate students. From the viewpoint of a busy professor, the research associate offers a number of advantages over the graduate student. He is more mature, independent, and experienced, and his experience is not lost—it remains a cumulative asset; more responsibility can be delegated to him, he requires less instruction and supervision, and his selection and retention is more completely under the professor's control.

The unfortunate feature of excessive reliance on research associates is, of course, the twofold loss to the educational process: the loss of a position previously filled by a graduate student (basic research agencies make much, in their budget justifications, of the educational assistance rendered to graduate students through the many research assistantships provided by grants and contracts); and the loss in the student's contact with the busy professor who delegates to the research associate much of the day-to-day counseling in the lab.

WHY RESEARCH STAFF ARE
INADEQUATELY USED EDUCATIONALLY

Increasingly, the research associate and postdoctoral fellow play an active part in graduate science education—helping students with their research problems, advising on their theses, participating in graduate seminars. Most important of all, perhaps, simply by being there, available for informal bull-sessions and scientific chitchat, the research associate provides the student with an invaluable bridge to the more inaccessible senior members of his profession and to the world outside.

This is good, but it could be better. The trouble is that few universities have managed to formalize the position of the research associate in the academic community in such a way as to give adequate recognition to, and make adequate use of, his educational contribution. There are several reasons for this.

1. The research associate is employed to spend full time on research, and any direct use of his time for teaching might be viewed by government contract administrators and auditors as a violation of the contract terms. Even grant administrators are handicapped on this point, although they have taken a broader view of what may be done under the terms of a "research" award. Senior and postdoctoral fellowships are administered more permissively, it being generally assumed that the fellow is adult enough to determine for himself how his time may best be allocated between independent research, study, and graduate seminars (whether he participates in or conducts one). It would be good to see government research programs move in the same direction, not informally and occasionally as happens today, but openly, consistently, and as the result of a clearly implemented policy. Research associates and research assistants on government research grants and contracts should be permitted and encouraged to participate in both graduate and undergraduate education, particularly in areas relevant to their research, so long as this does not interfere with the effective discharge of their research responsibilities.

Such a policy can be justified in terms of the benefits not only to education but to research, since the objective of research is not to bury knowledge but to unearth and transmit it and there is no livelier aid to both than the ceaseless fount of bright new students. (In physics and mathematics, we have heard it said in tones ranging from the humorous to the serious, anyone with a Nobel prize is played out and good only for administration; even the ordinary professor can't keep up with the game; and it is the ardent young graduate student who sets the pace for his busier, wearier, or more distracted professors—the "principal investigators" government agencies recognize.)

2. While the research associate is generally glad to participate informally in educational activities, he may be less interested in teaching, particularly when it is obligatory (as at some institutions), with no additional compensation and no recognition in terms of faculty

status. Surely, the last and worst way to deal with the shortage of teachers is to make teaching a burden that must be borne for the privilege of doing research. The problem will be solved only when the rewards and status of teaching are in balance with those of research, so that teaching becomes as attractive an avenue of professional and personal fulfillment. Faculty status of one kind or another is the main lure which is available and, often, the only one which is needed to get research associates to assume teaching duties.

3. However, faculty are reluctant to bestow this prize and to accept research associates as their professional equals. Associates are not appointed through the usual channels of departmental review to ensure their professional standing, but at the behest of a professor who has raised the money to employ them. Departmental and administrative approval of research appointments is far more perfunctory and restricted to more specialized qualifications than the broader and searching professional (and, at times, personal and social) inquiry that precedes normal faculty appointments, particularly to tenure ranks.

Research associates are generally paid more, year for year after the doctorate, than all regular faculty except some full professors; they are beholden to the government and to their patron professor, not to the professors in their field. The only things they do not have, departmental status and tenure, are precisely what they cannot readily obtain. For the granting of tenure—i.e., the pledge of permanent employment —to large numbers of research staff involves either the commitment of large financial reserves available only to a few of the wealthiest institutions or a general reduction in the per capita tenure reserve, reducing the security of established faculty.

Faculty resentment against the research career as a short cut to professional advancement is manifest in the following comment by a young assistant professor of biology.

> I think it unfortunate that federal programs supporting postdoctoral study create the following kind of situation:
> Two men graduate with a doctorate from the same institution. Each has equal academic ability and demonstrated research ability. Alpha accepts a teaching-research appointment at a university. Beta becomes a postdoctorate at a laboratory ideally geared for pursuit of research.
> After five years, Alpha has a research problem, has a reasonably adequate research laboratory, has five years of teaching experience, two babies named in his honor, and possibly a rank of assistant professor. In

the same time, Beta—who has been called a fellowship bum—has moved to two different, but well-equipped laboratories. He has publications from all three labs, though none of the work may have originated with him. He has continued his scientific education at an accelerated rate, whereas Alpha's rate has decreased as he has shared his knowledge with students.

Beta may now enter the institution where Alpha is employed. Beta seeking an academic appointment will command a higher salary than that of Alpha. He will probably do less teaching and more research than Alpha.

Although Beta may be better educated scientifically, he has no teaching experience. Whereas Alpha has in effect sacrificed salary and research opportunities to acquire his teaching experience, Beta lacks the teaching experience, has sacrificed nothing, and actually is rewarded for having resisted an earlier academic appointment.

While this account can be readily accepted as an accurate rendition of some career patterns, there is no immediate way of assessing just how typical these patterns are. The story has been recounted mainly to illustrate an attitude we believe to be widespread.

THAT MANY RESEARCH PERSONNEL are qualified to make a significant contribution to education is certain. A few with a penchant for teaching are, in fact, siphoned off into the regular faculty stream. A National Education Association study indicates that 1,300 of the 19,200 new full-time teachers employed by higher educational institutions in 1959-61 were previously engaged in research. However, if, as has been estimated, there are the equivalent of 40,000 full-time research personnel attached to academic institutions, this would represent an exodus of about 3 percent per year (even if all came from university research establishments)—hardly a mass movement.

The movement is no doubt greater from on-campus than off-campus research institutes, and at universities (rather than colleges), where former researchers constitute about 10 percent of all new faculty.[3] In the initial stages of a professional career, directly after the doctorate, a research appointment holds many attractions for a fledgling Ph.D.—

[3] See National Education Association, *Teacher Supply and Demand in Universities, Colleges, and Junior Colleges, 1959-60 and 1960-61* (1961), pp. 72-73. The estimate of 40,000 full-time equivalent professional personnel engaged in organized research is drawn from the Office of Education report, *Ten-Year Objectives in Education, Higher Education Staffing and Physical Facilities 1960-61 Through 1969-70* (January 1961), p. 13.

a higher salary, the opportunity to publish more, and freedom from teaching, especially from teaching the burdensome and professionally unrewarding lower-division classes. Subsequently, its charms diminish in comparison to the security and status of a faculty appointment with tenure.

For what it may be worth, it is our impression that there is little to choose between the quality of new research associates and junior faculty. The choice of career at this stage is probably determined less by intelligence than by temperament, length of outlook, and quite extraneous factors such as citizenship.[4] It appears clear, however, that at the other end of their careers, senior research associates rarely match and still more rarely excel the professional stature of senior professors at the same university. Where they do, the university is usually in a bad way. (This is obviously the case at one Group II university, where the administration is trying to strengthen the teaching staff by giving professorial status to research personnel in exchange for a limited amount of teaching.)

HOW THE SITUATION CAN BE IMPROVED

No simple formula will reconcile the conflict between research and teaching interests on campus and in Washington, and optimize the educational use of research personnel.

Better awareness of the nature of the talent available would be a helpful first step—that is, a fuller study and description of the professional qualifications and career pattern of research associates is indicated. A recent brief examination of postdoctoral fellows at graduate schools in the Association of American Universities was a useful start, but the larger and more significant population of full-time research personnel has not yet been carefully studied by any agency.

A second step has already been suggested—the establishment of more liberal policies by federal research agencies to promote the fuller

---

[4] Of the fifty-eight graduate deans giving a positive reply to Bernard Berelson's query, forty indicated that 21 percent or more of their postdoctoral students and fellows in 1958-59 were foreign; thirty-four, that 41 percent or more were. (Unpublished data from Berelson's survey for *Graduate Education in the United States*, McGraw-Hill, 1960.) It would be interesting to know the proportion of research associates who are foreign, although it could hardly run so high.

educational utilization of research personnel. This would be entirely in line with two excellent but somewhat less than explicit recent recommendations of the President's Science Advisory Committee.

It should be a general basis of policy and action that basic research and the education of scientists go best together; that they are inseparable functions of universities; that in graduate education the training of scientists involves research; and that the strength of scientific research grows out of research training in institutions of higher education. . . .

In the assignment of funds for basic research, the government should seek to promote the essential connection between the conduct of research and the training of scientists. Where it is feasible, new undertakings should be established in, or in close association with universities, and the great influence and effectiveness of basic research in existing government installations should be increased where possible by improving its connection to graduate education and to university scientists.[5]

This admirable pronouncement will have little effect until implemented by specific regulations governing the permissible—i.e., reimbursible—activities of scientists engaged in federally financed research. Should these scientists not only be permitted but encouraged to devote a certain fraction of their time to teaching? Should their services be donated, or should they be given leave without pay and be reimbursed by the institution? (Alvin Weinberg has suggested an arrangement whereby the institution reimburses the government, but at the *institution's* established rate.[6]) These issues have been glossed over, and, one suspects, deliberately avoided both by federal science agencies and educational institutions. Inevitably, some fudging of budgets and time records has ensued, so that research funds aid the teaching process.[7] Scientists

[5] *Scientific Progress, The Universities, and the Federal Government,* Statement by the President's Science Advisory Committee (The White House, November 15, 1960), pp. 28, 31.

[6] Weinberg, *op. cit.,* p. 30.

[7] Thus, the Comptroller General has reported "there are indications that Federal [NIH] research grants have been used, in some instances, to pay the entire salaries of faculty members engaged partly in nonresearch activities." He cited the cases of 44 medical faculty members whose salaries were charged entirely to research grants, although "the average estimated time spent by these 44 faculty members on nonresearch [teaching and patient care] activities was, according to the information supplied by the schools, 37.4 per cent." See *Report to the Congress of the United States: Survey of Policies Followed by Selected Medical Schools in Charging Faculty Salaries to Research and Training Grants Awarded by National Institutes of Health . . . November 1961,* by the Comptroller General of the United States (March 1962), p. 1 (of Letter of Transmittal); p. 9.

and educators tend to regard this as unavoidable and desirable; auditors, as illegal. The reluctance of federal science officials to raise the matter for open discussion and resolution presumably reflects a wish to avoid the political snares of subsidizing "teaching" ("training," and especially "training for research," being as far as the Washington lexicon has generally gone in that direction).

Finally, universities should review and improve their policies with respect to the status of research associates, and in most cases it would not be difficult to improve them. This type of review has recently been undertaken or is currently underway at a good many institutions. It would benefit from a fuller exchange of information on present practices, for which the National Council of University Research Administrators, the American Association of University Professors, or the National Science Foundation would provide a natural medium.

The equity and wisdom of research personnel policies at different institutions is related to the magnitude and duration of their research programs, the wealth of the institution, and the benevolent or exploitative outlook of administrative officers. Many peripheral benefits— vacations, contributions to retirement, health, accident, and life insurance, and severance notice—can be obtained from the government at little cost to the institution. Experienced university business officers and government negotiators versed in the compendious Armed Forces Procurement Regulation may know all the legitimate personnel charges on research budgets, but administrators at smaller institutions and research staff at any institution usually do not. Here again, a clear public statement of present practices would help in the formulation of fair policies by both universities and government agencies.

One has only to see a range of universities to appreciate how unjust and unnecessary are some present policies. The poorest practice is that which puts research associates in the same category as nonprofessional employees like janitors and secretaries. Far better and probably most common is their classification with administrative officers and other professional personnel without tenure who are employed twelve months in the year. Most difficult and most desirable is the formulation of a policy designed for their special professional status, rewarding length of service with additional benefits, security, and status. One solution to the status problem is the title "Research Professor" or the more equivocal "Lecturer," and one solution to the tenure problem, the granting of at least a year's notice to research associates who have served satisfactorily for a number of years. With increased recognition that research and the federal government are both here to stay, we can hope for more explicit assurances of this sort from university administrations, a greater sense of security on the part of research staff, and a greater acceptance by the faculty of the research intruders in their midst.

THIS DISCUSSION of the potential educational use of research associates may well close with a specific example in an area where the performance of professors has been amiss. This is in the continuing, informal, personal contact of senior staff with undergraduates, which now survives principally at good liberal arts colleges and small universities, the pressure of student numbers and other faculty activities having doomed it at most large schools. Even at Harvard, whose tutorials system was designed to achieve this type of contact, it has been found that senior faculty tended to drop out of tutorial instruction, leaving it to be handled by junior staff.[8]

Recently, however, Harvard has experimented with a new tutoring system in the biochemical sciences which has evidently been quite successful. In 1960-61, the twenty-one tutors ranged in rank from graduate students and teaching fellows to full professors, but their core was a number of mature professional staff engaged full time on research at nearby hospitals and on other projects who, as one informant put it, "are crazy to teach." Each tutor was assigned ten to twelve students who would remain with him for the two to three years until graduation, "and you can't separate them." Each was free to arrange the size of the group and the schedule of meetings to suit his convenience; most meetings were on an individual basis, but there were some group tutorials and some alternating group and individual sessions. In the senior year, tutoring was always on an individual basis for the 40 per-

---

[8] ". . . very few of the members of the faculty who have attained professorial rank have been willing to give more than a small fraction of their time to tutorial instruction. Only a minority, indeed, have been willing to make even a gesture in that direction. . . . [Most departments with large tutorial loads] have delegated the tutorial task primarily to teaching fellows, annual instructors, faculty instructors—to members of the staff who were not on permanent appointment." See *General Education in a Free Society*, Report of the Harvard Committee (1959), pp. 233, 235.

cent of students who did an honors thesis based on a review of the literature or, more commonly, on a laboratory problem. Tutors received one fourth of the instructor-level salary unless they were already on the teaching staff, in which case no additional pay was given.

Although the humanities and social sciences at Harvard have a long tradition of tutoring, the science departments were hostile to the idea; however, the new system has worked so well in biochemistry that the biology and chemistry departments are now adopting it. Students recognize the value of this contact with an experienced member of the profession they hope to enter, and the tutors appreciate the enlivening exchange with young students.

The Harvard experience suggests a particularly happy educational function for the research associate, because it uses part of the research system to remedy an educational deficiency (diminished professorial contact with undergraduates) largely caused by the same system. The Harvard practice will not be transferable to every institution, but imaginative examination of the situation on each campus should identify other ways by which research personnel can serve to improve the quality of education.

SUMMARY

Federal research programs have brought to many university campuses a large number of postdoctoral research scientists relatively divorced from normal departmental educational functions. Their involvement in teaching has been limited by the requirements and administrative restraints of the programs, faculty opposition, and their unsatisfactory academic status (not to mention their frequent disinterest in teaching). Explicit encouragement by the government, more favorable employment policies, and more imaginative educational methods can return to the educational community some of the talent which research programs have removed from it.

CHAPTER 6

The "Balance" of Federal Research Programs

ALTHOUGH THE EFFECT of federal research programs on the content—the ideas and knowledge—of instruction is probably their most important impact on higher education, we can say relatively little about it here. An adequate appraisal would require a review of the status of each discipline, and the extent to which its knowledge and theory has been aided, retarded, or channeled in special ways by the interests of federal agencies. These massive questions, of critical importance to the intellectual stature and integrity of each profession, can be answered only by each profession's best qualified scholars. The frequency with which such reviews, as well as surveys of the occupational status, teaching duties, and research interests of many professions have been undertaken in recent years testifies to the academicians' concern with questions of academic "balance" and their effort to get more support for neglected (and still more support for fashionable) areas. Such surveys have been conducted during the last decade in demography, engineering, applied and general mathematics, medicine, meteorology, oceanography, high energy physics, physiology, psychology, Russian studies, and many other fields.

MODIFICATION OF CURRICULA

Federal programs have unquestionably advanced knowledge in the sciences by giant strides. Although the advance has taken place initially at the highly specialized graduate and postdoctoral levels in which the frontiers of science are explored and extended, it has filtered down and is gradually transforming the content of undergraduate science as well. The progress of modern science is so rapid, however, that at many points gaps have opened between the level of undergraduate and graduate instruction. Special importance therefore attaches to the programs of the National Science Foundation which help to bridge these gaps by revising the undergraduate curriculum, texts, and laboratory materials; giving college teachers an opportunity to learn the latest findings in their field; and replacing traditional (and cheaper) lecture methods and laboratory demonstrations that communicate embalmed truths with continual exploration and with active participation in research by the best students.

Nevertheless, laboratory facilities and the opportunity to keep in touch with the latest experimental findings are more limited at the independent liberal arts college than at the undergraduate college of a large university. Several chairmen of graduate science departments remarked that their graduate students coming from independent colleges are not as well prepared as those coming from universities; and though the most able students can make up the deficiency, it presents more of a problem for the average student. This corresponds with Bernard Berelson's assertion that "the colleges are by all accounts inferior as a group to the universities in the [science] training they give" and his citation of a National Research Council study of National Science Foundation fellowship applicants in 1954 showing that "the candidates from large Ph.D.-granting universities did best and those from baccalaureate institutions least well."[1]

There is, of course, no simple correspondence between the nature of the nation's research effort and the nature of the curriculum in any discipline. The curriculum is broader and less volatile—"changing the curriculum entails all the physical and psychological difficulties of moving a cemetery"[2]—representing the residue of many generations of scholarly work, whereas research activity tends to be more focused on areas that are presently productive, financially supported, or simply popular. But, since a discipline can stay alive only by adding to its

---

[1] Berelson, *Graduate Education in the United States* (McGraw-Hill, 1960), p. 132.

[2] Logan Wilson, "A President's Perspective," in Frank C. Abbott, ed., *Faculty-Administration Relationships* (American Council on Education, 1958), p. 5.

corpus of knowledge and interpretation, with two major qualifications it may be assumed that, sooner or later, the curriculum will be modified to incorporate fruitful new facts and theories developed by the active finders and organizers of knowledge. The qualifications are:

1. The research must be academically acceptable and enter the discourse of the profession as defined by its leaders. Depending upon the particular discipline, it cannot be too "applied" or too "basic"; too foreign in subject matter, terminology, method, or theory; and so forth. (Richard L. Simpson noted that, in 1960, at least two active applied fields of postwar sociological research—military and medical sociology —were not represented at all in undergraduate course offerings; he concluded that "the trends in papers read [reporting current research at meetings of the American Sociological Association] and published run more nearly opposite than parallel to the trends in courses offered."[3])

2. The curriculum draws upon the results not only of American but also of other countries' research and scholarship and, to the extent that a discipline is truly international, balances the limitations of a nation with those of a generation.

BALANCE WITHIN FIELDS

Criticism can be readily multiplied of the lack of "balance" in the research programs of specific agencies or the federal government as a whole. Although the notion of "balance" is elusive and has a perceptibly utopian quality, it evidently betokens the "natural" or self-directed activity and interests in a field or profession. The normal play of forces upon an academic institution—the impact of benefactors, trustees, administrative officers, and students as well as of economic, political, and social developments—precludes the achievement of such "balance" at the best of times. The additional effects of federal programs may be summarized as follows.

1. The institutions least "imbalanced" by federal programs are the many colleges with little or no money, the institutes of technology geared to science and engineering, and the few rich universities with an excep-

[3] Simpson, "Expanding and Declining Fields in American Sociology," *American Sociological Review*, Vol. 23 (June 1961), p. 464.

tional range of government-financed work and at least some other sources of support for types of scholarship not aided by the government. Those which appear most adversely affected are the second-rank universities requiring project funds to hold their staffs and graduate students and unable to resist the attraction of contracts for work which is pedestrian in nature or of little academic interest.

2. The degree of "balance" in a field is directly related to its money requirements per person (engineers requiring more money for equipment than do mathematicians may be more often obliged to undertake work in fields of borderline interest to them), the size of appropriations particularly for the basic research agencies, the number of agencies financing research in the field, and the range of work in which they are interested. Thus, historians, limited to the small external research program of the State Department, are at one extreme; physicists, receiving massive support from virtually every science agency, are at the other.

3. The more experienced, well known, and eminent the man, the greater is the range of his choice and the easier is it for him to get money to do exactly what he wants. National leaders in a science are literally drowned in opportunities, while the neophyte can have hard going.

4. Recent periods of national emergency have been accompanied by an increase in applied research and development with practical and military applications. World War II, the Korean War, and the current "space race" brought an upsurge in various applied research programs, while the years immediately after 1945 saw the inauguration and slow expansion of basic research programs. Judging by the marked growth of their budgets after the Soviet launching of the first earth satellite in 1957, the "pure" research and education agencies (the National Science Foundation, the National Institutes of Health, and the Office of Education) have prospered from the cold war as well as from peace.

Let us review some of the most common complaints (some turning up in the course of our study, some from other sources) about specific imbalances within the sciences, social sciences, and humanities.

The Sciences

Several chairmen of engineering departments complained about the lack of money for basic research in engineering, one stating that this was due to the opposition of physicists "who control the dollars in basic science." This accords with the statement of Harold Work, Dean of Engineering at New York University, that "we should accept the fact that the NSF is for scientists and then try to have set up a national engineering foundation to meet the need for basic engineering research."[4] More broadly, it reflects the separatism of each profession and the dissatisfaction often expressed with programs whose administration is dominated by members of other professions.

Several biologists remarked that it was easier to get support for functional, molecular, and experimental approaches than for descriptive, and one chairman observed that, partly as a consequence, functional approaches are being extended to undergraduate courses.

The preference of government agencies for "safe" and "projectable" rather then venturesome research, and for experimental rather than theoretical work was noted by many observers; the aversion to theory was, however, stoutly denied by well-informed officials at the National Science Foundation and the National Institutes of Health. It is also said that, in order to guarantee at least some results, too much of the time of expensive machines is allocated to relatively routine work (which serves to fill in the precise contours of some known territory) rather than to riskier but potentially more productive inquiries.

Criticisms of a more specific order could be recounted at length—the polymer or rocket fuel emphasis of chemical research, the applied emphasis of mathematical military research programs, the purportedly poor quality work on cancer compounds financed by NIH, the lack of funds for drilling guided solely by the needs of geological science, and so forth.

ALL OF THE FOREGOING adds up to a simple conclusion: academic scientists would like more money for "basic research" to do exactly what they, or the leaders of their profession, want. This is true, but it may nevertheless convey a false impression of dissatisfaction and discontentment. The academic scientist is *not* generally discontented; quite the contrary, he is very pleased with present federal programs, and the

[4] See *Proceedings of the Twelfth National Conference on the Administration of Research* (Pennsylvania State University Press, 1959), p. 18.

more eminent he is, the more pleased he is likely to be. Again and again, leading scientists and federal officials will say that no first-rate man and no idea which is "really good" will fail to get support. While this is an overoptimistic view of the efficiency of the project system, it is probably true to say that the "best" scientists can generally get support for the work they want to do; the "average" scientists, for the work the government wants done.

Even the complaints about insufficient support for basic research are less frequent than they were some years ago, when the budgets of NSF and NIH were much smaller. Most scientists would welcome substantial further increases in the budgets of these agencies, and this certainly would be in the national interest, particularly in the case of NSF. (There has been criticism that the NIH budget has grown too rapidly, leading to a lowering of scientific standards and of administrative efficiency in some programs.[5]) However, their budgets are now large enough to foreshadow the day (if it has not already arrived in certain institutions and departments) when these agencies may compete *too* successfully with the military and other agencies that have practical missions for the time of the nation's best scientists. A future national emergency would then require either some budget curtailment or a redirection in the work of the basic research agencies.[6]

Despite limitations that have been enumerated, federal programs have evidently not produced an undesirable imbalance in most scientific fields but have, on the contrary, promoted work of an unprecedented variety, scale, and, in many areas and institutions, quality. There is every reason to believe that this has improved not only the content of

[5] See, for example, criticisms detailed in *Health Research and Training: The Administration of Grants and Awards by the National Institutes of Health,* Second Report by the House Committee on Government Operations, 87th Cong., 1st sess. (April 1961), *passim,* and *The Administration of Grants by the National Institutes of Health,* Hearings Before a Subcommittee of the House Committee on Government Operations, 87th Cong., 2d sess. (March 1962), *passim.*

[6] The National Science Foundation Act (1950) directs the Foundation "at the request of the Secretary of Defense, to initiate and support specific scientific research activities in connection with matters relating to the national defense," a provision which, to our knowledge, has never been implemented. The involvement of the Public Health Service in various aspects of civil defense and in measures to protect the population from radioactive hazards to health point to some important practical directions in which the work of NIH may subsequently expand.

scientific knowledge but also of scientific instruction, especially in the universities.[7]

The Social Sciences

The successes of the scientists have led to efforts by many social scientists and some humanists to emulate their technical—and political—methods. Although the stimulus, which may initially have been largely intellectual, long preceded the government's major intervention in the sciences, it has gained force from that intervention. Leading social scientists sought the mandatory inclusion of the social sciences in the National Science Foundation statute of 1950; after Congress resolved that NSF should be permitted, but not compelled, to operate in this area, they lobbied for larger budgets for its slowly growing social science activities and for the appointment of more social scientists to the National Science Board. Recently, a panel of the President's Science Advisory Committee has recommended expanded government support for the social sciences, and a broadening of social science representation in the National Academy of Sciences.[8] The National Defense Education Act of 1958 led to similar activity by humanists, whose relations with the government had previously been confined largely to participation in the administration of the Fulbright program and to counseling on special projects such as official histories of the war, area and language training for military personnel, and studies of certain strategic peoples.

The two social sciences which have been most successful on the model of the sciences are undoubtedly psychology and economics (some might also add the small but burgeoning field of scientific linguistics). Indeed, judging from interview impressions alone, the present condition of academic employment in these fields—the high involvement in research, low teaching loads, high salaries, shortage of qualified faculty, and the competitive demands of industrial and government employment

[7] However, relatively more scientists (as well as social scientists and humanists) in our colleges than in our universities stated that the quality of the education their department is giving has improved since 1955-56. (See Appendix A, Table A-10.) Is this because more improvement is possible and necessary in the colleges, to keep abreast of knowledge originating in the universities?

[8] See "Strengthening the Behavioral Sciences," *Science,* Vol. 136 (April 20, 1962), pp. 233-241.

—is akin to that in the natural sciences. The success of psychology (both as a business and a science) has come with its emphasis on physiological, experimental, statistical, and standardizing techniques; that of economics, also, with statistical and mathematical methods. Since World War II, psychologists have worked for military agencies on traditional problems of personnel selection, testing, and training, and on newer problems in human engineering and operations research. Federal support for research in clinical psychology was lacking until the National Institute of Mental Health entered the field.

NSF figures for federal obligations for research in various social sciences, fiscal year 1960, show a cleavage between the relatively substantial obligations for psychology and economics and the distinctly lower level for other social sciences:[9]

Psychology	$ 38.2 million
Economics	24.0
Sociology	4.1
Anthropology	2.3
Other Social Sciences	4.5
Total	$ 73.1 million

However, these data give a misleading impression of the scale of federal expenditures in departments of economics, for they include large research expenditures *within* the Departments of Labor, Commerce, and other government agencies as well as contracts and grants for work in agricultural economics at agriculture experiment stations. Unfortunately, information is not available on recent federal expenditures in individual social science departments at educational institutions. The only information we have to fall back on is eight years old, at which time federal expenditures in departments of psychology, sociology, geography, and political science exceeded those in economics (see Table 6-1).

Even today, federal funds probably finance relatively less university research in economics (outside of agricultural economics) than in psychology, sociology, or anthropology. This is suggested by our own survey, which found a decidedly larger proportion of not only psycholo-

[9] See National Science Foundation, *Federal Funds for Science*, X (1962), p. 106. The figures include obligations for research by government agencies and industry as well as academic institutions.

TABLE 6-1. *Social Science Research Expenditures at Universities and Colleges, 1953-54*[a]

Field	Total	Federal	Percent Federal
	(in thousands)		
Psychology	$6,352	$4,810	76%
Sociology[b]	2,234	591	26
Geography	575	528	92
Political Science	1,812	331	18
Economics	2,431	266	11
Area Studies	724	121	17
Other[c]	4,194	1,145	27
Total	$18,322	$7,792	43%

[a] Source: National Science Foundation, *Scientific Research in Colleges and Universities, Expenditures and Manpower, 1953-54* (1959), pp. 30, 94. Actually these data report expenditures for research "and development" (whatever that may mean in the social sciences). Agriculture experiment stations and federal research centers are excluded.
[b] Includes anthropology and archeology.
[c] A puzzle. NSF states only that "Quantitative breakdown by departmental class was not feasible." We have excluded $330,000 in history ($82,000 of which came from federal sources).

gists but also sociologists than of economists aided by the government (see Table 6-2). The extensive activities of economists are more likely to be financed by private foundations, industry, and financial institutions.

Faculty criticism of the "balance" of federal programs in psychology and economics is not uncommon, to judge from comments volunteered in response to our questionnaire. Some psychologists objected to the emphasis on mental retardation, mental health, and clinical applications in the work of the Office of Education and the National Institute of Mental Health, and to the choice of "clean" experimental design over new ideas and procedures. Economists objected to agency leanings to econometrics and quantitative work. But their criticisms were mild compared to those encountered in other social sciences.

Thus, sociologists complained about the restriction of government programs to quantitative, statistical, and computer analysis to the exclusion of qualitative and descriptive approaches; political scientists, about the shying away from political implications, which lie at the heart of their field. Anthropologists criticized the initial concentration of NSF

TABLE 6-2. *Government-Financed Work and Research by Various Disciplines, 1960-61*

"Since and including last summer, has any of your research, teaching, study, or consulting been financed by the federal government? (Do not include this coming summer.)"[a]

Percent of Faculty Replying "Yes"

Field	Total			Research[b]			Number Replying "Yes" or "No" in Institution Group		
	Institution Group			Institution Group			Institution Group		
	I	II	III	I	II	III	I	II	III
Total	48%	41%	22%	43%	33%	17%	1,812	1,097	535
Sciences[c]	78	71	51	76	64	38	798	439	173
Preclinical Biosciences	94	81	—	93	78	44	54	54	36
Physics	92	78	58	89	73	38	190	77	36
Chemistry	80	66	51	79	65	38	180	110	47
Biology, Zoology	74	73	55	74	66	53	182	110	49
Mathematics	61	59	41	53	37	12	173	78	41
Social Sciences[c]	39	38	18	30	27	17	491	296	125
Psychology	62	61	37	51	48	37	141	107	38
Sociology, Anthropology	44	43	14	33	26	14	124	70	22
Economics	26	15	11	19	13	8	133	68	37
Political Science	16	10	7	7	2	4	90	50	28
Humanities[c]	9	7	2	5	2	2	523	362	237
Foreign Languages	15	14	4	7	5	4	156	77	68
Philosophy	8	0	0	8	0	0	49	41	29
History	7	4	2	4	1	2	91	82	49
Classics	6	0	0	3	0	0	32	18	15
English	4	8	1	2	1	0	181	143	75

[a] Academic year 1960-61 plus the summer of 1960 but not the summer of 1961.
[b] For percent of faculty whose teaching, study, or consulting was financed by the government see Table 6-3.
[c] Includes a few cases which could not be categorized in the fields listed below.

upon archeology and physical anthropology, the politically "safe" areas, to the exclusion of social anthropology; like some of the psychologists, they complained also about the mental health emphasis of NIMH. (The president of the American Anthropological Association recently observed that "some 13 percent of anthropologists are now working in the field of mental health."[10])

Complaints about large projects and narrow, practical goals—contrasted with the lack of encouragement for individual scholars and intellectually significant problems—were leveled at private foundations as well as the government, and come with particular force in these fields with relatively small national research budgets. "We have the largest grant in behavioral sciences ever received in the institution," wrote one sociologist. "Though I am principal investigator, I am not convinced of its advantages for the development of our field." Unfortunately, this type of attitude is widespread in the social sciences.

The Humanities

If federal research programs have yet touched only selected areas of the social sciences, their direct effect on the humanities has been far more selective and, in most cases, negligible. Even at the major universities in Group I, only 5 percent of the humanists responding to our questionnaire received any federal research funds during the academic year 1960-61 or the summer of 1960, compared to 30 percent of the social scientists and 76 percent of the scientists (see Table 6-3). Aside from the small external research program of the State Department and the possibly larger program of the Central Intelligence Agency, which occasionally require the services of historians and authorities on foreign languages and cultures, and intermittent requests for "official historians" and other specialists, the only considerable current federal research program in the humanities appears to be that in foreign (particularly, "critical") languages and instructional materials under the National Defense Education Act. Some faculty charged these NDEA programs and their associated fellowships and institutes for language instruction with overemphasizing scientific approaches and laboratory work, which, it was said, has become something of a fad.

[10] See Margaret Mead, "Anthropology Among the Sciences," *American Anthropologist,* Vol. 63 (June 1961), p. 478.

TABLE 6-3. *Government-Financed Faculty Work by Field, 1960-61*

"Since and including last summer, has any of your research, teaching, study or consulting been financed by the federal government? (Do not include this coming summer.)"[a]

| Field and Institution Group | Percent of Faculty Replying "Yes" for | | | | | Percent Replying "No" | Total | Number |
	Research	Teaching	Study	Consulting	Subtotal[b]			
Total								
Group I	43%	8%	3%	9%	48%	52%	100%	1,812
Group II	33	11	2	7	41	59	100	1,097
Group III	17	6	3	2	22	78	100	535
Sciences								
Group I	76	12	4	13	78	22	100	798
Group II	64	19	5	8	71	29	100	439
Group III	38	18	9	5	51	49	100	173
Social Sciences								
Group I	30	7	3	11	39	61	100	491
Group II	27	8	1	12	38	62	100	296
Group III	17	1	1	3	18	82	100	125
Humanities								
Group I	5	4	1	3	9	91	100	523
Group II	2	5	1	1	7	93	100	362
Group III	2	—c	—c	—c	2	98	100	237

[a] Academic year 1960-61 plus the summer of 1960 but not the summer of 1961.
[b] Less than the sum of the four columns at the left, because some faculty received aid for more than one kind of work.
[c] Less than 0.5 percent (in fact, only one person).

The Politics of "Balance"

The question of "balance" within each field of research cannot be divorced from what may be called the "politics of balance" or, even, the "politics of knowledge." In establishing the scope of its research programs, each agency is naturally guided by the best advice it can get from leading specialists. But specialists' judgments cannot be solely technical; they are unavoidably also political, representing a judgment as to which types (and proponents) of knowledge should be encouraged. And there is a potentially endless fractionization of professional specializations, each subgroup believing that only colleagues in the same subspecialty are competent to evaluate their work. (What is worse from an administrative standpoint, much of the time they are probably right.) An interesting example of this sort occurred some years ago when surgeons complained of discrimination in the review procedures at the National Institutes of Health because their proposals were not being examined by surgeons; a panel of surgeons was subsequently established to meet their protest. Similar complaints are often heard from scientists in rare, newly emergent, or interdisciplinary areas.

The likelihood of support going to only one among several factions is enhanced where the volume of support is low and confined to one or two agencies. In general, this is the situation in the social sciences and humanities, and it is in these fields, therefore, that the government has been most guilty of fostering "imbalance." Particularly in the social sciences, federal programs have tended to support quantitative, statistical, and either real or mock experimental approaches which—partly for this reason, it may be argued—are more dominant than they were several decades ago. Judgment on the consequences will vary with one's evaluation of the fruitfulness and limitations of such methods in the study of human affairs. We believe that the social sciences have gained thereby in methodological rigor, in the volume of their data, and in the usefulness of their results in certain areas; but they have lost something in scope, historical perspective, and understanding.

BALANCE BETWEEN FIELDS:
THE SCIENCES AND HUMANITIES

We can hardly conclude this discussion of "balance" in federal programs without referring to the grossest imbalance of all: the heavy concentration on the sciences and neglect of the humanities, with most social sciences other than psychology falling somewhere in between. Comprehensive national figures are not available, but we can cite the situation at Harvard where, in 1960-61, federal agencies supplied the following sums for work conducted in various arts and science departments (excluding professional schools): $3,939 thousand in the sciences (but nothing in astronomy); $630 thousand in social sciences (including psychology, social relations, anthropology, and economics, but nothing in government or interdisciplinary centers); $62 thousand in humanities (including Far Eastern and Slavic languages, but nothing in other foreign languages, the classics, English, fine arts, history, music, or philosophy).[11]

The funds in the humanities went to establish a language and area center under Title VI of the National Defense Education Act. At a good many other universities, humanistic departments have benefited more from provisions of the NDEA, while social science departments have received proportionately less federal money; but the sharply different scale of financing for research, research facilities, research "training," or student stipends in the sciences, social sciences, and humanities is characteristic of current federal programs viewed as a whole. For example, the National Science Foundation reports federal expenditures in 1957-58 at colleges and universities "proper"—i.e., excluding research centers and agricultural experiment stations but including other professional schools—as $165.6 million for research and development in the physical and biological sciences compared to $8.9 million in the social sciences.[12]

Faculty Opinion on the Imbalance of Federal Programs

Faculty opinion on this state of affairs is divided. A small majority of scientists declared that the concentration of federal funds in the natural sciences and relative neglect of the humanities is in the present national interest, but over two thirds of the social scientists and a still larger proportion of humanists affirmed that it is not. Some 70 percent of the scientists, however, stated that the present pattern is neither

[11] Harvard and the Federal Government, A Report to the Faculties and Governing Boards of Harvard University, September 1961, p. 36.
[12] National Science Foundation, Review of Data on Research and Development, No. 19 (April 1960), p. 6.

in the long-run national interest nor in the best interest of their institution, and nine tenths or more of their colleagues in the social sciences
and humanities agreed (see Table 6-4).

Asked further, "If you could redistribute the federal funds presently
available, what would you do?" over 70 percent of respondents at all
three groups of institutions indicated that they would "Give the humanities somewhat more and the sciences somewhat less, but still the major
portion." (See Table 6-5.) It is worthy of special note that 67 percent
of the scientists at the Group I universities receiving the largest sums
from the federal government also subscribed to this position, and the
comments of many suggest that an even larger proportion would favor a

TABLE 6-4. *Faculty Opinion on the Imbalance of Federal Funds
Between the Sciences and the Humanities*

*"Do you regard the present concentration of federal funds in the natural
sciences and relative neglect of the humanities as*
1. *in the present national interest;*
2. *in the long-run national interest;*
3. *in the best interest of your institution?"*

Field and Institution Group	Percent[a] Answering "No" to		
	(1)	(2)	(3)
Total			
Group I	58%	84%	81%
Group II	64	86	83
Group III	68	91	89
Sciences			
Group I	42	74	67
Group II	48	74	67
Group III	47	80	73
Social Sciences			
Group I	67	88	87
Group II	68	91	89
Group III	75	93	92
Humanities			
Group I	75	95	93
Group II	81	97	96
Group III	78	98	98

[a] Percent of those who replied "yes" or "no," excluding the 3 to 23 percent who
replied "don't know."

policy which gave *both* humanists and scientists more money or at any rate did not penalize the sciences in order to help the humanities.

Additional written comments about this issue throw a good deal of light on faculty attitudes. A very few faculty, humanists as well as scientists, indicated that the humanities (or is it the humanists?) are just not good enough, not sufficiently scientific or socially useful to justify federal aid. Thus a professor of physics asserted that "the Ford Foundation could not find enough worthwhile projects to support in the humanities."[13] And a mathematics instructor said that the humanities are not "well enough developed . . . to warrant spending a lot of money on them," although he suggested that a little money is desirable "to encourage them to keep on trying to become respectable sciences." This condescending attitude is not radically different from the stern position of a professor of German that government aid to the humanities should be related to the degree of their scientific rigor, or to the view of an assistant professor of English that "until the people in the 'humanities' (by this they seem to mean disciplines with no practical application or visible, objective results) take on a more disciplined attitude to research, I feel that there should be no increase in funds to them . . . . The argument for federal funds to do research in teaching Freshman English to native speakers of English is particularly absurd."

Although the foregoing viewpoints are held by a distinctly small minority, they are significant as representing the intrusion of scientific criteria in the evaluation of the humanities. The government has not espoused this position, but many of its programs serve, nonetheless, to bolster it, because of their emphasis on scientific approaches in the social sciences (the buffer zone between the humanities and the sciences) and because the scientific contingent in the humanities (like the scientific linguists) has played an important role in existing programs.

A number of faculty who recognize the great value of the humanities were dubious about the desirability of federal aid either because they were apprehensive of resultant political pressures, potentially more

---

[13] Needless to say, the professor is mistaken. The Ford Foundation has spent many millions of dollars in the humanities through large grants to the American Council of Learned Societies, the university presses, the Council on Library Resources, the Princeton Council of the Humanities, and other channels. Its aid to the humanities has hardly been limited by the inability to find activities worthy of support.

TABLE 6-5. *Faculty Opinion on Redistribution of Funds Between the Sciences and the Humanities*

"If you could redistribute the federal funds presently available, what would you do?
1. *Retain the present relative distribution between sciences and humanities.*
2. *Give the sciences still more and the humanities less.*
3. *Give the humanities somewhat more and the sciences somewhat less, but still the major portion.*
4. *Give the humanities a great deal more and the sciences a great deal less."*

Field and Institution Group	Percent Responding				Total	Number
	(1)	(2)	(3)	(4)		
Total						
Group I	17%	3%	73%	8%	100%	1,732
Group II	15	3	73	9	100	1,059
Group III	13	2	73	12	100	494
Sciences						
Group I	27	3	67	2	100	772
Group II	28	5	64	3	100	424
Group III	25	5	66	5	100	163
Social Sciences						
Group I	11	3	78	8	100	470
Group II	12	1	76	11	100	287
Group III	15	1	73	11	100	114
Humanities						
Group I	6	1	77	16	100	490
Group II	3	1	82	15	100	348
Group III	4	—[a]	78	18	100	217

[a] Less than 0.5 percent.

dangerous to freedom of thought in the humanities than the sciences—"who wants loyalty oaths, etc., instituted in the humanities?"—or because there seems to be no objective way to determine who is worthy of support. "I do not think meaningful review of 'research in humanities' is possible in such a way as to satisfy needs for justification of spending federal funds." "In the sciences there are objective standards which furnish some guide to worthwhile projects and people . . . . A scientist needs money for equipment—and if he is good, he deserves it. A scholar in the humanities needs little besides brains—and it is very hard to assess those who have them and those who do not."[14]

Reasons for Aiding the Humanities

The majority of faculty appeared to favor federal aid to the humanities for one or more of the following reasons.

1. Sound science training itself requires a degree of literacy which too many scientists lack; as one philosopher wrote, "it is a waste of money to provide flashy facilities in the sciences for students who can neither read nor write. And isn't a rigorous course in logic and scientific method central in training scientific personnel?" And an English professor, "Everyone assumes that English is essential to all fields . . . and at the same time we do not have enough money to finance the efficient training of English teachers."

2. For the welfare of science and the nation, it was suggested that the danger of cultural barbarism is particularly great among those newly come to power, and the power of science should be tempered with the experience, the wisdom, and the mercy of the humanities. "Scientists untrained in humanistic disciplines and values, like other citizens similarly limited in their ethical training, can wield power they do not understand for ends and interests contrary to the good of a democratic society."

3. Finally, it was said that the humanities and social sciences are vital to the social health and, indeed, survival of the nation:

> Informed persons in the humanities can only remain in a state of silent dismay when they contemplate political and governmental debates focused upon issues which are not only secondary but, in fact, unreal in many cases. That our public life is now so largely contained within a dream-world is due mainly to the neglect of the humanities. (*From an English scholar.*)

> . . . neglect of the humanities . . . is one of our most crucial national problems . . . . We will lose all our scientific gains if we fail to take early and massive action on this aspect of our lives. (*From an English professor.*)

[14] However, an administrator at a federal science agency comments, "It is just as easy to develop a system of evaluating humanists as it is to evaluate scientists. We are at the stage of development where we are not yet ready for Federal aid to the humanists. When the time arrives a system will develop."

Our country must . . . begin to divert its resources into a study of ways and means of developing mature citizens . . . It is people who manufacture and set off bombs. (*From a psychologist.*)

I think the long-range national interest is seriously endangered by the imbalance between government funds used for the sciences and the lack of funds for the humanities. This imbalance merely accelerates the instability of a society that has failed to adjust to the impact of the industrial, technological, and scientific revolutions of the 20th Century. Neither scientists nor technicians will resolve the dilemma of the arms race, the meaning of human existence, and the nature of man's capacity for self-destruction. (*From a historian.*)

The preceding arguments display a rather frantic tone and excessive claims. More modest and more convincing are two other reasons.

4. Certain humanistic knowledge is useful:

The emphasis on science and particularly applied science has been a natural response to our national technological crisis, but for the long pull we had better have people trained in the languages, geography, and cultural traditions of the rest of the world. We must meet the challenge of world leadership by training leaders, not merely technicians. (*From a historian.*)

5. The humanities are important *in their own right,* regardless of any possible usefulness—indeed, despite the assured uselessness of most painting, poetry, and cuneiform inscriptions. They are important simply to our dignity and self-respect and to the quality of our civilization. As an English professor wrote:

Would it be altogether ridiculous to suggest that the study of language and literature, and specifically of American literature, might be as much in the national interest as the study of science and technology? Or, to put it another way, that the liberal arts *are* the civilization we are committed to support and defend?

There is, in addition, a powerful practical reason for some form of aid to the humanities and social sciences: to preserve the integrity and viability of higher educational institutions as presently constituted (or, in the words of Title X of the National Defense Education Act, to "strengthen the educational programs and objectives of the institutions of higher education"). Government research programs have cut university liberal arts faculties in two in terms of income, teaching load, and, most important, status and *esprit de corps.*

We cannot establish that the consequences have been bad for the quality of instruction in the humanities; although many people think so, we could find no clear evidence of this, nor did the humanists responding to our questionnaire believe this to be true. But they have been bad for morale, and bad for the faculty's sense of community and shared educational purpose. An institution, like a nation, cannot long endure half slave and half free. The breach between the humanists who teach more hours for less pay and the scientists who teach less hours for more pay has been opened by federal programs (or, to be more accurate, by historical forces which have affected federal programs and the academic market).

In the following two chapters, we will examine in more detail what has happened to faculty teaching loads and income in the sciences, social sciences, and humanities.

SUMMARY

The profound impact of federal research programs upon scientific knowledge and, hence, the scientific curriculum, can be evaluated only by specialists in each field. However, imbalances in these programs are manifest to any observer. Imbalances within fields affect the social sciences more than the natural sciences (which enjoy greater and broader aid) or humanities (where aid is negligible). The major imbalance within the social sciences has been a concentration on quantitative and putatively scientific approaches leading to a gain in rigor but a frequent narrowing of perspective and understanding.

Most faculty regarded the concentration of federal funds in the sciences and relative neglect of the humanities as against both the interest of their institution and the long-run national interest, but a majority of the scientists held this concentration to be in the present national interest. Among the reasons advanced for federal aid to the humanities, the more persuasive are their practical usefulness to the nation and their importance to the quality of our civilization. Aid is needed to preserve the integrity of liberal arts institutions as communities of scholars with equal status embracing with equal ardor the entire realm of knowledge.

CHAPTER 7

Teaching Loads

ALL THE EVIDENCE we have gathered by interview and questionnaire indicates that the average teaching load of university scientists is less than that of humanists. There almost seems to be an equation between scientific distinction or marketability and the smallness of teaching loads, and the stories of Nobel Prize winners being lured from one university to another by the promise of no teaching at all are not entirely without foundation.

The basic reasons are the stronger market position of the scientist, his greater interest in research, and his markedly greater success at getting money for it. When the government is prepared to pay for that portion of a scientist's time which he devotes to research, there is a natural incentive for the scientist and university administrators to work out an arrangement whereby he teaches less and devotes the time he has saved to government-financed research.

A scientist whose salary is $9,000 for the nine-month academic year and who does half-time work on a government project may receive $4,500 from the departmental teaching budget and the same amount from a National Science Foundation grant or an Office of Naval Research contract. The unused $4,500 in the teaching budget can be employed in one of three ways: a substitute can be hired for half-time teaching; if another $4,500 can be picked up in similar fashion from a colleague's research budget, the substitute can be hired for full-time teaching; or, most likely, the new teacher will also be engaged on a part-research, part-teaching schedule. The net effect of all variations is a larger staff that teaches, on average, less than is the rule in departments without government research funds.

RELATIVE TEACHING LOADS, 1960-61

The teaching loads prevailing in the academic year 1960-61 at the thirty-six institutions in our study are summarized in Table 7-1, which indicates that:

1. At the universities, scientists had a lower teaching load than humanists but at the liberal arts colleges, a higher load. In part, the higher load in the colleges is due to their lack of federal research money. However, the lack of research money is, in part, also due to the greater difficulty college scientists have in getting their teaching load reduced so as to conduct research, because of:

the colleges' greater emphasis on teaching as the scientist's principal obligation for his bread and butter;

the stricter controls operating against "special treatment";

the relatively greater number and power of humanists;

the lack of graduate assistants capable of taking responsibility for laboratory sections;

the greater difficulty of finding substitute teachers on a temporary basis and of ensuring a sufficiently steady flow of research funds into a small department to justify the permanent enlargement of the staff;

the lack of equipment, facilities, graduate students, and, perhaps, of the talent necessary for the kinds of research federal agencies sponsor.

2. The teaching load of social scientists was virtually identical with that of scientists at the universities and considerably lower at the colleges studied, so that, on this test, they emerged as the more favored group. We put this down partly to the large number of psychologists and economists in our population of social scientists, and of biologists and chemists (who are less highly priced and favored than physicists and mathematicians in the academic market) in our population of scientists. It is also consistent with other evidence showing that social scientists are younger and more active in research than scientists at Group III; are also younger, at all ranks, in Group II; and, in both Groups II and III, have

TABLE 7-1. *Mean Classroom Hours per Week, 1960-61*[a]

Field and Institution Group	Mean Classroom Hours		Percent Under-graduate
	Total	Under-graduate	
Total			
Group I	6.8	4.6	68%
Group II	8.6	6.1	71
Group III	11.5	11.3	98
Sciences			
Group I	6.0	3.8	63
Group II	8.1	5.0	62
Group III	12.7	12.4	98
Social Sciences			
Group I	6.4	3.9	61
Group II	7.9	5.4	68
Group III	10.1	10.0	99
Humanities			
Group I	8.3	7.4	77
Group II	9.9	7.8	79
Group III	11.2	11.2	100

[a] Representing replies to two questions: (1) "How many classroom hours per week do *you* teach, on the average?" (a previous question had specified "Exclude hours spent on thesis supervision and independent study courses") and (2) "How many of these are in undergraduate courses?"

Where different hours were reported in different semesters, an average value was calculated; courses admitting both undergraduates and graduates were weighted equally unless (as was often the case) additional information was supplied about the proportion of undergraduate and graduate students, enabling more accurate weighting; remedial courses which do not award graduate-level credit were classified as undergraduate courses even if taken by graduate students.

advanced more rapidly than scientists to upper ranks. Finally, university social scientists are about as heavily involved as scientists in graduate-level instruction, in contrast to humanists who are more fully engaged in undergraduate teaching (see not only Table 7-1 but also Appendix B, Table B-6, columns 1 and 2); and graduate instruction commonly brings a reduction in faculty classroom hours.

3. The disparity between the mean teaching load in universities and that in colleges is markedly greater in the sciences than in the social sciences or humanities. For example, college scientists taught, on average, 6.7 more hours a week than the scientists in Group I universities, whereas college social scientists taught 3.7 more hours, and college humanists only 2.9 more hours than their associates in Group I univer-

sities. Undoubtedly this partly accounts for the special difficulty colleges have had in recruiting scientists.

4. University humanists teach relatively more undergraduate classes than do scientists or social scientists.

5. Universities with a large volume of federal research funds have lower average teaching loads than universities with less federal money, and the latter, in turn, have lower loads than the colleges. The relation, again, is doubtless circular: universities with traditionally low teaching loads were more readily able to undertake major research expansion, and the money received from the government enabled them to reduce their teaching loads still further.

TEACHING LOADS OF 1954-55 AND 1960-61 COMPARED

Additional insight into recent changes in teaching loads is afforded by a question we asked faculty about the relation of current teaching loads in their departments to those prevailing in 1954-55. The percent of faculty resident in the institutions for at least five years who indicated that average teaching loads had been reduced in their department since 1954-55 was as follows:

Field	Group I	Group II	Group III
Sciences	40%	41%	52%
Social Sciences	35	32	35
Humanities	29	21	53
Total	35%	32%	45%

At the universities, it is evident that teaching loads had been reduced for relatively more scientists than humanists. However, teaching load reductions were reported far more frequently by college than by university faculty, particularly in the humanities and sciences. The picture in the humanities is most striking of all, for while roughly a quarter of the humanists at the universities reported a reduction in their teaching load, over half of those at the colleges did so. It may be surmised that the colleges have been forced into these reductions by the competition for faculty, but this explanation does not suffice, because as many college humanists as scientists reported teaching load reductions, and clearly the competition for faculty is keener in the sciences. Is this an instance of equity, and of the power of humanists outweighing strictly market forces?

IT MUST BE STRESSED that these statistics (for both 1960-61 and 1954-55) refer to formal hours of scheduled classroom teaching and not to the time spent on course preparation, thesis supervision, or independent study courses. The allocation of total faculty time between teaching, research, and other activities will be discussed subsequently. Nor do the statistics reflect the relative difficulty of different courses, the number of preparations required, the proper weight to be given laboratory hours, the total number of graduate and undergraduate students handled, and other factors important to the fair evaluation of what constitutes an equal amount of work in different departments.[1]

It should be repeated, therefore, and with emphasis, that the fact that a university scientist *teaches* less than a humanist does not mean that he *works* less. If anything, our impression is that he works more. This impression may be mistaken; lodged by its side is another impression of the overworked humanist, usually a junior member of his department, with piles of student themes and thankless chores delegated by his senior colleagues, who spend their time in ways more professionally and personally rewarding. (A humanist comments: "The scientist works as hard [as the humanist], but avoids more of the drudgery—freshman sections, grading exams, marking essays, etc.")

In any event, the model scientist seems to work around the clock and around the year, and to encourage his best students to work beside him in the lab. The model humanist is less interested in knowledge than in wisdom and, correctly or merely conveniently, is more relaxed about it. He may be interested in his students as persons, but not as workmates. His conception of a college education still retains something of the classical tradition of gentlemanly learning and "character building." The "gentleman" was accustomed to leisure and comfort and went to

[1] The relative time which the scientists and humanists devoted to teaching and research during the academic year 1960-61 is given most succinctly in Appendix B, Table B-6. This shows, for example, that at Group I institutions, scientists spent only 26.4 percent of their time on undergraduate teaching; humanists, fully 44.5 percent. But the scientists put in slightly more time on graduate teaching than did humanists (19.5 percent as against 17.8 percent) and much more time on research (35.5 percent as against 18.8 percent).

school to acquire, not practical knowledge but the acquaintances, manners, arts, and accent of his class. Even in the radically different contemporary American milieu, the humanist's attitude to the scientist still reflects a trace of the gentleman's aversion to the arriviste.

SUMMARY

Scientists teach fewer classroom hours than humanists at our universities, but more at our colleges; social scientists teach less than humanists at the colleges, and about as little as scientists at the universities. Classroom hours, however, should not be confused with *working* hours. University scientists probably work as many or more hours than university humanists; but they put in proportionately less time teaching (especially, teaching undergraduates), and proportionately more on research.

CHAPTER 8

Faculty Income

AT LEAST THREE COMPONENTS of faculty income have been significantly affected by federal programs: academic year salaries; summer salaries; and additional income from consultation, investments, and other sources. We will examine each of these sources of income in turn.

ACADEMIC YEAR SALARIES

Scientists tend to be paid more than humanists, to be hired at a higher rank, to be promoted more rapidly, and therefore to earn more at a given age even where there is a fixed salary scale for each rank. Actually, salary differentials start earlier, in graduate school, where science students receive more, larger, and better kinds of stipends than students in the social sciences and humanities. And the age/salary gap starts in graduate school too, since the dearth of fellowships and research assistantships in the humanities obliges students to accept teaching assistantships and other work that lengthens the time it takes them to get their Ph.D.'s and to start their academic careers.

In 1954 (the figures are deplorably old, but there are apparently none better and more recent) 18 percent of graduate students in the physical sciences but less than 0.2 percent of those in the humanities held a federal stipend; all together, 31 percent of physical science students but only 8 percent of those in the humanities held a fellowship or research assistantship from any source. (The fellowship picture has since been somewhat improved by the expansion of the Woodrow Wilson Fellow-

TABLE 8-1. *Mean Age of Faculty by Type of Institution, Field, and Rank as of May/June 1961*

Field and Institution Group	Mean Age				
	All Ranks	Professor	Associate Professor	Assistant Professor	Instructor
Total					
Group I[a]	42.3 (1,838)[b]	50.2 (795)	41.4 (397)	34.0 (451)	31.1 (194)
Group II	42.5 (1,105)	51.2 (382)	41.4 (315)	36.0 (301)	33.1 (107)
Group III	42.1 (536)	52.6 (179)	42.3 (136)	34.3 (151)	31.4 (70)
Sciences					
Group I[a]	41.4 (819)	48.7 (378)	40.2 (170)	33.4 (203)	28.4 (67)
Group II	42.2 (443)	50.1 (166)	40.3 (139)	34.8 (109)	33.2 (29)
Group III	41.7 (175)	53.1 (57)	41.7 (42)	34.0 (60)	29.7 (16)
Social Sciences					
Group I	41.8 (495)	50.3 (217)	39.6 (112)	32.7 (119)	30.7 (47)
Group II	41.1 (298)	49.9 (102)	39.2 (88)	34.7 (91)	32.2 (17)
Group III	41.0 (125)	51.3 (41)	40.3 (33)	33.4 (37)	32.5 (14)
Humanities					
Group I	44.1 (524)	53.0 (200)	45.0 (115)	36.2 (129)	33.5 (80)
Group II	44.1 (364)	54.0 (114)	45.4 (88)	38.4 (101)	33.2 (61)
Group III	42.9 (236)	52.9 (81)	44.0 (61)	35.1 (54)	31.7 (40)

[a] The figures for "all ranks" in Total, Group I, and Sciences, Group I, include one respondent not classified by rank.
[b] The number of cases is indicated in parentheses.

ship program and the initiation of graduate fellowships under the National Defense Education Act.) A 1958 study showed that 53 percent of graduate students in the physical sciences but only 7 percent in the humanities had received some financial support, such as a research assistantship, requiring work that contributed greatly to their degree.[1] As a result, six years is the median time elapsing between bachelor and doctoral degrees in the physical sciences, ten years in the humanities, and six years is also the difference between the median age of physical scientists (29) and humanists (35) upon receipt of the doctorate.[2]

While we do not have the data to check on salary differences between fields at a given age, we can report some data on the separate questions of ages and salaries.

Mean Age of Faculty, by Field

The data on age presented in Table 8-1 largely confirm our expectation that scientists are younger than humanists at each academic rank. At both Group I and Group II universities, the mean age of scientists was uniformly less than that of humanists (the sole exception occurring among instructors at Group II universities). A similar situation prevailed in the liberal arts colleges, although the age gap between the two fields was there reduced and, among full professors, eliminated.

In addition to age at completion of the doctorate, a major factor governing the average age of faculty is probably the relative stability of faculty and of departmental size. The average age of new and expanding departments will decline insofar as they hire relatively young men (who cost less and last longer), whereas stable departments can only age. This is very likely the explanation of why we found the social scientists to be younger than either the humanists or scientists at the middle ranks of assistant and associate professor. We know that the enrollment in the social sciences has been expanding relative to that in the humanities and the sciences (see Appendix A, Table A-6), and it is a fair inference that

---

[1] The 1954 figures are from National Science Foundation, *Graduate Student Enrollment and Support in American Universities and Colleges, 1954* (1957), p. 35; the 1958 figures, from a National Opinion Research Center study reported by Bernard Berelson in *Graduate Education in the United States* (McGraw-Hill, 1960), p. 149.

[2] National Research Council data cited by Berelson, *ibid.*, p. 157.

this expansion has been accompanied by a substantial expansion in faculty size.

Academic Year Salaries, by Field

The scattered available data on regular academic year salaries show a tendency for scientists to receive more than humanists, particularly at the level of full professor, but the differential is often slight and a careful study would identify many institutions, departments, and ranks in which the average salary of humanists was above that of scientists. The recent situation at two distinguished private universities in Group I is reported in Appendix A, Tables A-11 and A-12. At both institutions, full professors in the sciences received 5 to 6 percent more than those in the humanities, while at lower ranks the average salary of scientists was close to, or even slightly below that of humanists.

The top salaries paid by several major universities go not only to scientists but also to psychologists, economists, and a few humanists. Thus, the nine best-paid liberal arts professors at a leading private university were in the following departments: chemistry (two), physics, mathematics, economics (two), psychology, history, and international relations; the twenty-eight best-paid faculty at the same university included ten scientists (mathematicians, physicists, and chemists, one biologist, no earth scientist), eleven social scientists (all psychologists and economists), and seven humanists. These figures, of course, exclude the professional schools. Including them, the current hierarchy of top salaries appears to be: (1) clinical areas of medicine, (2) law, (3) engineering and physical sciences (mathematics, physics, chemistry), (4) economics and psychology, (5) other social sciences, earth sciences, and basic (nonclinical) biological sciences, (6) humanities. One graduate dean at a southwestern university observed:

> In general, you do pay more for scientists than for anyone else, whether they are first class or not; you pay as much for the first class people in the humanities as in the sciences, but by and large the people in the humanities are not so well off.

The federal government has, of course, influenced this picture by increasing the demand for scientists and hence the salaries they can command. In addition the government policy of allowing faculty to be paid from federal funds for that portion of their time which they devote to federally-financed research has served to raise the pay of scientists in two ways: (1) some institutions and some federal agencies permit research time to be reimbursed at a rate higher than teaching time; (2) even where higher rates are prohibited, as they often are, the fact that the university need not pay all of a scientist's salary but only half or three quarters (the remaining fraction being drawn from federal funds) probably tends to raise his basic academic year salary.[3]

The important policy implications of these practices will be discussed further in Part Three, Chapter 15. Here it may be useful to indicate something about their present extent.

HIGHER RATES OF PAY FROM FEDERAL FUNDS. Incremental payments are frequently condemned by both university and government spokesmen. A committee of the National Science Board recommended in 1958 "that no Federal agency agree to reimburse institutions for salaries of faculty members engaged in Government-sponsored research at a rate in excess of the university rate."[4] A similar policy statement was adopted in 1960 by both the Federal Council on Science and Technology and the President's Science Advisory Committee, and, subsequently, there has apparently been some tightening of Department of Defense regulations in this regard.

Nevertheless, payments in excess of an institution's rate are not uncommon in clinical medicine (where salary supplementation up to 100 percent is permitted from research funds as a substitute for clinical fees the faculty member is otherwise permitted to earn) and in engineering (where the formula for salary supplementation on research funds often represents the time a faculty member may devote to consultation). These practices in professional schools make it more difficult for the institution or the government to restrain similar demands from prized scientists in other graduate departments, and at least a third of the universities in our study occasionally permit some supplementation on federal research funds for *some* of these scientists.

The facts are difficult to determine with accuracy, for the definitions

[3] To put an extreme case: if a university had no scientists on federal projects in 1955, but by 1965 all of its scientists receive half their salary from federal funds, it could double the salary of every scientist in that period, without the expenditure of an extra penny (although any increase in the number of scientists occasioned by the reduction of teaching hours would require additional university expenditures).

[4] National Science Foundation, *Government-University Relationships in Federally Sponsored Scientific Research and Development* (1958), p. 24.

of basic academic year salary are highly varied, as are the methods of apportioning time between the teaching and research budgets and of calculating permissible additional compensation. Supplementation appeared to be more common at Group II than Group I universities, and at more penurious institutions of lesser prestige where it helps to compensate for low base salaries. Formulas cited include a 10 to 50 percent increment (25 percent is most frequent, particularly on classified military research) for "overload" above a "full-time" workweek of, for example, forty hours; or a one sixth (sometimes, one fifth) "time and energy" allowance deriving from an approved consulting time of one day in five or six (to which some enterprising professors add Sundays and holidays); this may also be translated into a quota of "thirty-five hours a month" or, at one Group II university, up to twenty hours a week which may be devoted to research or consulting; the latter quota can double a man's salary.

The opposition of influential government agencies and the improvement of academic salaries have evidently reduced the frequency of supplemental payments in recent years, at least among university faculty outside of professional schools. One well-informed university business officer suggested that only three or four of the leading fifty universities (leading in their volume of federal R&D funds) now continue the practice, but we believe this estimate is low. The "Harrell Formula" permits supplemental payments for faculty engaged in classified research, and even the National Science Foundation, which often represents the viewpoint of the "pure" scientist against the "applied" scientist and engineer (whose spokesman is more likely to be the Department of Defense) has sanctioned supplementation for faculty attached to research centers.[5]

[5] The ". . . 'Harrell Formula' developed in 1951 by representatives of thirteen universities . . . provided for *permissive* extra payment to those faculty members working on secret government contracts. A schedule of extra payments was developed, based on the individual's budgeted salary and with a maximum of $150 monthly." See Herbert E. Longenecker, *University Faculty Compensation Policies and Practices in the United States* (University of Illinois Press, 1956), pp. 108-109; see also p. 123. The National Science Foundation has specified that its recommendation against supplementary payments "should not apply to those faculty members granted leaves of absence to serve full time at research centers. In the case of faculty members serving part time at research centers [an arrangement that prevails at many centers located on or near campus], the rule should apply to that portion of time not charged to the center." (NSF, *Government-University Relationships . . .* , p. 24.)

REGULAR RATES OF PAY FROM FEDERAL FUNDS. Charging a faculty member's salary to federal project funds for the time he devotes to research has become more common as the budgets of federal science agencies have risen. It is ironic that Congress, during the years that it has been so averse to subsidizing teachers' salaries, should so readily have accepted the present system under which the government is paying part or all of the salary of an increasing number of faculty at leading educational institutions.

This practice is now common in some departments at all twenty-four universities in our study, but is firmly resisted by other departments and has not yet spread to half the colleges in Group III. Fortunately, there are several statistical measures of its prevalence.

At a private Group I university, which has made a careful study of the matter, the number of faculty whose salaries were charged in full or in part to federal agencies increased from 104 in 1953 to 151 in 1959; in the latter year, $805,000 in faculty salaries or 9 percent of the total faculty salaries of $8.6 million was paid by the government. At a smaller private university, $229,000 or 6 percent of total academic year faculty salaries was charged to the government in 1959-60 compared to 3 percent in 1949-50. At a large public university in Group I, on the other hand, only 1.4 percent of the teaching staff (excluding those at the medical school and agricultural experiment station) received any part of their salary from the government in 1960-61—but even that small fraction amounted to $24,000 a month.

Of the 10,468 full-time faculty members of the U.S. medical schools, 2,771 or 25.5 percent received some or all of their salary from federal research or training grants in 1959-60; a year later, 3,549 or 31.9 percent of the 11,111 full-time members of medical faculties received at least part of their salary from federal sources.[6] These figures turn out to be very close to those for Group I scientists, 24.6 percent of whom indicated that part or all of their regular salary during the academic year 1960-61 was drawn from federal funds. In contrast, only 4 percent of the humanists at the same institutions reported that any fraction of their salary came from the federal government. (See Table 8-2.) While

[6] *Journal of the American Medical Association,* Nov. 12, 1960, p. 1438, and Nov. 11, 1961, p. 633. The proportion of full-time medical faculty receiving half or more of their salary from federal funds rose from 13.4 percent in 1958-59 to 17.8 percent in 1960-61.

such responses to a general questionnaire in which detailed definitions of "salary" and "federal funds" were not given are not as reliable as the statistics an accountant might produce after examining the institutions' books, they do delineate the fields and types of schools where federal funds are having a direct impact on faculty salaries. (As Table 8-2 shows, at Group II universities as many social scientists as scientists—and at Group III colleges, relatively more—received part of their salary from the federal government. Is this partly because the small federal programs in these fields are relatively more dispersed than the larger programs in the sciences?)

TABLE 8-2.   *Proportion of Academic Year Salaries Drawn from Federal Funds, 1960-61*

"Was any of your regular salary during the academic year [1960-61] drawn from federal funds?"

Field and Institution Group	Percent of Faculty Replying				Number
	"Yes"			"No"	
	Half or More of Salary	Less Than Half of Salary	Total		
Total					
Group I	6.4%	9.2%	15.6%	84.4%	1,836
Group II	5.2	6.0	11.2	88.8	1,112
Group III	1.3	1.9	3.2	96.8	538
Sciences					
Group I	10.6	14.0	24.6	75.4	808
Group II	6.3	8.7	15.0	85.0	446
Group III	—	2.9	2.9	97.1	175
Social Sciences					
Group I	5.0	8.2	13.3	86.7	498
Group II	8.7	6.7	15.4	84.6	299
Group III	4.0	2.4	6.4	93.6	125
Humanities					
Group I	1.3	2.6	4.0	96.0	530
Group II	1.1	2.2	3.3	96.7	367
Group III	.8	.8	1.7	98.3	238

INSTITUTIONAL PAY SCALES AND FEDERAL INCOME. A final point which deserves a moment's attention is the relation between the

TABLE 8-3. *Median Salary of All Faculty at Three Groups of Institutions, 1959-60, by Rank*[a]

Rank	Eleven Universities in		Eight Colleges in Group III
	Group I	Group II	
All Ranks	$ 7,750	$7,250	$7,000
Professor	11,250	9,750	8,750
Associate Professor	8,750	7,750	7,000
Assistant Professor	6,750	6,250	6,250
Instructor	5,250	5,250	5,250

[a] Source: National Education Association survey of salaries and salary schedules in universities, colleges, and junior colleges, 1959-60. Salaries were restricted to full-time teachers on the basis of nine months of service. The median, of course, dampens extremes that would receive greater weight in an arithmetic mean.

Data were not available for one institution in both Groups I and II, and for four colleges in Group III. The inclusion of these schools would, in all probability, widen the disparity between salaries in Groups I and II, but would not significantly affect the medians in Group III.

amount of money received from the government and an institution's over-all pay scale. We cannot prove and do not assert that a direct or simple relationship obtains between these two factors. Historically, it may be that the wealthier private institutions and the public universities with more generous legislatures, by paying better salaries, attracted better faculty, who, in turn, were sought out by federal administrators and won out in competitive tests of talent. Probably it has worked both ways for different schools: the government has benefited from some schools' century-old investments in learning, while both these schools and others have benefited from the government's more recent and narrower interest in knowledge. There is also the simple fact of size that tends to be positively correlated with both salaries and federal funds.[7]

Be all of this as it may, the institutions with the largest volume of federal funds now pay the highest salaries at all ranks but instructor, and particularly at the levels of associate and full professor. To the facts set forth in Table 8-3, we should add two points manifest in the

[7] Louis D'Amico notes that in 1959-60, "The size of average faculty salaries was directly related to the size of the institution." See "Salaries of College and University Professors by Rank, Institutional Size, and Control," *The Educational Record*, Vol. 41 (October 1960), p. 305.

supporting data: the top salaries in each rank tend also to be highest at Group I universities; and the salaries at the wealthier and better-known colleges compare very favorably with those at Group II universities.[8] On this evidence, if the best independent liberal arts colleges are losing out to the universities in salary competition (as is frequently charged), they are losing only to a very small and select group of universities.

THE PRECEDING DISCUSSION of salary differentials resulting from federal programs may be summarized briefly.

Supplementation due to salary payments by the federal government at a higher rate than the faculty member's basic academic salary is frowned on but, in fact, permitted by the government. The practice is confounded by the intricacies of measuring an academic man's "full-time" obligation to his institution. Nevertheless, it is probably sanctioned in most, if not all, departments of engineering and clinical medicine and, outside of such professional departments occurs occasionally at more universities than is generally realized, but usually then affects few persons.

Paying part or all of the salary of faculty from federal funds, which is increasingly prevalent at major universities, tends to raise the salary of these and other faculty. This practice and market pressures have opened a gap—but a surprisingly small one—between the academic year salaries of scientists and humanists at each academic rank. (Analysis of salaries by age would probably show a wider gap.)

SUMMER SALARIES

The point at which the scientists' income shoots ahead of humanists' is in the addition to their nine months' academic year salary they com-

---

[8] In 1961-62 the average nine-month salary of full-time faculty at Groups II and III was virtually identical—$8,887 and $8,889, respectively; the comparable figure for Group I was $10,141. Source: American Association of University Professors, *The Economic Status of the Profession, 1961-62: Annual Report by Committee Z* (April 28, 1962, mimeo). Salaries included specified fringe benefits; the data excluded faculty in medical and dental schools, evening colleges, extension programs, and summer sessions. The averages are based on data for eleven institutions in Group I—the mean salary for two being derived by extrapolation from 1960-61; eleven institutions in Group II; and nine in Group III. Inclusion of the missing schools would probably serve to raise slightly the average for all Groups, particularly Group III.

monly draw from the government for engaging in "full-time" research during the summer months. The quotation marks are not intended to indicate that scientists do not actually put in full time. Indeed, most of them put in much more than the forty hours accepted in many occupations as a full-time workweek, not only during the summer but throughout the year (despite the jokes about the man who "lives it up" on a grant or the mathematician who does his research at the beach). But there is something nominal and unmeasurable about "full-time" service in any profession, and it often appears that summer compensation is, in fact, simply a convenient way to increase a scientist's salary without breaking existing pay scales.

The scientist is, then, engaged on his research in the summer, but, in many cases, he has also been working at it (perhaps at a reduced pace) throughout the academic year; the humanist, of course, who is similarly engaged in summer research generally gets no money for it. Only at colleges do the bulk of scientists confine their federally-financed work to the summer months. We asked faculty if, during the summer of 1960 or the 1960-61 academic year (excluding the summer of 1961) any part of their work—research, teaching, study, or consulting—was "financed" by the federal government, a question broad enough to embrace personal salaries, stipends for student assistants, equipment, and other forms of help. The scientists replied "yes," as follows:

Institution Group	Summer 1960	Academic Year 1960-61	Both	Total	Number
I	21%	11%	68%	100%	630
II	21	13	67	100	312
III	60	4	36	100	89

Summer Salary Formulas Reflect Market Forces

The fictive or, should we say, market aspect of summer reimbursement is particularly clear when an institution with a general rule (for instance, permitting extra compensation for two summer months, or two ninths of a man's academic year salary) is forced to break its own rule and allow more generous compensation (say, three ninths) for members of a department who are in a particularly strong bargaining position. Several instances of this sort were recounted in our interviews.

Physicists at a well-known public university were said to have forced a change from two tenths to two ninths in their summer compensation by threatening a mass move; at a famous private institution with a general two ninths formula, mathematicians were permitted three ninths; and at a poorer private university where a two tenths formula prevailed, some scientists were permitted to get more, because, as the research administrator frankly stated, "We have to do what is necessary to meet outside offers." Departmental differences in summer reimbursement may be reflected in—or reflect—similar differences in agency policy. Thus the Atomic Energy Commission's Division of Biology and Medicine has generally paid only two months' salary for summer work, while the Division of Research (which deals with physical scientists) has paid three months'.

Extra compensation for summer research occurs at all institutions in our study, except where salaries are already on a twelve-month basis. Reimbursement "up to three months" or three ninths of the academic salary is the formula employed by seven institutions in both Groups I and II and by six colleges in Group III; two months or two ninths is the second most common rule; and other fractions like ten weeks or two tenths follow with diminishing frequency.

Manipulation of the academic year to raise the formula for summer reimbursement on government projects is another way to raise salaries. Assuredly, this is not the only motive for such changes: a shift from a year-round operation to a conventional semester system was natural after the war, and it is claimed that the shift to a quarter system from semesters allows an institution to handle more students per faculty member. But the former change also enables an institution to charge the government for two months' summer salaries where no charges had been made before; and the latter, to charge for three summer months instead of two. Arguments are also made for raising the amount of summer compensation by adding academic holidays, and, where a man is on a twelve-month appointment, to permit compensation for his one-month holiday. The following summary of a discussion among University of California faculty could be echoed on many campuses:

> The request was . . . made that supplements for summer research in addition to basic salary be approved in the amount of three ninths rather than two ninths of the annual pay, and that the right of those on eleven-month contracts to receive an additional one eleventh of their salary for summer research be reaffirmed. It was noted that this small amount of

extra pay is often the deciding factor in obtaining or holding young faculty members in competition with employers outside this University.[9]

Such changes in the formula for summer salaries tend to have one thing in common: they increase, not decrease, scientists' yearly income.

Summer Opportunities Vary Markedly by Field

All universities and many but not all colleges in our study have programs of summer instruction which provide employment and additional income for some of their faculty. However, only part—on average, little more than a third—of the regular faculty are needed to staff these programs; the programs generally run for a shorter period than that for which reimbursement is permitted on research projects; and the rate of reimbursement for teaching may be less than that for research.[10]

The lack of summer research opportunities on campus leads many scientists at smaller institutions to spend their summers working on research projects at large universities or at such government-owned installations as the Oak Ridge Institute for Nuclear Studies or the Argonne or Brookhaven National Laboratories which operate special programs to encourage summer participation by faculty. One unfavorable consequence of this, and of the fact that science faculty can generally get more money for summer research than for summer teaching, is the difficulty which some institutions report in adequately staffing their regular summer teaching program or special summer teaching institutes in the sciences. The problem is particularly acute at institutions with a low pay scale for summer teaching, as in the South. In this respect (and others) federal research programs compete too successfully for manpower and conflict with the goals of federal science education programs. Much good would be accomplished by a smoother meshing of the policies and goals of these rival programs, which might

[9] *The University in a Period of Growth,* Proceedings of the University of California Sixteenth All-University Faculty Conference, University of California, March 1961, p. 40.

[10] The foregoing observations are based upon replies to several questions about summer teaching opportunities and salaries in the National Education Association's survey of salaries and salary schedules in universities, colleges, and junior colleges, 1959-60. Eight universities in Group I and five in Group II indicated that summer teaching was paid for at the same rate as during the academic year; one university in Group I and five in Group II, that their summer rate was lower.

well start *within* agencies operating both types of programs—notably, the National Science Foundation and the National Institutes of Health.

We did not collect statistics on the relative number of scientists, social scientists, and humanists drawing summer salaries from federal funds, as the point was so obvious it did not seem necessary to prove it. It may be noted that in fiscal year 1960, 65 percent of principal investigators on NSF grants received reimbursement for their summer salaries. A leading private university which examined the situation on its campus as of 1960 found that 67 percent of its scientists but only 14 percent of its social scientists and none of its humanists received two ninths additions to their academic year salaries that summer. Another study at the same university showed that the percentages of faculty (rank of assistant professor and up) holding summer 1960 research appointments for at least a month were: scientists, 59 percent; social scientists, 29 percent; humanists, 4 percent. (For percentages in selected departments, see Appendix A, Table A-13.)

For some reason, we were impressed most of all by a chart we only glimpsed, which showed the relative salaries of another university's physical scientists, biological scientists, social scientists, and humanists, at each rank. This was briefly exhibited by the university president who, to protect the confidentiality of his salaries, said, "I don't *want* you to study it." Its immediately striking point was the scientists' advantage in yearly income over humanists, in part because of their academic year salaries, but in greater measure because of the summer research stipends they alone received from the government. The president had had it prepared for his trustees, to impress them with the importance of raising a special sum to provide summer stipends for faculty not aided by the government, a direction that other earnest administrators have taken in an effort to preserve the harmony and integrity of their liberal arts faculty.

Some who see little amiss in prevailing salary differentials suggest that where scientists lead, humanists follow to the ultimate benefit of all. This is frequently but not invariably true; where it is true, it is attributable not to any iron law, but to concurrent market pressures, faculty pressures, and the good judgment and financial exertions of administrative officers and trustees. The everpresent danger remains of a rupture in the income, the status, and hence the mutual educational function of scientists and humanists. Abraham Flexner's remarks about medical faculty decades ago are applicable to the present situation of scientists:

> To the extent that the medical faculty command salaries at a higher level, the good fortune of the teacher of anatomy or pathology is a wholesome influence; for it tends to elevate the general level. On the other hand, the medical faculty cannot be permitted to become an aristocracy; it cannot advance too far ahead of other faculties without creating ill-feeling on the part of colleagues, and such difficulties for administrators as may in the end make them as keen to drop medicine as they once were to take it up. The rest of the university cannot be forgotten.[11]

CONSULTING AND OTHER INCOME

From the Government

Clearly, there are far fewer faculty involved in paid consulting for the government (either directly for a federal agency or indirectly, on a federally-financed project at their own or another institution) than in government-sponsored research. Still, consulting opportunities are much more common for scientists than humanists and, to that extent, add to the disparity in yearly incomes traceable to federal programs. It was a surprise to learn from our survey that the frequency of consulting among social scientists was similar to that among scientists (see Chapter 6, Table 6-3). This must reflect the extensive consulting by economists (at federal agencies with economic, regulatory, and manpower functions), and by clinical psychologists (often at nearby hospitals, on funds derived from the Veterans Administration and the Public Health Service).

"Indirect" consulting on federal projects is limited by institutional regulations. Consulting on a research project of a colleague in the same department was sanctioned by only one university in Group I but by four universities in Group II; on a research project of another department, again by only one Group I university but by six Group II universities. Most institutions placed no restrictions of principle—only of time or money—upon consulting at another university or industry. The poorer universities in Group II, it will be noted, here again were some-

[11] Abraham Flexner, *Medical Education* (Macmillan, 1925), pp. 321-322.

what more lenient than the wealthier institutions in Group I in their rules on additional compensation. Rules on consulting tended to be less formalized at Group III institutions because of the colleges' lack of experience with the matter.

Formal limits set by the institution on the time a professor may devote to consulting ranged from one day a month to one day a week, but there was scope for maneuver within any regulation. One college physics professor, for example, interpreted a "day in two weeks" rule to permit two and one half days a week—half of one working day plus Saturday and Sunday. What actually transpires on a campus, of course, is determined not so much by any rule as by the working relationship between a professor and his department chairman and dean, and the degree to which outside activities enhance or reduce the professor's value to the institution.

From Other Sources

Additional income of faculty from (1) consultation with profit-making and nonprofit concerns with a large volume of government contracts, (2) direct contracting with the government through their own nonprofit or profit-making organization, and (3) private investments in the stock market is much bruited in gossip but little studied in fact. Statistically, (1) and (2) affect relatively few members of liberal arts faculties, but, since these few tend to be eminent and influential in their professions, their activities are important in defining the public image of the scientist at some universities as that of a businessman as much as an academician. And the image, of course, is not only the public's—it is shared by many scientists and their students.

At one university, it was observed that this new-won prosperity led many scientists to prefer the company of other successful professional and business people—doctors, lawyers, and businessmen—to that of less affluent academic colleagues, and that scientists' social conversation was more apt to involve the stock market and income tax than intellectual problems. The conflict in attitude and interest between scholars who are business-oriented and those who are academically-oriented is one of the most fundamental cleavages which federal programs (and, of course, our business-oriented society) have engendered on many campuses, and it is a cleavage which divides scientists from their fellow scientists as well as from humanists. (In one interesting case at a private college, the business aspirations of some humanists have served, in a similar manner, to divide the faculty into two hostile factions.)

In November 1961, a subcommittee of the House Armed Services Committee announced an investigation to determine:

> . . . whether university consultants . . . are able to use their inside knowledge on research contracts for personal stock speculations.
>
> Another objective of the inquiry will be to establish whether scientists serving as consultants and advisers to the Government are using their influence and information to help their own universities or industrial employers. . . .
>
> The President's Science Advisory Committee and its numerous subcommittees and panels, for example, have spent much of their time considering individual research projects and making influential recommendations on weapons development. . . .
>
> The result has been to place the scientific advisers and consultants in a position where they can, if they wish, use their advice and information to profit their universities or industrial employers or to make personal gain through stock speculation.[12]

The conflict-of-interest aspect of this investigation is somewhat removed from our present subject. It does, however, point up how far some scientists have moved from their academic isolation of the 1930's (an isolation in which most of their colleagues in the humanities still languish), ostensibly indifferent to and patently unheard by political leaders, to their present position of military, industrial, and political influence. It is only natural that, in their visits to Washington and Wall Street, they should encounter the same conflict-of-interest problems that representatives of other special interest groups, such as businessmen and farmers, have experienced while in public service.

SUMMARY

Just as federal stipends have raised the average income of graduate science students above that of graduate students in the humanities, so federal research funds have raised the average yearly income of science faculty above that of faculty in the humanities. The universities have

[12] *New York Times,* Nov. 19, 1961, Section 1, pp. 1, 57.

managed to maintain a surprising degree of comparability between the academic year salaries of scientists and humanists (yet, even where these are identical, scientists still earn more than humanists by a given age, for the scientists are several years younger at most ranks). However, the universities have been unable to match the supplemental income received by some scientists from government research programs during the academic year and by most scientists from the same source during the summer months. Additional income which many scientists receive from consulting work for the government as well as for nongovernmental organizations (and, in all likelihood, from their greater investments in science-based industry and business) enlarges the difference between the average yearly income of the two groups. Varied lines of evidence suggest that the added income derived by university social scientists from government sources falls in between that received by scientists and humanists, upon whom our discussion has focused.

CHAPTER 9

A Brief Review

THE EFFECTS OF FEDERAL PROGRAMS on the quality and nature of higher education have been varied and uneven—pronounced in some areas but virtually undetectable in others where one would expect them to be marked. On the whole the effects have been decidedly beneficial.

They have been most striking and direct in scientific research and education at a few leading graduate and professional schools and institutes of technology, and most imperceptible and indirect in scholarly work and teaching in the arts and humanities at four- and two-year liberal arts colleges. We have not explored either the tenuous effects at the latter institutions or the pronounced effects at professional schools of medicine, engineering, and agriculture, but have focused on the impact on liberal arts education at two groups of universities, illustrative of those which have received relatively large and small sums, respectively, from the government, and a group of good private colleges.

Federal programs have aided these institutions to improve the quality, increase the numbers, improve the salaries, and reduce the teaching loads of their faculty in the sciences and some social sciences. They have also served to concentrate the number of scientists at leading universities, and one may infer that this has aggravated the difficulties which small colleges are experiencing in attracting new Ph.D.'s in the sciences to their staffs.

Surprisingly, there is no sign that the large sums which the government has invested in the sciences have yet led, nationally, to an increase in the proportion of faculty or students in the sciences, or to an undue concentration of the ablest minds in these fields. However, there are signs of a concentration of the best students at a few famous private universities, and of scientists at leading universities and their affiliated research installations.

By greatly advancing knowledge in the sciences and in some aspects of the social sciences, federal research programs have greatly improved the content of instruction in these fields. Indirectly, however, they have had other and less favorable effects, particularly on undergraduate science education. Their emphasis on research has accelerated the long-standing depreciation of undergraduate education at large universities and the reduction of personal contacts between lower classmen and those professors who are heavily engaged on research. And the numerous attractive stipends that federal research and fellowship programs offer have left only the less able graduate students to instruct undergraduate laboratory and other science sections.

Perhaps the most unfortunate consequence of federal science programs has been the cleavage they have engendered between the status and rewards of faculty in the sciences and humanities. Surely this is the major problem posed for educational institutions by the unbalanced nature of present federal policies and expenditures, and it suggests the desirability of either counterbalancing programs in the humanities or broader forms of institutional aid.

PART TWO

Should Present Funds
Be More Widely Dispersed?

¶ PREFACE • This question has the advantage of dealing with dollars, which are more measurable and less perplexing than educational "quality." However, the jump from the realm of numbers to that of policy—from a description of the present distribution of funds to a statement about how they *should* be distributed—can hardly be made by a set of mathematical procedures which eliminate the need for individual judgment about our scientific, educational, and even our social goals. The function of inquiry, after all, is not to eliminate judgment but to base it on a sounder body of fact.

It should be emphasized that the discussion in Part Two relates to *present* federal programs—which, on a dollar basis, are primarily programs of scientific research and development. The question is, essentially: Should the funds in present federal research and development programs at universities and colleges be distributed more broadly?

This study has not been designed to examine the question of whether the federal government should establish various *new* programs to aid all institutions of higher education or all college-level students. That question has been discussed in a recent Brookings report (1961) by Alice M. Rivlin, *The Role of the Federal Government in Financing Higher Education,* which concludes that expanded federal support for higher education is desirable in the national interest.

Nor can we say anything very constructive about whether federal funds should be more broadly dispersed in order to increase the number of universities of the first rank, a goal said by many to be in the national interest. The President's Science Advisory Committee has stated that "over the next fifteen years the United States should seek to double the number of universities doing generally excellent work in basic research and graduate education."[1] But years ago, James Bryce observed, "There has been much waste of effort and of money in planting several weak colleges where one strong one would have rendered better service,"[2] and there are many today who fear that a broader dispersion of funds may result, not in the creation of additional centers of the highest quality, but in a weakening of the highest standards now maintained by very few institutions.[3]

We will approach the question of the dispersion of funds in established federal programs in three ways.

First, the degree of concentration to be found in these programs, considered both as a whole and individually, will be reviewed (Chapter 10). The objective here is a description of the present situation, together with an analysis of major postwar trends.

Then such objective indices of the quality of students and faculty at our three groups of institutions as we could secure will be examined (Chapter 11). The logic here is that if significant quality differences do indeed emerge, particularly between the universities in Groups I and II, the argument that the concentration of research funds is a consequence of the agencies' emphasis on quality will be substantiated (although this

[1] *Scientific Progress, the Universities, and the Federal Government*, President's Science Advisory Committee (The White House, Nov. 15, 1960), p. 28.

[2] James Bryce, *The American Commonwealth* (Macmillan, 1910), Vol. 2, p. 759.

[3] Cf. the 1960 statement of the Problems and Policies Committee of the American Council on Education (*The Price of Excellence: A Report to Decision-Makers in American Higher Education*, p. 3): "A great waste in higher education comes from the unnecessary duplication of programs, both among and within institutions. Educational costs increase not only with the rise in the number of students but also with the number and kinds of educational programs. A prime source of waste is the initiation of new programs or the continuation of ineffective ones, particularly of a professional and graduate character, while already successful and useful programs are not being employed to their maximum.

"Institutional imperialism and special-interest pressure are among the forces which contribute to such duplications of effort. . . . Additional . . . [programs] which are educationally unnecessary and economically unsound should be resisted by all leaders of opinion."

would not necessarily justify the present *degree* of concentration). If, however, no significant quality differences can be shown between Groups I and II, some interesting further questions can then be posed about the rationale of the present concentration, and the quality argument can be turned around to justify a broader dispersion of funds. This is primarily a statistical inquiry into various indicia of institutional quality, supplemented by some direct quality ratings of the institutions in our study by department chairmen and scientists at two federal agencies.

Thirdly, the academic and administrative factors that appear to be associated with a high degree of involvement in federal research programs will be discussed (Chapter 12). In the course of our interviews and questionnaire analysis, an attempt was made to identify these factors, so that a policy of promoting a broader dispersion of funds could be more realistically formulated.

The conclusions resulting from these three approaches to the question are set forth in Chapter 13.

CHAPTER 10

The Concentration of Funds in Present Federal Programs

CERTAIN INFORMATION necessary to an adequate analysis of the institutional concentration of federal funds is, unfortunately, either nonexistent or unpublished. Federal agencies concerned with higher education are organized to fulfill specific statutory functions, and, as no agency has cognizance of all federal activities affecting educational institutions, none has the information necessary to evaluate these activities on a continuing basis. Indeed, many agencies do not even keep central records of their own activities at particular institutions. Consequently, the National Science Foundation has repeatedly asked almost two thousand educational institutions for some information on federal research and development expenditures that should have been obtainable from a dozen federal agencies.

More reprehensible is the deliberate withholding by some agencies of information about their expenditures at individual institutions that should be published or available for public inspection. It is noteworthy that in the flood of federal financial statistics flowing from the U.S. Office of Education and the National Science Foundation, the two main public sources of information on the volume of federal educational and scientific activities at colleges and universities, the former agency has eschewed reference to the total federal income of any named institution (other than land-grant schools), and the latter, to the total federal expenditures for research and development—or even its own total expenditures—at

138

any named institution.[1] Information on the allocation of federal research funds at a particular institution between salaries, equipment, overhead, and other expenses is more readily obtainable from the institution's financial statement than from government sources.

This policy is, we believe, misguided and contrary to the public interest. It is all the more misguided because federal science funds have, in general, gone to schools well qualified to receive them, and their distribution has been made on scientific and professional grounds singularly divorced from political considerations. The volume of federal expenditures at educational institutions is so large and growing that a systematic public accounting of these expenditures is in order. Primary responsibility for the accounting plainly rests with the U.S. Office of Education and the National Science Foundation.

Let us review the available information on the concentration of federal funds at institutions of higher education.

POSTWAR TRENDS
IN THE CONCENTRATION OF FUNDS

Although the statistics are incomplete, the pattern of federal expenditures has probably shifted at least twice in the last two decades toward and away from a heavier concentration at a few great universities.

Marked concentration was the rule during World War II when the Office of Scientific Research and Development invested large sums in high-priority projects at laboratories managed by a few institutions—including the Massachusetts Institute of Technology, the University of Chicago, and the University of California—whose scientists had pioneered in vital fields of atomic physics and electronics. In its 1945 re-

[1] In its annual reports, the National Science Foundation lists the individual grants awarded to investigators at particular institutions, but these are arranged by scientific field and are not summed by institution. Such a list of total Foundation research grants at named institutions in fiscal year 1960 was published by the House Committee on Science and Astronautics (*Annual Review of the National Science Foundation*, 87th Cong., 1st sess., May 1961, pp. 8-14, and June 1961, pp. 31-37). The House Committee on Appropriations published a list of Foundation grants for research and scientific manpower in fiscal 1959 (*Independent Offices Appropriations for 1961, Part 3: National Aeronautics and Space Administration, National Science Foundation,* Hearings Before the Subcommittee of the House Appropriations Committee, 86th Cong., 2d sess., March 1960, pp. 44-65).

port to Vannevar Bush, director of OSRD, on plans for the peacetime development of science, the Bowman Committee observed that "the large wartime university research laboratories have drawn upon the intermediate universities for staffs" and therefore urged special financial support to "the 25 universities just below the first half dozen in size and resources" to help them recover and rebuild their scientific staffs.[2] Broadening the geographic distribution of federal science funds was much discussed, also, in connection with postwar legislation to create the National Science Foundation, which Congress eventually directed "to strengthen basic research and education in the sciences . . . throughout the United States . . . and to avoid undue concentration of such research and education."

However, it was 1950 before the Foundation was established and July 1957 before its budget reached $50 million, and, although the other agencies financing research and development at universities probably distributed their funds somewhat more widely in the immediate postwar years than during the war, the decisive dispersion was achieved by federal payments for veterans' education which reached a peak in 1947-48 when veterans' tuition and fees accounted for $365 million or 70 percent of all federal income reported by institutions of higher education. As these payments declined thereafter, those of the federal research agencies rose, particularly after the outbreak of the Korean war in June 1950 and again after the launching of the first earth satellite by the Soviet Union in October 1957, with the net effect of again heightening the concentration of federal funds at a few leading institutions.

Thus, between the academic years 1947-48 and 1957-58, the proportion of the federal income of all colleges and universities received by the top 20 institutions rose from 32 to 61 percent, and the absolute

[2] See Vannevar Bush, *Science—The Endless Frontier* (Office of Scientific Research and Development, 1945; reprinted by the National Science Foundation, 1960), p. 93.

Russell I. Thackrey, executive secretary of the Association of State Universities and Land-Grant Colleges, has very reasonably argued that "the effect of the 'concentration of research' policies followed during World War II was substantially to weaken the research staffs of many universities in order to build up those at a few centers. If this was a war necessity, it seems to me that there also was and is at least some obligation on the part of the government to help correct the imbalance which it thus created." See excerpt from Thackrey letter in *Sponsored Research Policy of Colleges and Universities,* A Report of the Committee on Institutional Research Policy (American Council on Education, 1954), p. 72.

amount by $270 million, while that received by over 1,700 other institutions declined $85 million. (See Appendix A, Table A-14.) In 1948, 107 institutions reported $1 million or more income from the federal government; in 1954, only 70; in 1958, 92. During the same ten years, federal funds tripled at Group I universities, declined slightly at Group II universities, and dropped tenfold at Group III colleges.

It should be borne in mind that certain federal appropriations serving in one way or another to aid higher education (such as additions to plant, or cost of education payments made directly to students) do not show up in these figures. Some of the steep increase at leading universities may also be attributable to a fuller reporting in later years of federal contracts at large, mainly off-campus laboratories. National Science Foundation statistics which exclude these laboratories (the so-called "research centers") and agriculture experiment stations indicate a slight dispersion of federal research and development funds from fiscal 1954 to fiscal 1958.[3] Of all federal R&D expenditures at colleges and universities in those two years, the percent going to leading schools (arrayed by volume of funds) was as follows:

Leading Schools	Percent of Federal R&D	
	1954	1958
6 schools	33%	28%
14 schools	56	49
20 schools	66	54
36 schools	81	73

The passage of the National Defense Education Act in 1958 and the large increases in the budgets of the National Science Foundation, the National Institutes of Health, and other science agencies have undoubtedly again broadened the base of federal expenditures, although not to the extent that prevailed during the high tide of veterans' education in the late 1940's.

[3] Herbert Rosenberg's view of similar NSF data is that they show "increasing concentration of research expenditures in fewer institutions: about 6.5 percent of the institutions accounted for 57 percent of the total in 1958 as compared with 45 percent in 1954." However, the correct statement should be, not "fewer" institutions but "relatively fewer"—or "absolutely more," as decidedly more institutions received some federal R&D funds in 1958 than in 1954. See Herbert H. Rosenberg, "Research and the Financing of Higher Education," *Higher Education*, Vol. 18 (October-November 1961), p. 5.

VARYING DEGREES OF CONCENTRATION
IN DIFFERENT PROGRAMS

The great range in the degree of concentration and dispersion of current programs is indicated by an examination of the proportion of funds which went to the twenty institutions receiving the largest sums in various programs in fiscal year 1960. In the tabulation below, Column A represents the percent of total obligations in the program going to these twenty institutions (determined separately for each program).

A	Agency	Program
89%	AEC	Research (including research centers)
88	NASA	Research (excluding research centers)
83	DOD	Research (including research centers)
83	NSF	Regular graduate fellowships
78	NSF	Graduate research laboratories
60	DOD	Research (excluding research centers)
58	AEC	Research (excluding research centers)
54	NSF	Research
54	NIH	Research
50	NSF	Cooperative fellowships
50	NIH	Training grants
32	OE	Graduate fellowships
22	HHFA	College housing loans
11	OE	Student loans

The figures indicate orders of magnitude, but are not all precisely comparable. It is difficult to get a complete and exact list of the awards in many programs and to ensure that every branch and affiliated research institute of complicated, multicampus institutions is defined identically in every list. But they do demonstrate the marked variation in the institutional concentration of different programs.

The multimillion-dollar research centers of the Atomic Energy Commission and the Department of Defense markedly accentuate the concentration of federal research funds at a few leading institutions. Indeed, the budgets of centers administered by a few institutions—particularly the Universities of California and Chicago, and the Massachusetts and California Institutes of Technology—are so large as to significantly affect the national statistics of federal expenditures at educational institutions. Each of these centers represents a unique national enterprise which can hardly be duplicated on every campus; its financing must be justified in terms of its individual purpose, rather than the criteria of programs involving a multitude of institutions.

Excluding these research centers, the general-purpose research programs of the National Institutes of Health and the National Science Foundation are dispersed little more broadly than the more specialized research programs of the Atomic Energy Commission and the Department of Defense. The Commission and the Office of Naval Research had major, intelligently administered, basic research programs going a good many years before the two granting agencies received comparable appropriations. Starting with modest budgets, the granting agencies tended to emphasize quality, and the best quality is to be found at relatively few institutions. However, there is a visible tendency for both contract and grant research programs to broaden their institutional base as their budgets grow (Table 10-1).

TABLE 10-1. *Number of Institutions with Federal R & D Funds, 1952 and 1960*

Agency	Number of Institutions with Federal R & D Funds[a]		R & D Obligations (in millions)	
	1952	1960	1952	1960
All Agencies[b]	225	450	$294.7	$782.8
DOD	173	250	155.7	234.0
PHS	147	290	14.4	151.3
AEC	115	250	105.3	243.2
NSF	53	240	1.0	56.0

[a] The 1952 figures are derived from National Science Foundation, *Federal Funds for Science, I* (1953), p. 41; the 1960 figures are estimates, from information supplied by agency representatives.
[b] All federal agencies, including those not listed below.

The dispersion associated with a budget increase results from a variety of factors. We would not care to say flatly that a lowering of standards is invariably one of the factors, but it is certainly common enough. The more abundant the support in a given field, the more likely is the ordinary man to be supported. Cancer research in particular, and health research in general, afford good examples: "As the available funds for [medical] research increase . . . the quality of those undertaking research as well as that of the research they perform is diluted and the standards are inevitably lowered."[4] Between 1956 and 1960 the proportion of NIH research grants rated by reviewers in the highest quality class declined from 40 to 24 percent.[5] Concomitantly, there has been a visible change in the philosophy of NIH staff, and those who once spoke of supporting quality now state that they are not "awarding prizes" but building a great scientific structure in which each brick is important to the whole; criteria of scientific "excellence" are yielding gradually to criteria of mere "competence."

A broadening of the scope of programs is another pattern demonstrated by the expanding fields supported by NSF, and the extension of NIH grants to graduate schools and the social sciences, following the initial concentration on schools of medicine. Generous congressional appropriations will soon expand the scope of the National Aeronautics and Space Administration's programs at educational institutions from the aeronautical and engineering sciences to the physical and life and some social sciences as well. Ultimately, the limits of "defense," "health," or "space" sciences are set less by academic than by political and budgetary considerations. The increased competition of different agencies for the same recognized scientists at the same recognized institutions has driven many program directors to lesser institutions and less eminent (but sometimes more cooperative) men.

Research programs utilizing the prevailing distribution of talent and facilities have gradually been supplemented by programs for the training of new talent, the purchase of equipment, and the construction of facilities that serve to increase the number of institutions able to conduct research; and a number of programs have been initiated in recent years specifically to counter criticism of concentration leveled at earlier programs. Examples include the graduate fellowships of the National Defense Education Act, the $250,000 ceiling on the capital sum available to any one institution for student loans under the same act, NSF's cooperative fellowships, and its new program of matching grants for undergraduate science equipment.

[4] Max Finland, of the Harvard Medical School, testifying before a U. S. Senate committee; quoted in *Saturday Review,* Vol. 43 (Oct. 1, 1960), p. 38.
[5] See *Health Research and Training: The Administration of Grants and Awards by the National Institutes of Health,* Second Report by the House Committee on Government Operations, 87th Cong., 1st sess. (April 1961), p. 28.

The dominant factor governing the present concentration of federal funds is, of course, the objective for which they were appropriated. Veterans' benefits affected students at every accredited institution of higher learning; the NDEA student loan program extended to some 1,400 institutions in fiscal years 1960 and 1961; the housing loans of the Housing and Home Finance Agency have involved more than 600 institutions from 1951 through 1960.[6] Whatever these programs may be criticized for, it is not lack of institutional dispersion. However, most federal fellowship and training programs are geared either by statutory or administrative requirements to the graduate and often the doctoral level, and most research programs, to the kind of men, equipment, and environment found more frequently at the 200 or so doctorate-awarding institutions than at the 1,800 other institutions of higher education.

[6] The exact number cannot be readily determined. From 1951 to 1960, 1,138 loans were made to educational institutions, but many institutions received more than one loan. J. Kenneth Little has reckoned that over 600 institutions received loans through 1960.

CHAPTER 11

Relative Quality of Institutions with More and Less Federal Money

MUCH MATERIAL pertinent to a quality comparison of our three groups of institutions has already been presented in Part One (see especially Chapter 1, Table 1-1, and Appendix A, Tables A-1, A-2, A-5). The main additional statistics to be reported in this chapter are given in Tables 11-1 to 11-7, which are concerned with various comparisons of undergraduates, of graduate students, and of faculty. As the three groups of institutions were not selected from a homogeneous universe and the data for one group cannot meaningfully be added to the data for another, ratios rather than percentages have been adopted as a means of comparison.

STUDENT QUALITY

Undergraduates

In attempting to compare the quality of undergraduates, we have sought measures both of the average quality of the entire student body and of certain select groups of students. We do not know of a more widely available measure of the quality of an entire student body than the Scholastic Aptitude Test scores. However, in addition to limitations already discussed (see the first section of Chapter 2), the major disadvantage of this test is that state institutions do not use it as often, or require it of as large a proportion of their applicants, as do private institutions.[1] But it is the best available.

The mean verbal and mathematical scores of freshmen entering the undergraduate college of liberal arts and sciences in the fall of 1960 were obtained from eight schools in Group I, nine in Group II, and ten in Group III. These show that the average verbal and mathematical aptitude of undergraduates at Group I universities was decidedly higher than that of students at Group II universities, but only a little above that of students at Group III colleges. However, scores were available for only two of the six state universities in Group I, but for five of the six in Group II (see Table 11-1). Judging from the scores of students at institutions of known reputation, it is likely that, were the scores of all institutions available, the over-all average for Group I would be reduced somewhat below that for Group III, while still remaining well above that for Group II institutions.

It is also evident from an examination of these scores that, with few exceptions, the average score of students at private universities was above that of students at public universities in both Groups I and II. (Two of the three exceptions among private institutions are urban universities with a large proportion of part-time students, and the highest-scoring public institution is one of the nation's greatest.) Some admissions officers at our great public universities concede that the average ability of their undergraduates is lower than that of undergraduates at the private university with which they are competing most keenly, because of their larger "tail" of inferior freshmen—admitted as state residents, and often flunked out before their junior year—but affirm that their best students are as good as any anywhere. There is a growing concern in the academic community lest, under current conditions and because of their social cachet, the private universities corner an undue proportion of exceptionally talented students.

With few exceptions, the indices of various select groups of undergraduates (see Table 11-2) lead to the same general conclusion as that drawn from SAT scores: relative to either the number of students enrolled or the number of degrees awarded, undergraduates and alumni from Groups I and III received the enumerated distinctions more often than did those from Group II. This is true of the number of alumni

---

[1] A number of institutions, particularly in the Midwest, have begun to employ tests of the American College Testing Program.

TABLE 11-1. *Mean Scholastic Aptitude Test Scores of Entering Class, Fall 1960, at Twenty-Seven Institutions*[a]

	Mean Verbal Score Ranked by Group			Mean Mathematical Score Ranked by Group			Mean Mathematical Score Corresponding with Verbal Score in Group		
	I	II	III	I	II	III	I	II	III
	650	620	681[b]	728	665	670	728	635	667[b]
	641	577	641[b]	675	635	667[b]	675	665	658[b]
	635	550	638	642	554	658[b]	637	554	670
	631	505[c]	626	637	538[c]	637	642	510[c]	628
	597	505	612	596	520[c]	628	596	489	637
	550[c]	497[c]	575	553[c]	518[c]	571	553[c]	518[c]	566
	528	494[c]	566	526	510[c]	566	526	469[c]	571
	501[c]	493[c]	551	510[c]	489	565	510[c]	538[c]	565
		480[c]	535		469[c]	542		520[c]	534
			521			534			542
Median	614	505	594	617	520	600	617	520	600
Mean	592	525	595	608	555	604	608	555	604

[a] Source: The institutions. Scores were restricted, wherever possible, to students in the college of liberal arts and sciences.
[b] Median.
[c] Public university.

TABLE 11-2. *Comparisons of Three Groups of Institutions: Undergraduates*

	Group			Ratio of		
	I	II	III	I:II	II:III	I:III
Undergraduate Enrollment, Fall 1957	146,238	82,978	13,773	1.8	6.0	10.6
Fall 1947	95,633	41,659	14,721	2.3	2.8	6.5
Bachelor Degrees, 1958-59	32,428	13,891	2,836	2.3	4.9	11.4
Bachelor Degrees, Sciences, 1956-59[a]	29,489	10,192	2,441	2.9	4.2	12.1
Entering Class, Fall 1960						
Verbal SAT Score[b]	614	505	594			
Mathematical SAT Score[b]	617	520	600			
National Merit Scholars, 1955-60	632	137	235	4.6	.6	2.7
Undergraduate Alumni:						
Receiving Ph.D., 1936-56[c]	13,786	3,796	2,233	3.6	1.7	6.2
Sciences[d]	7,814	1,945	935	4.0	2.1	8.4
In *American Men of Science*, 1960[e]	9,118	2,193	963	4.2	2.3	9.5
Starred Scientists, 1903-43[f]	417	94	102	4.4	.9	4.1
In *Who's Who in America*						
Vol. 27, 1952-53	10,105	2,807	1,636	3.6	1.7	6.2
Added in Vols. 28-31, 1954-61	5,713	1,612	1,030	3.5	1.6	5.5
	4,392	1,195	606	3.7	2.0	7.2
NSF Fellows, 1960-61[g]	167	56	49	3.0	1.1	3.4
Woodrow Wilson Fellows, 1945/46-1961/62	755	287	284	2.6	1.0	2.7

[a] Source: National Science Foundation. Sciences include agriculture, engineering, and psychology as well as physical and biological sciences.
[b] The median of the mean Scholastic Aptitude Test scores of the freshman class entering in fall, 1960; mean scores obtained for eight schools in I, nine in II, and ten in III.
[c] Source: National Academy of Sciences, *Doctorate Production in United States Universities 1936-1956* (1958).
[d] Sciences include engineering, physical and biological sciences.
[e] Vols. A-E and F-K, 1960 (analysis courtesy of H. E. Zabel).
[f] Source: Stephen S. Visher, *Scientists Starred 1903-1943 in "American Men of Science"* (Johns Hopkins Press, 1947), pp. 151-153.
[g] Count restricted to first-year awards in NSF regular graduate fellowship program.

TABLE 11-3. *Comparisons of Three Groups of Institutions: Undergraduates; Mean Intelligence Scores of 1958 and 1959 Ph.D's, by Baccalaureate Institution and Field*

Field	Mean Intelligence Scores of Ph.D's by Baccalaureate Institution in Group[a]					Number of Cases in Group				
	I	II	III	X[b]	Y[c]	I	II	III	X[b]	Y[c]
Total[d]	66.4	64.6	69.2	67.0	64.2	1,078	314	179	1,968	4,789
Sciences	66.9	64.2	69.5	67.2	64.5	479	135	67	854	2,081
Social Sciences[e]	66.7	64.0	68.6	66.7	65.1	214	54	47	377	827
Humanities[f]	67.6	65.0	69.3	67.5	65.5	121	36	32	236	652
Engineering	67.1	67.4	72.7	68.0	66.5	127	39	7	251	254
Education	62.9	62.6	64.2	62.8	60.2	77	28	19	125	636
Selected Departments										
Physics	69.7	69.0	69.9	70.2	68.1	93	22	16	174	264
Chemistry	66.8	63.1	68.3	67.4	64.9	135	54	23	237	760
Psychology	66.8	65.6	70.5	67.0	65.0	108	39	27	183	490
English	67.8	63.5	73.5	67.5	66.2	34	10	8	73	179
History	66.3	66.7	68.6	67.4	65.4	31	6	12	63	178

[a] Intelligence scores measured in various tests in American high schools for those who received Ph.D's in calendar years 1958 and 1959. All tests transmuted to a common scale with a mean of 50 and standard deviation of 10, based on the general population (*not* on high school graduates only). For Ph.D's in general, the mean on this scale is 65.4, standard deviation 8.5, range from 35 to 85. Multiplied by two, these scores are comparable to the Army Standard Scale which assumes a mean score of 100 and standard deviation of 20. See Lindsey R. Harmon, "High School Backgrounds of Science Doctorates," *Science*, Vol. 134 (March 10, 1961), pp. 679–688, for further detail on method of derivation and comparability with Stanford-Binet and other scales.

[b] All (twenty-five) institutions which received $4 million or more from federal government in 1957–58.

[c] All other institutions.

[d] Source: National Academy of Sciences. Total includes fields not itemized below.

[e] Social Sciences: anthropology, economics, geography, political science, psychology, public administration, sociology, statistics.

[f] Humanities: area studies, English, fine and applied arts, foreign languages, history, international relations, philosophy.

listed in *Who's Who in America,* of the number with doctorates in any field and in the sciences, of those listed in the 1960 *American Men of Science* or starred in that publication during the years when that practice was used to designate scientists of distinction.

Relative to the number of bachelors' degrees awarded in the sciences, the number of undergraduates receiving regular National Science Foundation first-year graduate fellowships was virtually identical at Group II and Group I universities. This point is of special interest, because of the heavy preference of these fellows, thereupon, to use their awards to attend graduate schools at Group I institutions. And there can be no doubt that, given a free choice at either the graduate or undergraduate level, a student will prefer most (*not* all) Group I to most Group II universities, as is indicated by the markedly higher preference of National Merit Scholars for the former institutions. Group II undergraduates also scored almost as well as those at Group I in the relative number of Woodrow Wilson fellowships they have won, although not quite as well in the relative number of NSF fellowships—since the appropriate base of comparison for Woodrow Wilson awards is *all* baccalaureate degrees awarded (line 3, Table 11-2), not all baccalaureate science degrees (line 4).

The appropriate base line for comparing certain achievements of undergraduates of Group I universities and Group III colleges is critical, as enrollment in the former has skyrocketed, particularly since the war, while remaining relatively stable at the latter (actually declining slightly from 1947 to 1957). If the fall enrollment of 1957 is taken as the base, Group III alumni excel in all distinctions noted; but if the fall enrollment of 1947 is the base, they lag behind Group I alumni in three respects: listings in the 1960 edition of *American Men of Science,* listings in the 1954-61 editions of *Who's Who,* and the number of science doctorates received 1936-56. This should serve as a warning against drawing drastic conclusions from isolated indices; were more time available in which to extend the analysis, it would be desirable to explore other and perhaps more appropriate base lines of comparison for our three groups.

Table 11-3 reports the mean intelligence scores in high school examinations administered around 1947, 1946, or earlier years, of undergraduates at the thirty-six institutions in our study who went on to re-

ceive Ph.D.'s in the calendar years 1958 and 1959 from any U.S. graduate school. The data represent a further analysis for our institutions of
the material reported in 1961 by Lindsey Harmon for various fields.[2]
As these data are of unique value, we undertook an additional analysis
of the mean intelligence scores of the entire crop of 1958 and 1959
Ph.D.'s (for whom the information was available) broken into two
groups: those who attended the twenty-five institutions receiving $4
million or more from the federal government in 1957-68, and all other
U.S. institutions. (This analysis also permits a test of the representativeness of our data on Group I institutions, which constitute a selection
from the same twenty-five institutions, and it will be noted that the over-
all means for the two groups diverge by only 0.6 scale points.)

The results support the conclusion derived from the analysis of mean
SAT scores. The average performance of undergraduates at our three
groups of institutions who subsequently obtained Ph.D.'s was consistently highest at Group III colleges, next highest at Group I universities,

[2] Harmon, "High School Backgrounds of Science Doctorates," *Science,* Vol.
133 (March 10, 1961), pp. 679-688. The method of deriving these data and,
hence, their meaning, is sufficiently complicated to warrant further elucidation.
The point of departure was a record at the National Academy of Sciences of
persons who received their doctorate from any U.S. institution in 1958 (the same
procedure was repeated the following year). Thereupon, "a questionnaire form
was prepared for each holder of a 1958 doctorate, to be mailed to his former high
school. All forms for a given high school were assembled and sent, together with
a letter, to the principal, informing him of the relative standing of his high school
in the state and nation with respect to the number of graduates in the 1958 doctorate 'crop.' For each of its graduates who held a 1958 doctorate, the school was
given information on all degrees held and was asked to supply information from
the school records" (pp. 679-680).

Now, taking 1958 as the date of the doctorate, 1950 was the medial year when
most students received their baccalaureate, eight years being the median period
elapsing between bachelor's and doctor's degrees; see Bernard Berelson, *Graduate
Education in the United States* (McGraw-Hill, 1960), p. 157. Allowing only four
years to complete college, these students were in college, then, from the fall of
1946 to the spring of 1950. The senior year of high school was the modal year in
which the intelligence tests were administered, but a good many were administered
earlier—some, even, in elementary school. Therefore the modal year for obtaining the intelligence scores of students who received their Ph.D. in 1958 was the
academic year 1945-46.

This long reach back should be borne in mind in interpreting these data; but it
may also be noted that, in most cases, these intelligence test scores are the only
objective record of ability other than grades available in student high school
records for the guidance of educational counselors. It is believed that, if anything, the scores underestimate the average ability of the students.

and lowest at Group II universities. Expressed on the Army Standard Scale, their mean intelligence scores were as follows:

Field	Institution Group		
	I	II	III
All Fields	132.8	129.2	138.4
Sciences	133.8	128.4	139.0
Social Sciences	133.4	128.0	137.2
Humanities	135.2	130.0	138.6

An examination of the data by individual institutions (see Appendix A, Table A-15) shows that the mean intelligence score of these students at *every* private university in Group I exceeded that of students at public universities in Group I; the mean score of students at private institutions in Group II, taken as a group, was also above that of students at public universities in Group I. The rank order was as follows:

Institution Group	Mean Intelligence Scores	
	Individuals	Institutions
Group III	138.4	134.6
Group I, private schools	137.0	137.4
Group II, private schools	132.4	130.6
Group I, public schools	128.8	128.8
Group II, public schools	125.8	126.6

Graduate Students

The indices of the quality of graduate students, although sparser, again favor Group I students over Group II (Table 11-4). However, the difference between the mean intelligence scores of recent Ph.D.'s (1958 and 1959) at the two groups of institutions was less at the graduate than at the undergraduate level, and in the key field of physics, the mean intelligence score of Ph.D.'s was greater at Group II institutions (Table 11-5).

Examination of the mean intelligence scores (Army Standard Scale) of these Ph.D.'s by the institution from which they received their doctorates again shows the private universities in Group I ranked first, private

TABLE 11-4.   *Comparisons of Two Groups of Institutions: Graduate Students*

	Group I	Group II	Ratio I:II
Graduate Enrollment, Fall 1957	48,823	11,992	4.1
Fall 1947	20,980	6,749	3.1
Graduate Students in Sciences, April 1958[a]	16,220	3,493	4.6
Doctorates, 1936-56	29,993	6,669	4.5
Sciences[b]	16,627	3,160	5.3
Percent in Sciences	55.4%	47.4%	
Science Doctorates, 1956-59[c]	4,669	900	5.2
National Science Fellows, 1960	520	44	11.8
Woodrow Wilson Fellows, 1959/60-1961/62	1,229	143	8.6
Ph.D's and M.D.'s starred in *American Men of Science*, 1903-43[d]	603	35	17.2

[a] Source: National Academy of Sciences, *Census of Graduate Students in Basic and Applied Natural Sciences* (1958). Sciences include engineering, psychology, and anthropology, as well as physical and biological sciences.

[b] Source: National Academy of Sciences, *Doctorate Production in United States Universities 1936-1956* (1958). Sciences include engineering, physical and biological sciences.

[c] Source: National Science Foundation. Same fields as in footnote b, with addition of psychology.

[d] Source: Stephen S. Visher, *Scientists Starred 1903-1943 in "American Men of Science"* (Johns Hopkins Press, 1947), pp. 270-271.

universities in Group II second, public universities in Group I third, and public universities in Group II last:

Institution Group	Mean Intelligence Scores	
	Individuals	Institutions
Group I, private schools	133.0	133.6
Group II, private schools	130.2	129.6
Group I, public schools	129.0	128.4
Group II, public schools	127.2	127.2

Again, the distinction between the mean intelligence scores of students at public and private institutions was less sharp at the graduate level; two public universities in Group I and three in Group II ranked among the first six schools in their respective groups. (See Appendix A, Table A-16.)

We should not leave this discussion of student quality without intro-

TABLE 11-5. *Comparisons of Two Groups of Institutions: Graduate Students; Mean Intelligence Scores of 1958 and 1959 Ph.D's by Doctoral Institution and Field*

Field	Mean Intelligence Scores of Ph.D's in Group[a]				Number of Cases in Group			
	I	II	X[b]	Y[c]	I	II	X[b]	Y[c]
Total[d]	65.4	64.3	65.8	64.0	1,998	483	3,676	2,911
Sciences	66.0	64.9	66.2	64.2	917	219	1,618	1,230
Physical	67.3	66.1	67.6	65.6	609	149	1,070	743
Biological	63.4	62.5	63.5	62.1	308	70	548	487
Social Sciences[e]	65.2	63.9	65.8	62.6	360	85	719	469
Humanities[f]	65.4	63.7	66.3	66.0	232	66	501	359
Engineering	68.1	66.2	68.1	66.1	205	33	361	157
Agriculture	61.1	61.0	61.2	62.5	68	3	113	69
Education	61.1	61.5	60.6	60.8	143	54	243	511
Selected Departments								
Mathematics	70.6	66.8	70.7	67.8	90	21	134	70
Physics, Astronomy	69.2	69.7	69.7	67.4	157	32	286	158
Chemistry	65.7	64.9	66.2	64.6	303	87	534	453
Sociology	66.5	62.6	66.7	65.5	50	9	121	61
Psychology	65.2	64.4	66.0	63.4	187	64	377	302
Economics	64.3	63.9	65.6	65.0	75	9	117	42
Foreign Languages	67.6	64.3	67.5	66.6	35	10	60	43
English	65.4	65.7	66.8	66.6	70	19	146	105
History	65.3	64.9	66.4	65.8	72	12	149	99

[a] For notes a to f, see Table 11-3.

TABLE 11-6. *Comparisons of Three Groups of Institutions: Faculty*

	Group			Ratio of		
	I	II	III	I:II	II:III	I:III
Faculty, 1957–58[a]	22,097	8,254	1,222	2.7	6.8	18.1
Full-time	15,418	5,158	1,094	3.0	4.7	14.1
Faculty Scientists, 1957–58[b]	13,434	4,215	554	3.2	7.6	24.2
Non-Faculty Scientists, 1957–58[c]	20,116	2,166	54	9.3	40.1	372.5
Faculty, Thirteen Core Fields, 1960–61[d]	3,656	2,097	756	1.7	2.8	4.8
Four Sciences[e]	1,480	778	221	1.9	3.5	6.7
Faculty:						
In *American Men of Science*, 1960[f]	3,788	1,275	140	3.0	9.1	27.1
Starred in *American Men of Science*, 1937[g]	363	68	14	5.3	4.9	25.9
Members, National Academy of Sciences, 1960	167	9	0	18.6	—	—
Nobel Prizes (as of Feb. 1961)	15	2	0	7.5	—	—
Members, American Philosophical Society, 1959	126	7	1	18.0	7.0	126.0
Receiving from ACLS, 1958–62:[h]						
Distinguished Scholarship Prizes	14	1	0	14.0	—	—
Postdoctoral Fellowships	20	4	2	5.0	2.0	10.0
Grants-in-Aid	41	22	4	1.9	5.5	10.3
Guggenheim Fellows, 1960–61	69	11	3	6.3	3.7	23.0
Former Woodrow Wilson Fellows (as of 1960–61)	53	8	11	6.6	.7	4.8
Receiving American Philosophical Society Grant, 1959	26	8	4	3.3	2.0	6.5

[a] Source: Office of Education. Full and part-time faculty, instructor or above, in resident instruction in degree-credit courses. [b] Source: NSF. Full or part-time faculty in engineering, physical, life, and social sciences. [c] Source: NSF. Full or part-time scientific professional staff (including salaried graduate students) other than faculty, in fields listed in footnote b; research centers included. [d] Full-time faculty, instructor or above, teaching at least one course, in 1960–61, in fields surveyed by our questionnaire. [e] Biological sciences, chemistry, mathematics, and physics. [f] Vols. A-E and L-R (analysis courtesy of H. E. Zabel). [g] Source: National Resources Committee, *Research—A National Resource* (1938), Vol. 1, p. 174. [h] American Council of Learned Societies, *Newsletter* and *Annual Report, passim*.

ducing a strong methodological caution. The comparisons of institutions and groups have been conducted largely on the basis of mean scores on certain tests. Thus, the mean SAT scores of entering students at Groups I and II differed substantially, whereas the mean intelligence scores of graduates who received the doctorate were quite similar. But a single central measure like the mean or median is hardly a sufficient basis for the satisfactory description and comparison of large populations. It should, of course, be supplemented by frequency distributions, and there can be no doubt that these distributions would overlap for large numbers of students—that many students at Group II universities would score higher than many at Group I. However, two experienced students of education have suggested that the continuation of present trends of selectivity may create, not an overlapping, but an essentially bimodal distribution of student bodies:

> In one group there will be the more selective private colleges and universities, whose students average at about the 85th percentile or above on scholastic aptitude. There will be a few students in these colleges whose intellectual abilities are only average for all college students, but who have other special abilities which make them desirable. In the other, larger group, will be most of the state and municipal colleges and universities, together with the less selective private institutions. Their students will average between the 60th and 70th percentile in scholastic aptitude, with no more than 15 or 20 per cent of them above the mean of students in the more selective group of institutions.[3]

FACULTY QUALITY

Statistical Indices

There can be little doubt about the superiority of Group I to Group II faculty in virtually every significant test and, unlike so many indices for students, most of these tests and the bases of comparison are up to date (Table 11-6). After all, there are only three times as many faculty in Group I as in Group II; indeed, a count of 1960-61 full-time faculty in thirteen fields, undertaken for our survey, showed only 1.7 times as many faculty in Group I as in Group II. The former ratio is exactly

[3] Robert J. Havighurst and Bernice L. Neugarten, *Society and Education* (Allyn and Bacon, 1962), p. 270.

matched by the relative number of faculty from the two groups listed in the 1960 edition of *American Men of Science,* a mark of competence but hardly of distinction. Most of the distinctions go overwhelmingly to Group I faculty: starred names in the 1937 edition of *American Men of Science,* Nobel prizes, Guggenheim and Woodrow Wilson awards, and American Council of Learned Societies' prizes and postdoctoral fellowships. Two honors—membership in the National Academy of Sciences and the American Philosophical Society—are weighted so heavily in their favor, one wonders if some restrictive principle is not at work. The same cannot be said of the latter society's small grants for research and scholarship, or the small ACLS grants-in-aid, the one award examined in which faculty in Group II clearly did better than those in Group I.

TABLE 11-7. *Comparisons of Three Groups of Institutions: Faculty; Articles in Leading Journals, 1957-58*[a]

	Group		
	I	II	III
Articles in Leading Journals	929	193	30
Authors	1,614	348	39
Authors per Article	1.8	1.8	1.3
Authors per 100 Full-Time Faculty	10.5	6.7	3.6
Total, Selected Fields	37.7	16.8	4.6
Sciences	64.4	26.0	6.8
Chemistry	101.7	29.1	11.1
Biology	89.9	39.6	12.9
Physics	67.3	27.1	—
Mathematics	9.8	2.2	1.6
Social Sciences	23.2	15.2	3.5
Psychology	49.8	33.9	7.5
Sociology	22.0	11.5	—
Economics	9.8	2.4	4.0
Political Science	8.8	2.3	—
Humanities	5.8	3.8	3.3
Languages	6.7	4.1	2.2
Philosophy	6.1	6.7	7.3
History	4.0	1.4	2.9

[a] Procedures employed in this count and the list of journals included are given in Bernard Berelson, *Graduate Education in the United States* (McGraw-Hill, 1960), pp. 271-274; worksheets at the Bureau of Applied Social Research, Columbia University, were used to obtain tables for our institutions; full-time teaching faculty, as of 1960-61, were derived from catalogues and faculty lists.

A re-analysis of data on faculty publications in leading professional journals originally compiled by Bernard Berelson shows a higher rate of output by Group I than Group II faculty, with Group III bringing up the rear (Table 11-7). On this measure, Group I faculty excel more in the sciences than in the social sciences or the humanities. In philosophy, the relative output of faculty in Groups III and II surpassed that in Group I, although the absolute number of articles involved is small. College faculty are also notably less addicted than university faculty to multiple authorship: is this due to inclination or, more likely, opportunity?

The superior record of Group I faculty in journal publications may be due, in part, to the choice for analysis of the leading or "core" journals in each field. Examination of journals with more specialized or regional audiences might yield results more favorable to Group II faculty, particularly in certain disciplines.

Direct Quality Ratings

Not being satisfied to hold Group I faculty superior in quality to those at Group II simply on the basis of the kinds of statistics that have been presented, we checked this conclusion against various direct quality judgments of scholars in numerous fields. These consistently agreed in rating most (*not* all) Group I universities ahead of most Group II universities in every field examined.

Two such sets of judgments have already been reported. (See Chapter 1, second section, and Appendix A, Table A-2.) As noted, in 1925 and 1957 department chairmen throughout the nation were asked to rank the leading graduate departments in their field. The findings have been conveniently summarized by Hayward Keniston.[4] (Institutes of technology were excluded from these rankings, whereas one is included in both Groups I and II, but there is no reason to believe that this has changed the findings in any significant way; inclusion of these institutes would merely add another institution in Group I to the number of leading departments in most sciences, and a Group II institution to the number of leading departments in some sciences.)

The conclusion is clear and striking, and virtually identical in both

[4] Keniston, *Graduate Study and Research in the Arts and Sciences at the University of Pennsylvania* (University of Pennsylvania Press, 1959), pp. 119-150.

1925 and 1957: 4 or 5 institutions in Group I, but none in Group II, were ranked among the top 10 in the nation in each of six major fields of science; and an average of 4.1 institutions in Group I, but only 0.3 in Group II, were ranked among the leading 10 in four fields of social science and six of humanities.

Faculty in Group II generally agree in rating their departments below those in Group I. It is true that there is a tendency to inflate the quality of one's own institution and department. Examining the replies of 432 faculty at 46 colleges in Paul Lazarsfeld's 1955 interview survey of a national sample of social science faculty, David Riesman found that 53 percent ranked their college "among the top ten percent of colleges in the country" while 42 percent said of their department that "there are few better in the country."[5] But pride is not the same thing as complete self-deception. Berelson's 1959 survey of 1,821 university faculty included the question, "How would you rank your department among other graduate departments in your field in the U.S.?" Respondents at our twenty-four universities rated their departments as follows:

	In top 5	6th-10th	11th or lower	Number
Group I	57%	25%	18%	208
Group II	23%	26%	51%	119

As a final check, rankings of the twelve best universities of the twenty-four in Groups I and II were secured from a number of department chairmen in the course of our interviews, and a limited attempt was made to check their judgment against that of program officers and scientists in two government science agencies.

Of the several ways by which the resultant rankings can be totted up, all put Group I departments overwhelmingly ahead of Group II; despite the occasional contention of a Group II department for national notice, and the good repute of most and excellent repute of some Group II institutions, Group II, considered as a whole, is completely outclassed by Group I. The rankings in the fields for which ratings were obtained from six or more chairmen are given in Table 11-8.

We commend for another investigation a more thorough comparison of quality rankings by government and university representatives than time permitted in this study. With the kind cooperation of agency offi-

[5] David Riesman, in Paul Lazarsfeld and Wagner Thielens, *The Academic Mind* (Free Press, 1958), p. 325.

TABLE 11-8. *Rankings of Group I and II Graduate Departments by Department Chairmen*

Field	Raters	Number of			
		Ratings in Top 6		Schools in Top 6 at Least Once	
		Group		Group	
		I	II	I	II
Total	80	442	38	12	5
Biology	11	62	4	11	3
Chemistry	14	79	5	10	4
Physics	15	89	1	9	1
Economics	9	50	4	8	2
Psychology	12	59	13	8	2
Sociology	6	31	5	8	1
English	7	37	5	9	3
History	6	35	1	9	1

cials, ratings were obtained from thirty-four representatives of the National Science Foundation and the National Institutes of Health, but only in psychology and biology were the ratings numerous enough to be worth reporting. (The few other ratings, in chemistry, mathematics, and physics, would probably yield correlations similar to that found for psychology.) Through a simple weighting system, individual ratings were combined into the over-all rankings indicated in Table 11-9.

The lower correlation in biology is not surprising, as biology is one of the least uniform departments in the liberal arts and sciences in terms of curriculum content or even title. College departments of biology are often divided at universities (especially land-grant universities) into separate departments of botany and zoology, and bacteriology or microbiology, biochemistry, biophysics, and genetics may be broken out as well. This, plus special agency interests, may explain why a few departments received such divergent ratings by university and government representatives. Thus, one department was probably rated lower by chairmen than by agency scientists because the former were considering the whole spectrum of biology, whereas the latter had in mind modern molecular and other specialized approaches.

The similarity in the ratings of chairmen and representatives of grant-

TABLE 11-9. *Composite Rankings by Academic and Government Staff of the Twelve Best Departments at the Twenty-Four Universities in Groups I and II*

| | Psychology Departments[a] | | Biology Departments[a] | |
	Academic Ranking	Government Ranking	Academic Ranking	Government Ranking
	1	2	1	1
	2	1	2	2
	3	8	3	4
	4	3.5*	4	7
	5*	6*	5	5
	6	5	6	3
	7	7	7	11
	8*	3.5*	8	10
	9	10	9	6
	10	11	10*	14*
	11	9	11*	12*
	12	14	12*	13*
	14	12	13	8
			18	9
Number of Raters	12	8	11	17
Correlation[b]	.83		.58	

[a] In the columns below, the asterisk connotes a department in a Group II university; all other departments are in Group I Institutions.
[b] Spearman rank order correlation.

ing agencies with a highly academic orientation is scarcely surprising; lower correlations might well be found between chairmen and government scientists in the more applied research agencies.

SUMMARY

At the undergraduate level, the rank order of mean student quality at our institutions was found to be: (1) Group III colleges; (2) Group I, private universities; (3) Group II, private universities; (4) Group I, public universities; (5) Group II, public universities. At the graduate level, the same sequence prevailed (minus, of course, Group III colleges), but the gap between students at different groups of institutions was noticeably reduced.

Faculty in Group I were clearly superior to those in Group II. We are not inclined to extend this ranking to faculty at Group III, because of the thinness of the data embracing both university and college faculty, the different functions of the two faculties, and the uncertainty as to precisely which university population is represented—the college of liberal arts and sciences alone, or the professional schools and affiliated research institutes as well. Nor have we attempted to rank the faculty in public and private institutions within Groups I and II, because of the statistical hazards of doing so with the data in hand; however, for whatever value a guess may have in such a treacherous business, the sequence of over-all faculty quality, with notable exceptions at individual institutions, might well be: (1) Group I, private universities; (2) Group I, public universities; (3) Group II, public universities; (4) Group II, private universities.

It should also be observed that the quality of faculty and students at Group III institutions varied quite sharply between those at a select group of six schools nationally recognized for their high educational (and in two instances, at any rate, social) standards, and another six which, while good, serious institutions above the average for independent liberal arts colleges, do not reach this level of achievement. Faculty and students at the six best schools (and there are not more than a dozen or two in the nation to match them) were responsible for most of the honors and distinctions recorded in preceding tables.

In sum: the heavier volume of federal funds at Group I institutions coincided with the superior quality of both the faculty and students in Group I over those in Group II; but not with the superiority of students at private universities in Group II over students at public universities in Group I in indices that have been enumerated.

CHAPTER 12

Academic Factors Associated with a High Volume of Research

THE CONDITIONS which make for a large volume of research are not mysterious: good salaries to attract good people; good administrators favorably disposed to research; low teaching loads; some money with which to get started, space in which to work, and equipment with which to work; and, as one government official suggested, "a critical mass of high-quality individuals." In all of these respects Group I institutions are generally superior to Group II. These conditions all cost money, and most of the leading research institutions are also well-supported institutions, through the beneficence of private donors or the state. Indeed, an analysis undertaken in terms of institutional wealth would probably correlate highly with our analysis in terms of federal income. Evidence for this is afforded by Alexander W. Astin and John L. Holland, who contrasted various characteristics of wealthier and poorer institutions.[1] They demonstrate a pattern of association between wealth, research funds, and faculty and student quality similar to that we have found for institutions in Groups I and II. (See Appendix A, Table A-17.)

There is also the inescapable influence of history. Group I institutions did not embark on research simply because the government was supporting it, although government money has expanded their operations enormously. They were famous and research-oriented before the inception of government programs during World War II, as is shown by

[1] See Astin and Holland, *The Distribution of "Wealth" in Higher Education* (National Merit Scholarship Corp., 1961; multilith), Tables 2 and 4.

the following estimates of research expenditures prepared in 1938 by the National Resources Committee.[2]

Number of Schools		Estimated Research
Group I	Group II	Expenditures, 1937-38
3	0	$ 2 million or more
4	0	$ 1 to 2 million
5	2	$ 0.3 to 1 million
0	10	Under $ 0.3 million

THE MATTER OF SCIENCE DOCTORATES

Much has been made of the relation between the volume of federal research funds and the number of science doctorates awarded by an institution, and with good reason. The Ph.D. is a research degree, and an expensive one, and the factors that go into its production and mass production are closely related to those that make for a large volume of federal research. The institutions with the largest volume of federal research funds are, without exception, major producers of science doctorates, and it is easy enough to produce statistics along the lines: X percent of federal research money went to institutions awarding X percent (or, more frequently, X-Y percent) of science doctorates.

One author noting the relation between engineering college research expenditures and the number of graduate engineering degrees conferred even suggests that "an appropriate index of research activity [in fiscal year 1958] is of the order of $10,000 annual research expenditures per M.S. degree conferred and $30,000 per Ph.D. conferred."[3] But there is no invariant relation between the number of science doctorates awarded and the volume of federal research funds received, as an examination of major participants in the research programs of several agencies indicates (see Table 12-1).

[2] National Resources Committee, *Research—A National Resource*, Vol. 1 (1938), pp. 190-191.
[3] Ross J. Martin, "Impact of Engineering College Research on Graduate Programs and Faculty Development," *Journal of Engineering Education*, Vol. 51 (April 1961), p. 640.

Thus, Rensselaer Polytechnic, which ranked sixty-second nationally in the number of science doctorates awarded, was ninth in research and development funds received from the Atomic Energy Commission; the California Institute of Technology and Johns Hopkins University received far more for R&D from the Department of Defense than did such

TABLE 12-1. *Leading Recipients of Research Funds from Four Federal Agencies, Fiscal Year 1960*[a]

	Atomic Energy Commission			Department of Defense	
X	Institution	Y	X	Institution	Y
1	California	1	1	MIT	4
2	Chicago	15	2	Johns Hopkins	30
3	Princeton	23	3	Columbia	9
4	Iowa State	11	4	Michigan	6
5	MIT	4	5	California	1
6	Rochester	29	6	Cal. Tech.	26
7	Columbia	9	7	Stanford	14
8	NYU	12	8	Illinois	2
9	Rensselaer	62	9	Chicago	15
10	Michigan	6	10	Texas	18

	National Science Foundation			National Institutes of Health	
X	Institution	Y	X	Institution	Y
1	California	1	1	California	1
2	Harvard	10	2	Harvard	10
3	Chicago	15	3	NYU	12
4	Michigan	6	4	Columbia	9
5	MIT	4	5	Johns Hopkins	30
6	Columbia	9	6	Michigan	6
7	Wisconsin	3	7	Minnesota	8
8	Pennsylvania	24	8	Pennsylvania	24
9	Yale	16	9	Wisconsin	3
10	Illinois	2	10	Yale	16

[a] X column: national rank order of research and development funds received, fiscal year 1960. Information supplied by the agencies; research centers are included in the case of the AEC and DOD.

Y column: national rank order of doctorates awarded in the natural sciences, 1956/57-1958/59. Source: National Science Foundation. Fields include agriculture, biological sciences, engineering, forestry, geography, mathematical subjects, physical sciences, psychology, and general science programs.

universities as Wisconsin, Purdue, Ohio State, Minnesota, or Harvard, each of which awarded more science doctorates than those two institutions combined; Chicago and Pennsylvania ranked three times as high in grants received from the National Science Foundation as in science doctorates awarded; and so forth. Indeed, there was a *negative* correlation of — 0.64 between the rank order of the twenty leading institutions receiving most R&D money from the federal government and their national rank in the number of science doctorates awarded.[4]

Now, it may well be that a more precise analysis of doctorates awarded in the fields of special interest to each agency would explain some of these divergencies; but it is unlikely to explain them all, nor is an ultimate explanation of the distribution of federal research funds to be found along these lines. We may come closer to such an explanation by examining some of the institutions which have been leading participants in various federal programs.

THE PROMINENCE OF A
FEW PRIVATE INSTITUTIONS

A striking point, and a significant political issue, is the allocation of so much money to so many private institutions (as the allocation of such large sums inevitably involves political as well as scientific issues). This is scarcely explicable in terms of the science doctorates we have just been discussing, for while private institutions may claim pride of place in the humanities, public institutions have been more prominent in the development of graduate education in the sciences. Of the ten leading institutions in terms of science doctorates awarded, seven are state universities—but of the ten leading institutions in terms of federal funds received, only three![5]

[4] Rank order Spearman coefficient computed from the rank order of research funds received in 1957-58 (as reported to the U.S. Office of Education) and the rank order of science doctorates awarded in the academic years 1956/57-1958/59 (as reported by the National Science Foundation).

[5] Science doctorates as reported by the National Science Foundation for the three years 1956/57-1958/59; federal funds, as reported to the Office of Education, 1957-58. It is true that the Ph.D. production of public universities has been concentrated in the life sciences; that of private universities, in the physical

The public and private institutions involved can virtually be named by determining which institutions gained and lost by the inception of the National Science Foundation cooperative fellowship program. The regular NSF graduate fellowships, which entitle students to choose whichever institution they wish to attend, resulted in such a heavy concentration at Harvard, Massachusetts Institute of Technology, Berkeley, California Institute of Technology, Princeton, and Stanford (54 percent of the 1,200 fellows choosing these six schools in 1960) that the Foundation instituted a program of "cooperative" fellowships in which the number of fellowships was assigned to each institution in proportion to the number of science doctorates it awarded.[6] Now, if we first rank the leading twenty institutions in order of the number of their regular NSF fellows in fiscal year 1960, and then in order of the number of their fellows under the cooperative program, the following institutions (listed in order of their rank in the regular fellowship program) will be found to drop in rank under the new program: Harvard, California Institute of Technology, Princeton, Stanford, Chicago, Yale, Johns Hopkins, Carnegie Institute of Technology, Pennsylvania, Northwestern, Wash-

---

sciences. Thus, in 1957-58, public institutions awarded a majority of doctorates in agricultural, biological, chemical, and earth sciences; private institutions, in physics and engineering. See U.S. Office of Education, *Earned Degrees Conferred by Higher Educational Institutions 1957-1958* (1959), pp. 10-19. The ten institutions awarding the largest number of Ph.D's in the biological sciences from 1950-56 were all public universities, if we regard Cornell as public in this area; whereas four private institutions ranked among the top ten in physical science doctorates awarded during those years—Massachusetts Institute of Technology, Harvard, Columbia, and California Institute of Technology. See National Academy of Sciences-National Research Council, *Doctorate Production in United States Universities 1936-1956* (1958), pp. 20-52.

[6] State universities have, of course, criticized fellowship programs which result in this kind of concentration and commended those which lead to a broader dispersion of students. Thus, they have declared themselves "strongly opposed to expansion of the [National Defense Education Act] fellowship program along lines which would increase the present tendency of several existing programs to further concentrate fellowship holders in a very few institutions. We commend the National Science Foundation for recognizing the problem of concentration (which it has in part created) by awarding a portion of its fellowships through institutions." (*Recommendations on Desirable National Action Affecting Higher Education* by the Association of State Universities and Land-Grant Colleges and the State Universities Association, January 1962, p. 10.)

ington (Seattle). In short, ten private institutions and one public institution. The following gained in rank in the cooperative program: Illinois, Michigan, Wisconsin, Purdue, Columbia, New York University, Minnesota, Cornell, Ohio State, Iowa State, Michigan State, Pennsylvania State, UCLA, Texas. In short, eleven state and three private institutions. (Two schools—Massachusetts Institute of Technology and the University of California at Berkeley—retained the same rank in both programs: second and third respectively.) There could be worse starting points than this second list for a planned dispersion of federal research, as well as fellowship, funds.[7]

Dean John Burchard of MIT has observed that private institutions got a head start in vital research and development work because of their ability to act quickly during the war. "Private institutions were almost without exception the first of the universities to enter into the war research program on any large scale. This was implicit in their type of management, which made rapid change of policy and rapid decision on details as easy as it is for a private corporation." He adds that private institutions were also able to gamble their money, committing funds with no guaranty of repayment, while a contract with the government was being worked out, action that would be difficult or illegal for many state institutions.[8] The point is probably truer for some state universities than for others like California, Michigan, or Minnesota with substantial endowment funds that can be committed speedily with the approval of their president and board.

The key question is: is the *present* concentration of federal research and development funds at a few great private institutions due to their unexcelled experience and quality (and therefore justified) or, to a cer-

---

[7] Actually a policy under which the rank order of the amount of federal money going to each institution was the same as the rank order of science doctorates awarded in 1956/57-1958/59 (which we do *not* advocate) would result in the following changes among major institutions: (1) those whose rank in federal funds received would rise more than one place over that which they actually held in 1957-58—Illinois, Wisconsin, Purdue, Ohio State, Minnesota, Iowa State, Michigan State, Yale, and Cornell; (2) those whose rank in federal funds received would be lowered one or more places—MIT, Cal Tech, Johns Hopkins, Columbia, Chicago, Pennsylvania State, Princeton, Pennsylvania, and Rochester; (3) those whose rank would not change more than one place—California, Michigan, Harvard, New York University, Stanford, Texas, and Washington (Seattle).

[8] John Burchard, *Q.E.D.* [*M.I.T. in World War II*] (Wiley, 1948), p. 128.

tain extent, also to their unexcelled prestige and influence (and, to that extent, not so justified)?

One may like or dislike it, but it would be foolish to disregard the halo of prestige which surrounds institutions like Harvard and Princeton or Cal Tech and MIT. Harvard is not only great because it attracts great scholars; a scholar somehow appears greater because he is at Harvard. This factor—the certification of intellectual quality by some clearly visible sign like a Ph.D., publication of a book or journal article, the letterhead of a great university—is particularly important in the United States, especially when men without scientific training or the possibility of forming an independent judgment of scientific distinction must allocate large public sums for work of national importance. It has played a part in the present concentration of federal funds, although it is a part that can never be exactly defined. The cause of public higher education would be greatly advanced by the creation of a few elite state institutions with standards of faculty and student selection as high as Harvard's, and no student masses to depersonalize education and drag down the average quality of the student body. Perhaps the new campus of the University of California at La Jolla will afford a prototype.

FACULTY OPINION ON INSTITUTIONAL CONCENTRATION

Our questionnaire sought the views of faculty on the current concentration of federal funds. In their replies, scientists agreed that the concentration at a few well-known institutions reflected the distribution of faculty talent, institutional prestige, research equipment, graduate students, and advisory panels of scientists (see Table 12-2; the judgments of social scientists and humanists were similar to those of scientists, although, as a larger proportion are untouched by federal programs, fewer expressed an opinion about them). A large majority of faculty at all three groups of institutions agreed to these propositions, but the minor differences in the size of that majority at different institutions are instructive. In Group I, more scientists attribute the concentration of funds to the distribution of "faculty talent" than to the distribution of

TABLE 12-2. *Scientists' Opinions on the Concentration of Federal Funds at a Few Institutions*

"The current pattern of federal financing of research and training in the sciences tends to concentrate funds at a few well-known universities. Do you think that this distribution is fundamentally:

Question	Percent of Scientists Replying "Yes"[a] In Group		
	I	II	III
"a. a reflection of the present institutional distribution of:			
faculty talent?	92%	85%	75%
research equipment?	75	72	88
graduate students?	66	62	87
advisory panels of scientists?	57	72	70
prestige?	87	91	87
b. in the present national interest?	69	44	46
c. in the long-run national interest?"	38	17	18

[a] Among those replying "yes" or "no"; "don't knows" eliminated.

"institutional prestige," whereas in Groups II and III, more scientists attribute it to "institutional prestige"—which is natural enough, as neither group wishes to depreciate their own talent. Similarly, more college scientists are prepared to attribute the concentration of funds to equipment and graduate students (which they clearly do not have) than to faculty talent. Scientists in Groups II and III, who are less represented on advisory panels than are Group I scientists, are more prone than the latter to hold that panel membership influences the concentration of funds.

Over three fifths of scientists in Group I and over four fifths of those in Groups II and III believe that the present concentration of federal funds at a few institutions is not in the *long-run* national interest, but there is a significant difference of opinion about whether it is or is not in the *present* national interest. Some 70 percent of Group I scientists, who are the principal beneficiaries of present federal policies, assert that it is; about 55 percent of scientists in Groups II and III assert that it is *not*.

Who is right? The answer cannot be found in any or all of our statistics. It can only represent a judgment based upon knowledge of the present academic scene and upon hopes about how it should develop. Our judgment will be set forth in the next chapter.

CHAPTER 13

No, Yes, and Moot

IN EVALUATING the present concentration of federal funds for research and development, three separate questions must be considered:

1. the concentration of R&D funds at major research centers;
2. the concentration of *other* R&D funds at doctoral-level institutions;
3. the concentration of R&D funds, among doctoral-level institutions, at a few eminent schools.

The answers we will give, successively, to each question about the desirability of a broader dispersion of federal funds, are foretold by the title of this chapter. But let us consider each question in turn.

CONCENTRATION OF FUNDS AT RESEARCH CENTERS

Although our study was not designed specifically to deal with this question, and a special study of the matter would be useful, we see no reason to challenge the essential soundness of the judgment that placed the great national laboratories at a few institutions now receiving several hundred million dollars a year from the federal government. There was only one Fermi and one atomic pile, and they were at Chicago; one Lawrence and one cyclotron, and they were at Berkeley; one Wiener, and he was and is at MIT. In work of such critical national importance as these men and their colleagues and successors have undertaken, only the best will do, and it would be folly to draw and quarter the Radiation Laboratory, the Argonne National Laboratory, the Lincoln Laboratory,

173

and the Jet Propulsion Laboratory and distribute the segments among other campuses to promote a broader institutional dispersion. So long as these laboratories remain where they are, and until the volume of other federal expenditures for higher education rises far above the current level, a marked concentration of funds at a few institutions will *and should* continue.

Is it, however, necessary for these great laboratories not only to be associated with great institutions (which is clearly desirable) but also to be managed by one institution exclusively?

An attractive alternative is management by a group of institutions as is the case with the Brookhaven National Laboratory, the Institute for Defense Analyses, and the two new installations financed by the National Science Foundation, the National Radio Astronomy Observatory and the National Center for Atmospheric Research.[1] Cooperative management escapes the problem of using public funds to benefit only one of several rival institutions and extends the educational advantages of the facility to many institutions, while yet locating it at whichever site may be best from a strictly scientific standpoint. One problem posed by such management is presumably administrative; as the diffusion of authority hardly expedites decisions, it is important for participating institutions to delegate adequate responsibility to their representatives on the governing board and to the laboratory director.

Before a major new facility is established, it should be incumbent on the responsible agency to give claimant institutions a full hearing, to examine the alternative of cooperative management, and to justify publicly its final decision. In seriously contested cases, it might be well to put the decision to a panel appointed by an impartial arbiter like the President's Science Adviser or the president of the National Academy

---

[1] Cf. the 1954 recommendation of the Hancher Committee: "In the event that further large-scale defense research projects become necessary, the Committee suggests that the government should give consideration to the desirability of establishing additional central laboratories involving the multiple participation of institutions. A good geographical distribution of such facilities . . . may provide one of the most satisfactory ways for meeting the government's needs while at the same time meeting the special requirements of colleges and universities." The Committee also suggested that some research centers "might, by subcontracting procedures, distribute some of their work among a variety of institutions without loss of effectiveness and coordination." See American Council on Education, *Sponsored Research Policy of Colleges and Universities,* A Report of the Committee on Institutional Research Policy (1954), p. 17.

of Sciences. It seems reasonable, also, to ask that the management of existing centers be periodically re-examined to ensure that it continues to serve the public interest. Such re-examination has led to changes in the management of a good many centers, including the Operations Research Office, the Oak Ridge National Laboratory, the Sandia Laboratory, the Mitre offshoot of the Lincoln Laboratory, and the Systems Development offshoot of Rand.

CONCENTRATION OF FUNDS AT
DOCTORAL-LEVEL INSTITUTIONS

The order of concentration of National Science Foundation research funds in fiscal year 1960 was 91.9 percent at institutions awarding one or more science doctorates, 6.4 percent at institutions whose highest degree in the sciences was the master's, 1.7 percent at institutions whose highest science degree was the bachelor's, and nothing at all at the remaining 984 two- or four-year institutions of higher learning.[2] This came to approximately $47.8 million to under 139 institutions awarding science doctorates, $4.2 million to over 104 institutions awarding lower science degrees, and not a penny to either the remaining 801 institutions awarding one or more master's or (in most cases) bachelor's degrees in the sciences, or to the 593 institutions below the four-year level, most of which presumably give instruction in mathematics and some other fields within the purview of the Foundation. It is reasonable to assume that the degree of concentration of other agencies' research funds at doctoral-level institutions was at least as great and, in most cases, greater.

Such facts establish a prima facie case against the preponderant omission from present federal research programs of liberal arts colleges and other institutions that do not award the doctorate. This conclusion is supported by our visits to Group III colleges, and the analysis presented in Chapter 11 which showed the average quality of students at this

[2] Data from the National Science Foundation. The number of institutions awarding a doctor's, master's, and bachelor's as their highest level degree in the sciences was determined by an NSF analysis of Office of Education data on degrees conferred during the three academic years 1956/57-1958/59; the 984 institutions conferring no science degrees included 391 four-year institutions and 593 junior colleges.

select group of colleges to be superior to that of students at Group I universities, and the average quality of faculty to be comparable to that at Group II institutions.

There were no Nobel Laureates and probably no members of the National Academy of Sciences at the 1,785 institutions of higher education receiving no research funds from the National Science Foundation or the 1,600 receiving no research funds from any federal agency. Many who teach science at these institutions do not hold the doctorate and, at junior colleges, are trained to about the level of a good high school teacher. The environment and objectives of many institutions are avowedly inimical to research. Nevertheless, it strains credulity to imagine that not *one* member of the staff of these institutions has the capacity and opportunity to conduct research of a quality comparable to that of the dullest scholar now receiving federal research funds.

Because, unhappily, some dullards are supported, it does not follow that more should be; or as Leo Szilard's dolphin puts it, ". . . if we accept, as the basic tenet of true democracy, that one moron is as good as one genius, is it necessary to go one step farther and hold that two morons are better than one genius?"[3] A policy of dispersing research funds to institutions and individuals not now receiving any must *not* be founded upon the pork-barrel principle of the least common denominator, but rather upon the principle of quality which present science programs espouse but do not always exemplify. This means the avoidance of statistical formulas for the allocation of funds, and, in general, the continuation of present methods of evaluating quality by the use of advisory panels, referees, and intelligent staff (the responsibility assumed by staff should probably increase, if efficiency is to be maintained in expanding programs). But, as present programs have not succeeded in dispersing funds widely, new programs might well be established specifically for this purpose, with their own standards and guidelines.[4]

[3] Szilard, *The Voice of the Dolphins* (Simon and Schuster, 1961), p. 43.

[4] Cf. the recommendation of the House Committee on Government Operations that the National Institutes of Health "initiate for a limited time a special developmental-type grant as a direct means of stimulating research capability in those universities and professional schools which have training responsibilities in scientific fields related to health, but are not actively engaged in health research." See *Health Research and Training,* Second Report by the Committee on Government Operations, 87th Cong., 1st sess. (April 1961), p. 74. Whereas the committee appears to advocate a one-time or short-term program with reduced standards

Program directors and panel members at NSF and NIH often say that they lean over backwards to favor an unknown man at a small institution. This is true—but it demonstrates that different standards are required in judging proposals from a Nobel Laureate at Berkeley and a fledgling instructor at Podunk College. Different standards can still be standards of quality; but to be equitable, they should be explicitly formulated and published, and, to be effective, they should be implemented in a special program.

The kind of work that can be undertaken at a small institution may require more brains and less equipment. It may lean to theory, synthesis, and the analysis of published data. Experiments must be modest in scale. And this is all to the good. The small institution provides a natural environment for independent thinkers and independent approaches which, properly supported and encouraged, might provide a desirable counterbalance to the large-scale experiment and teamwork that dominates the major universities.

A new program of small matching grants for the purchase of scientific equipment for undergraduate instruction, recently initiated by NSF, is the sort of thing which is needed not only to improve science instruction but to stimulate research at small institutions. Other examples of programs geared to the needs of the liberal arts college are the AEC grants for equipment to aid instruction in nuclear physics, the NSF grants for research participation by undergraduate science majors, and the small grants program of NIH (which, unfortunately, is evidently in decline). The beauty of such programs is how much they accomplish for small sums that can pass unnoticed at large universities.

In addition to its value in its own right, research brings important practical benefits to the college community. It serves to lower teaching loads—and the teaching loads of scientists at small colleges are now the highest of any group of faculty examined in the present survey. It should help to attract and retain scientists in institutions where they are in short supply. It will improve the status of college scientists, the vitality of science instruction (particularly where students are actively involved in the research), and the physical resources of the college.

But the success of programs to foster research at liberal arts colleges

---

of quality, we would prefer a long-term program that maintains normal quality standards but encourages small-scale, independent, and highly varied kinds of work.

does not rest with federal agencies alone. It requires a degree of cooperation from college presidents and trustees that many have not shown. They must be prepared to lower the teaching loads, to provide space and facilities, to invest institution funds, to withstand criticism from faculty in other fields, and, above all, to provide support and encouragement to the isolated scientist. There is a price tag on educational vitality that too many institutions are unwilling or unable to pay.[5]

CONCENTRATION OF FUNDS AT
A FEW EMINENT INSTITUTIONS

The third and final question about the desirability of the present concentration of research funds, among doctoral-level institutions, at a few eminent schools, is also the most difficult.

If 59 percent of the funds which the National Science Foundation awarded to institutions conferring one or more science doctorates went to 20 of the 139 schools in this class (as it did, in fiscal year 1960) was this too much or too little? If the concentration of federal funds coincided precisely with the institutional concentration of science doctorates (and we have shown that, contrary to common opinion, it does *not*), would this be good or bad? Should research funds follow or enlarge the present institutional concentration of quality?

Nothing would be more damaging than to give a single answer to these questions, a single formula for the redistribution of hundreds of millions of dollars derived from many different budgets and serving radically different purposes.

The agencies contracting for research and development necessary to the fulfillment of their mission, like the Department of Defense, the Atomic Energy Commission, and the National Aeronautics and Space Administration (whose research program will spread to many new institutions in the next few years), must reserve the right to pick the in-

---

[5] A further discussion of the problems of encouraging research at liberal arts colleges, including recommendations for action by faculty, college presidents, private foundations, and government agencies will be found in two reports: *Research and Teaching in the Liberal Arts College,* a Report of the Wooster Conference, held at the College of Wooster, June 22 to July 2, 1959; and Howard Lowry and William Taeusch, *Research, Creative Activity, and Teaching* (Carnegie Foundation for the Advancement of Teaching, 1953).

stitutions and individuals best qualified to do their work. However, Charles J. Hitch's admonitions about the tendency of military research to be over controlled and over centralized, directed though they were primarily to military contracting in industry, may be equally relevant in the present context:

> . . . the basic trouble with military research and development is that it already leans too far in the direction of centralized bureaucratic solutions to its problems.
> 1. It is too highly centralized. Detailed decisions get made at too high a level. Detailed budget control is exercised at too high a level. There is too little delegation to the contractor and to the official on the spot.
> 2. Precise paths—with far too little flexibility—are dictated by administrators to researchers.
> 3. There is too little duplication, especially at the level of exploratory development, where it is cheap.
> 4. There is not enough competition among laboratories and contractors, or even among the services. There are not enough competitive purchasers of new ideas, or enough competition in exploiting them. Where there is competition among services or agencies, the record shows that we tend to make rapid progress. Where we suppress it, trying to decide the optimal path and contractor in advance, we do not do well.[6]

The military have another problem: how to interest not just good, but the very best scientists and the very best institutions in their work. Harvard and Yale, for example, have been noticeably less involved than Johns Hopkins and Texas in the research programs of the Department of Defense, or than Iowa State and Rensselaer Polytechnic in those of the Atomic Energy Commission. Is this solely an historical accident which will change in time with the construction of new facilities currently being financed by the AEC at Cambridge and New Haven? Does it simply represent a wish to be different from MIT and Princeton—or, also, a certain aversion to military bureaucracy, contract controls, and work which is too practical? (Harvard has refused to accept classified work on campus.) As the budgets of the granting agencies increase, affording more and more scientists the opportunity to engage in research entirely of their own choosing and with no restrictions as to direction or the need to meet onerous reporting requirements, a contest that would hardly be in the national interest could develop between the con-

---

[6] Charles J. Hitch, "Character of Research and Development in a Competitive Economy," *Proceedings of a Conference on Research and Development and Its Impact on the Economy* (National Science Foundation, 1958), pp. 137-138.

tracting and granting agencies for the time of key scientists. This danger adds a further incentive to those agencies whose mission requires a primary emphasis upon applied research and engineering to establish or enlarge granting programs of their own, as many have done under new statutory authority, and to broaden the number of universities involved in their programs.

What the net effect of such a broadening of institutional contacts would or should be on the concentration of R&D funds, it would be folly to say on the basis of abstract considerations. In some applied programs attacking urgent problems, it may be desirable to concentrate funds further; in broader and longer-range work, perhaps, to disperse them more widely. The test in each case must be effectiveness in achieving the agency's objective.

Primary responsibility for promoting a dispersion of scientific research and education rests with the U.S. Office of Education, the National Institutes of Health, and, above all, the National Science Foundation, which is instructed by statute "to strengthen basic research and education in the sciences, including independent research by individuals, throughout the United States, including its Territories and possessions, and to avoid undue concentration of such research and education."

The following considerations may be suggested in implementing such a policy:

1. Quality must come first. Even at the most eminent institutions, there is constant danger that intellectual standards will deteriorate from the too ready availability of too much money. The danger will be greater at lesser institutions if programs are established solely to hand out dollars on the basis of a mechanical formula. Whatever the program, high professional standards should be set, and selective judgments made by the best qualified professional men available to make them. The bane of our time, of professional journals, and of higher education is not too much research but too much meaningless research. If, as is likely, there are good men, at good and poor institutions, untouched by present research programs, a greater effort should be made to find and encourage them. It need not be an expensive effort—relatively little money is required and, if the effort fails, little money will have been lost. A redirection of these funds into other scientific and educational enterprises would then be preferable to a program of research for the sake of re-

search and regardless of quality or purpose—a direction in which, all too often, we veer.[7]

The quality institutions with a low level of research were readily identifiable in our study. Among the universities in Group II, for example, three public and three private institutions stood out as obvious candidates for expanded programs of research and education. Their faculty accounted for virtually all the honors won by any faculty in the Group; their students had the highest records of achievement; and (in five of the six cases) campus visits revealed a sense of purpose and confidence on the part of the faculty and wise leadership on the part of the academic administration.

2. However, institutions of high quality which do not wish to expand should not be pushed into it. There will always be enough institutions eager to grow and too few which combine the special educational virtues of smallness and quality. Those that succeed in maintaining both their low enrollment and their high quality should be lauded and not dragooned into fulfilling some planner's statistic.

3. One type of institution that merits support for broader reasons of national policy is the school which, while not up to the standards of Berkeley or the California Institute of Technology, stands alone, like a monadnock on the plains, representing the best that higher education has to offer to the population of a vast region. It is easy to pick out the few universities of this type in the southern and the mountain states; they fulfill a vital function for their regions and the nation, and warrant special consideration from granting and contracting agencies.

4. Another type is the institution—or, rather, the department—of any size whose present capacity is not being fully utilized. Despite its many pioneering accomplishments, the graduate fellowship program of the National Defense Education Act has been rightly criticized for fostering new and weaker graduate programs in fields—for example, German language and literature, history of the U.S. South, Latin American history—in which long-established departments of greater strength

---

[7] It is worth noting that this criterion of quality is *not* endorsed by all. Indeed, there has been a marked tendency to substitute standards of "competence" for "excellence," as the budgets of science agencies rise. "One can establish a plausible case that adequate support of all competent people is a rational, national objective," one federal official suggests. Perhaps one can. So much mediocrity is supported under present standards of "excellence" that one can only shudder at what would transpire under the avowed reign of "competence."

did not have enough students. Since this NDEA program is the government's most broad-ranging recent effort to promote a dispersion of graduate education, a careful study should be made of its experience. This should include not merely a recital of the satisfaction of recipients and the displeasure of nonrecipients of funds, but an appraisal by each profession of the quality of the new programs established under the Act and their effect upon already established programs. If institution X rises and institution Y falls, because the former pirates good students and staff from the latter, the nation has gained nothing. The dispersion which is needed is the kind that raises the capacity and quality of X while maintaining that of Y.

5. Finally, special attention should be given in the highest reaches of educational and scientific diplomacy to maintaining and strengthening the quality of our leading state universities. Mounting enrollments and the penuriousness of state legislatures have exercised a braking effect on the improvement of many state institutions, while leading private universities have benefited from their strategic advantages in an affluent, free-enterprise society (in prestige, salary scales, the political and financial support of wealthy patrons, and their powerful position in federal research undertakings). As a result, there is danger of a disastrous breach opening up between the quality of our greatest public and private institutions. The breach appears most evident at present in the average quality of undergraduate and graduate students at the two types of institutions, but it may be followed by a corresponding breach in faculty quality if salaries at leading private universities rise too far above those at state universities.

Precisely this danger was foreseen by a committee of the American Association of University Professors in its report on 1961-62 academic year faculty salaries:

> . . . probably the most serious and, from the national point of view, most ominous, aspect of the report is its summary of the lack of progress of state and municipal universities.
>
> Whereas five private independent universities were in the highest [salary] category, no state university reached the very top level.
>
> But even this is not as serious as the fact that almost half of all public universities are in category D on a scale that ranges from AA to F. Only 3 per cent of the independent institutions range as low. . . .
>
> If the gap between private and public universities thus becomes wider, the trend toward academic excellence which marked public institutions in

recent years would be reversed. And this would inevitably mean that students who cannot afford the rising tuition costs of private institutions would be condemned to an education of lower quality than can be afforded by their wealthier contemporaries.[8]

In terms of doctorates awarded and graduate students enrolled, it is the great state universities and *not* the great private institutions which are now the bulwark of higher education in the sciences. For the crassest practical reasons as well as the loftiest democratic principles, the nation cannot afford to see the quality of their research and education impaired.

A nonacademic factor which will increasingly have to be considered as R&D expenditures mount is their economic implication for the regional employment of scientists and engineers, the growth of science-based industries, and the degree of regional prosperity. In justification of the recent pattern of geographic concentration, it is said that science is national and international in scope, and scientific gains made anywhere are immediately available everywhere. But eminent scientists

[8] From the account by Fred M. Hechinger in the *New York Times* (April 29, 1962, Section 4, p. 9) of the report "The Economic Status of the Academic Profession, 1961-62," by Committee Z of the American Association of University Professors. The eleven institutions—one public university, eight private universities, and two technical institutes—reporting for 1961-62 an average nine-month faculty compensation of $11,000 or above (including fringe benefits averaging 6.3 percent) were: Harvard, Cal Tech, Duke, Johns Hopkins, MIT, Princeton, Columbia, Cornell, Northwestern, California, and Rochester. Average salaries of all reporting universities and technical institutes were:

	All Ranks	Professors
29 private independent universities	$9,473	$12,959
9 private independent technical institutes	8,556	11,493
62 public universities	8,384	11,295
7 church-related universities	7,811	9,942
6 public technical institutes	7,790	9,812

Salary data reported by the National Education Association for 1961-62 showed far less of a cleavage between public and private universities—indeed, on certain measures, faculty at public institutions were better paid, particularly at the ranks of associate and assistant professor. This is probably due to the fact that the NEA data are reported in terms of quartiles and medians, which reduce the weight given to the highest salaries that are more common at private universities and technical institutes. See William J. Baumol and Peggy Heim, "The Economic Status of the Profession, 1961-62: Report on the Self-Grading Compensation Survey" (American Association of University Professors, 1962; multigraphed); and National Education Association, *Salaries Paid and Salary Practices in Universities, Colleges, and Junior Colleges, 1961-62* (February 1962).

are not equally available everywhere, and their concentration in certain schools is a distinct asset to that area's industry. The concentration of Department of Defense R&D funds at universities in the Northeast and in California has been accompanied by a great rise in defense procurement of missiles and electronic equipment produced by the industries of these regions, and a proportionate decline in the procurement of wheeled vehicles, weapons, ammunition, and equipment produced by Midwest factories.[9]

The perennial discussions of dispersion have a certain air of unreality, for they attempt to pose and to resolve in strictly objective terms issues that are irreducibly political in nature. If, as the President's Science Advisory Committee states, the nation "urgently" needs thirty or forty "first-rate academic centers of science" instead of the "fifteen or twenty" of today[10] (and what government leader will dare to name the institutions which are *and are not* now "first-rate"?), there is no intrinsic difficulty in creating more (other than the difficulties of locating, importing, or educating the necessary brainpower).

We have examples all around of mighty scientific and educational enterprises created rapidly—the wartime laboratory at Los Alamos, the peacetime laboratory at Brookhaven, the Rand Corporation, the institutes of advanced study at Princeton and Palo Alto, the La Jolla campus of the University of California come readily to mind. The new Graduate Research Center of the Southwest and other cooperating and competing enterprises it will evoke in the region may visibly change the

[9] Ohio, Indiana, Illinois, Michigan, and Wisconsin, collectively, received 32 percent of military prime contracts during World War II but only 12 percent in fiscal 1961. "It must be recognized that the Midwest, with its great university resources, and with its heavy annual production of Ph.D.'s and other professionals, did not in FY 1961 obtain a share of defense prime contracts awards, either for production, for general RDT&E [research, development, testing, and evaluation], or for non-profit research proportional to its share of the nation's scientific and technical skills." See Office of the Secretary of Defense, *The Changing Patterns of Defense Procurement*, (June 1962), pp. 12, 10. Angus Macdonald, director of engineering at the Chicago branch of the Motorola Company, has observed that "midwestern universities and colleges . . . graduate large numbers of qualified scientists and engineers, but they take jobs in other areas where . . . the atmosphere is more conducive to research and development work . . . . Neither industry nor schools can long survive such a situation." See "Midwest Called Science 'Desert,' " *New York Times*, June 3, 1962.

[10] *Scientific Progress, the Universities, and the Federal Government*, President's Science Advisory Committee (The White House, Nov. 15, 1960), p. 14.

national distribution of federal research funds in a few years. All that is needed is the will, the money, and the man to do the job. The money and the leadership are available. What is lacking is the will—the resolution by the Executive and the Congress that more Berkeleys and more MITs are needed.

Or is that all? To pose the question this way suggests both the possibilities and the limitations of public action. The government can, by a resolution it has not shown, create more centers of strength in existing or new institutions. It cannot, by any effort, duplicate, and it should not, by any measure, weaken, what is unique.

The realism of our educational goal will condition our success in attaining it. It is realistic to improve standards throughout our educational system, to improve the curriculum, to improve the training and pay of faculty, to encourage good students, good research, good teaching, good scholarship, and independent thinking. Is it realistic to broaden the peak of the research and education pyramid? We can level down, no doubt, but how many institutions can be brought to the peak of achievement? How many Einsteins can any effort produce? Fortunately, these questions need not be answered immediately. Improving the quality of our research and education is a large and urgent enough goal for public policy, within which the ultimate limits of our talent can be explored.

OUR FINAL ANSWER to the third question about the desirability of dispersing more broadly among doctoral-level institutions research funds now heavily concentrated at a few universities must, to a certain extent, be moot, because the calculus of factors involved in diverse programs cannot yield a simple "yes" or "no" answer. The analysis presented in Chapter 11 demonstrates that the present concentration of federal funds at certain universities coincides with the concentration of both faculty and student talent at these schools—so much so, that there is ground for concern at the excessive concentration of the ablest talent at a few institutions. Primary responsibility for broadening this distribution of scientific talent clearly rests with the U.S. Office of Education, the National Institutes of Health, and the National Science Foundation. Of the broad objectives which they should seek, the most important, we believe, is to strengthen our major state universities without impairing the strength of our great private universities.

PART THREE

The Schools' Administrative Experience

¶ PREFACE • An appraisal of institutions' experience with the administration of federal programs is the easiest of the three tasks set for this inquiry, since records of the experience are plentiful and both academic and government spokesmen will readily supply additional observations. Special insight can be gained from the observations of academic representatives about agency operations, and of agency representatives about academic institutions. Thus, a trip to Massachusetts, Illinois, or California can sometimes be the best way to learn what is going on in Washington, and, in turn, key agency staff may know more about certain institutional practices than anyone on campus. The main difficulty we faced, therefore, was not the lack of information but its superabundance, and the need to limit and define the issues worthy of major attention.

Our resolution of this difficulty is presented in the next seven chapters. Chapter 14 reviews the extent of faculty contacts with government agencies and some of the problems that have arisen in faculty relations with government and university administrators. The next two chapters examine two pervasive financial issues—the payment by federal agencies of faculty academic year salaries (Chapter 15), and the payment of the full indirect and direct costs of federally financed research (Chapter 16)—with important implications for the economics and the philosophy of federal-university relations, and even, as we shall see, for the relationship of faculty to their own institution.

187

Chapter 17 moves to a less controversial subject—the availability of information on federal programs, about which agency performance has been something less than could be desired. Chapter 18 deals with the administrative core around which, since World War II, so much of the government's relations with educational institutions has been elaborated: the project system. Finally in Chapter 19, we will touch on the perennial and critical issue of institutional independence and on the danger of federal control, which we are not inclined to dismiss as lightly as do many advocates of federal aid.

CHAPTER 14

Faculty-Administrator Relationships

FACULTY CONTACTS WITH FEDERAL AGENCIES

AT ONE TIME OR ANOTHER about half of the members of the liberal arts departments surveyed at our twenty-four universities had submitted an application to a federal agency for a research grant or contract. Surprisingly, there was little difference in the proportion at Group I and Group II universities, the major cleavages arising between university and college faculties and, of course, between faculty in different fields (see Table 14-1). Even at Group I universities, home of some of the nation's most distinguished humanists, less than a fifth of the faculty in the humanities had ever applied for federal research funds

TABLE 14-1. *Applicants for Federal Research Awards*

"Have you ever submitted an application to a federal agency for a research grant or contract?"

Field	Percent of Faculty Replying "Yes" in Institution Group			Number Replying "Yes" or "No" in Institution Group		
	I	II	III	I	II	III
Total	52%	47%	29%	1,825	1,106	531
Sciences	75	73	56	809	445	172
Social Sciences	48	43	23	493	297	124
Humanities	19	16	12	523	364	235

189

(and included in their number were many applicants for Fulbright awards, which should more properly be regarded as fellowships). In contrast, about half of their colleagues in the social sciences and three quarters of those in the sciences had made application. The proportions were very similar at Group II universities. The application rate of college faculty (Group III) was not only markedly lower, but also varied more widely among individual schools. As these are a select group of colleges, it may be surmised that there are many other colleges with conditions so inimical to research that their faculty have never had the time, the talent, or the motivation to submit an application.

As to frequency of applications, there was, again, little distinction between the proportion of faculty at Group I and Group II universities applying various numbers of times to federal agencies. (See Appendix A, Table A-18.) This is puzzling, in view of the vast difference in the sums actually received by faculties at the two groups of institutions. In 1957-58, federal agencies awarded the liberal arts faculty (that is, faculty outside of the research centers and professional schools of agriculture, education, engineering, and medicine) at Group I universities $42.2 million for scientific research and development, while those at Group II received only $6 million. The explanation lies in a number of cumulative factors, all serving to favor the Group I faculty:

1. The slightly larger proportion applying for funds.
2. The larger proportion applying *very* often—ten or more times in the sciences, six or more times in the social sciences, and three or more times in the humanities—for it seems clear that these are successful, not stubborn, persons. This factor, incidentally, also distinguishes applicants in the sciences at *each* of the six private universities from those at the six public universities in Group I.

TABLE 14-2. *Percent of Applicants Receiving Various Numbers of Federal Research Awards*

Institution Group	Number of Awards					Number of Applicants
	0	1–2	3–5	6 or more	Total	
Group I	11%	50%	22%	17%	100%	931
Group II	17	50	23	10	100	509
Group III	22	56	16	6	100	155

3. The smaller proportion of applicants who had never been successful and larger proportion of those who had been successful very often (Table 14-2). In brief, the higher frequency of *successful* applications. (For further detail on the number of awards received by applicants from different liberal arts fields, see Appendix A, Table A-19.)

4. The larger size of individual awards. While we did not gather new data on this, it is a reasonable surmise from the different scale of research operations noted on visits, and from previous studies which show that the average size of federal awards rises with the total volume of federal research and development expenditures at an institution.[1]

5. The larger number of applicants and the larger proportion who were well informed about agency programs and acquainted with agency staff (see Chapter 17, Table 17-1).

6. Institutional conditions more favorable to research and, therefore, to the proportion of cogent research proposals. Setting aside the question of the intrinsic merit of proposals and their proponents (and, on the evidence presented in Part Two, Group I faculty would presumably come out ahead), not only do faculty in Group I devote more time to research than do those in Group II; they usually have more and better equipment and graduate students, and more petty cash with which to explore new ideas, and they receive more institutional assistance in the preparation of proposals. Successful proposals are more mature, and have been subjected to more severe, more helpful, and more experienced intellectual and administrative scrutiny. This is certainly the case at one private Group I university with an exceptionally low proportion of rejected proposals. Proposals are referred to a faculty committee for review prior to submission, and it is not unusual for the committee to recommend that they be revised or that further exploratory work be done (and a special fund had been provided for the purpose, which has proved of particular help to younger faculty).

Frequency of Application to Various Agencies

The agencies most frequently applied to are listed in Table 14-3. Of these, the National Science Foundation is the one to which the

[1] Thus, in 1953-54, the average size of federal awards was $7,000 at institutions receiving $25,000-$100,000 a year, compared to $31,000 at those receiving $5 million and over. See National Science Foundation, *Scientific Research and Development in Colleges and Universities* (1959), p. 37.

TABLE 14-3. *Proportion of Applicants and of All Faculty Who Have Applied to Various Federal Agencies for Research Funds*[a]

			Percent of			
Applicants in Group			Faculty in Group			Applying to
I	II	III	I	II	III	
100%	100%	100%	52%	47%	30%	All Agencies[b]
73	76	71	38	36	21	NSF or PHS
39	33	12	20	16	4	Department of Defense
33	33	28	17	16	8	Other Agencies[b]
56	54	60	29	26	18	National Science Foundation
35	42	26	18	20	8	Public Health Service
25	18	8	13	9	2	Navy
19	16	2	10	8	1	Air Force
15	14	3	8	7	1	Army
14	11	4	7	5	1	Atomic Energy Commission
10	10	19	5	5	6	State Department
6	10	4	3	5	1	Office of Education
			Number			
950	524	159	1,825	1,106	531	

[a] Percentages add to more than total for all agencies as many faculty have applied to more than one agency.
[b] Including agencies not itemized below.

largest proportion of university science faculty have applied, and its position in the colleges is even more dominant: of the ninety-seven respondents at our college science departments who had applied for federal research funds, eighty-two had applied to the Foundation. Within the Department of Defense, the Navy (primarily the Office of Naval Research) received more applications from science faculty than either of the other services.

The third rank of the Public Health Service among the agencies to which Group I science faculty had applied is partly due to the exclusion of medical schools from our survey, except for a few basic biological science departments. However, in the social sciences, the Public Health Service replaced NSF as the agency to which the largest number of faculty turned. The National Institute of Mental Health has for years granted substantial sums for research in psychology, sociology, and anthropology, whereas NSF grants in the social sciences were originally confined largely to psychology. Subsequent program and budget expansion enabled NSF to finance a broader spectrum of research, but, to this day, NSF remains more limited to experimental and quantitative approaches in psychology and sociology than NIMH.

Applications for federal research funds in the humanities have gone mainly to the State Department and, secondarily, to the U.S. Office of Education. Although the State Department administers a small program of support for research in foreign affairs and diplomatic history, most applications were for Fulbright fellowships for overseas teaching and research. The Office of Education cooperative program of research in education was instituted in 1956, and its broader program of research in new educational media and foreign language instruction, in 1958.

Faculty Opinion About Agency Fairness and Efficiency

Most applicants indicated that they had been treated "fairly and equitably" by agencies reviewing their research proposals. Some who had been turned down naturally felt otherwise; accordingly, relatively more applicants from Group II than from Group I institutions believed they had been treated unfairly by the Defense agencies and the two major granting agencies, NSF and PHS. The agencies with the unenviable distinction of having the largest proportion of critical applicants were, in order of frequency, the Office of Education, the Air Force, and the State Department, but it should be emphasized that the dominant tenor of faculty comment was favorable, no more than 14 percent of those commenting stating that any agency was "unfair."

The sense of inequity arose principally from the belief that the applicant and his proposal was as good as or better than others who have received research funds; some were also critical of the agency's failure to explain why a proposal was rejected. And some successful as well as unsuccessful applicants expressed apprehension that their idea might be exploited by agency staff, members of reviewing panels, or authorities to whom a proposal is sent for evaluation. Occasional incidents have lent some substance to this concern, although most agency staff and panel members undoubtedly behave with discretion. The fear of being beaten to a good experiment or of not receiving credit for a good idea is more pronounced in America than in European countries where, since every scientist in a particular field knows every other scientist and what he is doing, there is less pressure to publish and less opportunity to capitalize on someone else's ability. Some experienced American scientists take such steps as they feel necessary to protect their priority, withholding from proposals and early publications critical information that would permit too early replication of their work.

The opinion that government agencies were inefficient was more prevalent than that they were unfair. One in every five faculty replied "No" to the question "Reviewing your experience with the agencies with which you have dealt in connection with research proposals, do you feel that you have been treated efficiently, without undue delay or red tape?" Among the agencies frequently dealt with, three stood well ahead of the others in citations for inefficiency (relative to those for efficiency): the State Department, Air Force, and Army; most efficient and least bureaucratic, by this test, were the Public Health Service, National Science Foundation, and Navy. Reasons given for the charge of inefficiency included excessive delay in decisions, unnecessary reports and paperwork (frequently associated with the use of contracts instead of grants), and a "civil service mentality"—rather than the quicker and more informed judgment of professional scientists. Thus a physics professor commented:

> A major difficulty with some of the federal agencies is their lack of ability to make a decision. I believe this reflects essentially second-rate technical people who basically are afraid to make a decision. They therefore "bend with the breeze". . . . A technical program should be judged by capable people, in positions of responsibility, on the basis of an understanding . . . of the technical problem.

Occasional delays of six to nine months or more were charged, however, even against the popular NIH and NSF, which exemplify the model of agencies guided by panel members attached to, and scientists on leave from, educational institutions.

CAMPUS ADMINISTRATIVE STAFFS

Despite Veblen's delightful analysis, over forty years ago, of "the intrusion of business principles in the universities," no one in his right mind can contend that these principles have yet triumphed in universities' transactions with the government. The administrative chaos, absence (or, what can be equally uninformative, creation) of records, the inconsistency in and mutual ignorance of practices of different schools, laboratories, departments, and professors at some of our greatest institutions are simply astonishing. Even the president, research administrator, or dean frequently does not know what actual faculty practice is, while many faculty are either oblivious or disrespectful of central institution "policy."

The situation in Washington is better only by comparison, there being great divergence not only among but within agencies about rules for overhead and salary payments, reporting requirements, and so forth. The frequent absence of information vital to intelligent policy formulation has already been noted. It is said that one Secretary, appalled at the lack of a central list of funds dispersed by his department to various institutions, ordered one to be prepared; it is not said that this was ever completed. The main compensating factor is the inverse relationship frequently obtaining between the readiness of an administrator to make decisions and the quality of the information he requires before acting.

Withal, as the scope and scale of federal programs and research expenditures have grown, there has been a growth in the administrative apparatus and an increasing attempt to strengthen policy-making and policy-enforcing machinery in Washington and on campus. On campus, many special-interest groups affected by federal programs are organized nationally to exchange experience and gain strength—the professional associations (physicists, chemists, mathematicians, psychologists, etc.), medical deans, and engineering schools, and, recently, business officers, research administrators, and graduate deans. The degree to which the university presidents can weld their professional and graduate schools and the undergraduate college, their fat and lean departments, into an integral institution with consistent rather than adventitious policies remains to be seen.

Similarly, it remains to be seen when more consistent policies will emerge from the Bureau of the Budget's long-term pressure for a coherent, nonduplicative federal science budget, congressional demands for the effective direction and public accounting of science programs, and the need for more rational management of the vast research and development enterprise that yearly consumes a larger fraction of the nation's resources. Steps in this direction since the Russians' launching of the first earth satellite include the appointment of a presidential science adviser, the formation of the National Aeronautics and Space

Council and the Federal Council on Science and Technology, and, most recently, the establishment, in the Executive Office of the President, of an Office of Science and Technology one of whose objectives is "to advise and assist the President in achieving coordinated Federal policies for the promotion of basic research and education in the sciences."[2]

Many institutions have established separate research offices to advise faculty on the rewarding art of proposal writing and project budgeting, to maintain financial, property, and even time records required by government regulations, and to provide a central source of information about both federal and institutional programs and policies. One vice president of a major university noted that whereas a few years ago "one girl and a half" could handle the paperwork involved in medical research projects, six persons are now needed, headed by a $12,000-a-year man. Similar developments are characteristic on other campuses. As of March 1962, representatives of eighty-eight universities and institutes of technology and three colleges (Dartmouth; Adelphi College, New York; and Concord College, West Virginia) were members of the newly formed National Council of University Research Administrators. It was the fifty schools with a yearly research volume of $2.5 million or more which pledged funds to establish the new Washington office of the National Federation of College and University Business Officers Associations. When a difference of 1 percent in an institution's overhead rate can mean $35,000-40,000 in its annual income on a research budget of $5 million, a president and his trustees will deem it prudent to hire the best-qualified business officer they can find and give him the staff necessary to defend the institution's interests in interminable negotiations with government auditors.

The growth of administrative staffs has generally been encouraged by government agencies—or, to be more exact, government administrators (since there is a perceptible cleavage between the attitudes and, to an extent, the interests of administrators and scientists, be they in government or at educational institutions). They furnish controls for the disbursement of public funds and accounting for government property,

[2] Reorganization Plan No. 2 of 1962, Sec. 3 (1). See House Report No. 1635, *Approving Reorganization Plan No. 2 of 1962 (Office of Science and Technology— National Science Foundation),* Government Operations Committee, 87th Cong., 2d sess. (April 1962), p. 2. Note the stronger wording than Sec. 3(a)(1) of the National Science Foundation Act of 1950 which directs the Foundation "to develop and encourage the pursuit of a national policy for the promotion of basic research and education in the sciences."

and information for budget and program purposes, and, by satisfying the (real and imagined) needs for *some* procedural uniformity, greatly simplify the task the government would otherwise face of having to deal individually with university faculty members about every administrative detail. It is presumably partly for these reasons that the National Science Foundation has done little to implement that section of its statute instructing it "to strengthen basic research and education in the sciences, *including research by individuals*" and that most other government agencies have signally failed to develop small-scale research awards to individuals on or off campuses.[3] William H. Whyte has made the same observation about large private foundations.[4]

The government can and should institute programs of this sort, and take other steps to simplify research financing and thereby eliminate controls that waste the scientist's time and the taxpayer's money. However, as will be argued more fully in Chapter 18, such steps are needed to improve and supplement, not replace, the present "project system." As long as this system endures, and is supplemented by massive, individually negotiated, operating and capital outlays at universities, so long will special administrative staffs of a kind and number previously unknown on most campuses be required. These staffs do not appear to have reached their optimum size for handling the increasing volume of government expenditures, and they have certainly not reached their optimum mode of operation and of rapport with the faculty.

A brief schedule we distributed to our thirty-six institutions shed a little light on their patterns of research administration. Only two of the twelve colleges had a special office, most indicating that the volume was too small to justify one, the business officer or dean handling such problems as arose. The fractionation of functions between research office, special large laboratories, and the graduate and professional schools (the undergraduate college is least likely to be involved) was common at Group I and Group II universities.

One graduate dean observed that, as extensive graduate work at the great eastern schools long antedated the postwar research boom, their

---

[3] Thus, although private medical practitioners are presumably qualified to conduct independent research, only 39 of 11,572 research grants made by NIH in fiscal year 1960 went to private individuals. See Department of Health, Education, and Welfare, *Public Health Service Grants and Awards by the National Institutes of Health Fiscal Year 1960, Part I* (1960), pp. 394-444.

[4] Whyte, *The Organization Man* (Simon and Schuster, 1956), Chap. 18.

graduate deans were more likely to be concerned with student stipends, and research administration would be handled by another official; in the newer western institutions, where the growth of graduate education and research have been closely linked, the graduate deans were more actively involved in research questions.

An admirable function that can be served by the graduate dean is that of protecting the interests of graduate students. At one university, the dean reviews proposals before submission to Washington, and, if necessary, meets with the students who are to serve as research assistants to ensure that they are interested in the work, know the range of alternative choices open to them, and can judge the acceptability of the problem as a dissertation topic.

FACULTY-ADMINISTRATOR RELATIONS

Federal programs have frequently served to exacerbate the perennial conflict between faculty and "administration." As a general policy, the federal government has tried to minimize, or to stand aside from, any such conflict, requiring that faculty research proposals bear the additional signatures of "the relevant department head(s), and . . . an official authorized to commit the institution in matters involving business and financial affairs"[5] (indicating thereby that the proposal has institutional approval with regard to the nature of the work as well as salary and budgetary detail). Nevertheless, because the principal investigator deals with his scientific counterpart in Washington, while the university business officer deals with the administrative staff in a different office of the same agency, two distinct streams of information, advice, instruction, and reporting flow between Washington and the campus. Lack of harmony between the scientific and the administrative side either in the agency or at the school will quickly be manifested in contradictory instructions—or divergent interpretations of the same instruction—in arguments over deadlines, advance approvals, budget alterations, travel authorizations, salary charges, and so on.

At the level of "rules and regulations," the best-liked administration is one which relieves the faculty of paperwork and helps them to do what they want, with no taint of dictation; the most criticized, that

[5] National Science Foundation, *Grants for Scientific Research,* (1960), p. 3.

which creates unnecessary paperwork of its own, compounding delays originating in Washington. And there are a good many which come in for criticism. Thus, the chairman of a leading psychology department remarked, "We have more red tape in our own business office than in Washington," and a research administrator noted with regret that his university required advance approval of budget changes in NSF grants, thereby "losing on the local level freedom won in Washington."[6] Some government administrators have been known to complain about the rigidity of certain large university research offices, and the resultant loss of informality and flexibility in their relations with university scientists.

At a higher level, the administration best liked by faculty researchers is not necessarily the best administration. For the conflict between faculty and "administration" reflects not so much issues of academic freedom which, when all is said and done, are relatively rare, as the more common issues of money, students, the relative status of different individuals and fields, and the future direction of institutional growth. An administration which does not impose scholarly standards on the type of research it will permit, which is drawn toward money and does not encourage work in academically important but moneyless fields, which rewards faculty in terms of the size of their contracts rather than the quality of their work, is one which has forfeited the respect of intellectuals for that of entrepreneurs.

The availability of federal funds only in certain fields and types of work therefore poses a difficult dilemma for the university administrator. (The dilemma is less serious at colleges, as funds are less abundant there; but even small benefits—reduced teaching loads, new equipment, funds for publication and for travel to professional meetings—restricted to science faculty can produce aggravating problems in a tight-knit college community where everyone knows what everyone else is doing.) If he is too strict about not permitting his scientists and engineers to undertake lines of work which he regards as inappropriate for an edu-

[6] Although NSF takes a lenient attitude toward budget changes after a grant has been awarded, its policy, as usual, is carefully worded so as to take no sides between the principal investigator and the university: "The Foundation believes that the principal investigator, *operating within the established policies of the grantee institution* . . . is best qualified to determine the manner in which the grant funds may be used most effectively to accomplish the proposed research. Therefore, once the grant has been made, the grantee may use the funds for the proposed research without strict adherence to the original budget estimates." (*Ibid.*, p. 12; our italics.)

cational institution (e.g., routine testing, or work requiring a delay in publication to protect a company's commercial advantage) he may lose them to a rival and more lenient institution. But at least he approaches *that* problem with a clear idea of what kind of work is and is not appropriate at his institution.

More intractable is the problem of setting a limit to the volume of research in a legitimate academic area. The traditional conception of a balanced community of single and equal scholars can be maintained in form by limiting the number of tenured faculty appointments. But it is lost in substance when a professor of physics manages a laboratory with a staff of secretaries, purchasing clerks, technicians, senior postdoctoral associates, and a flock of graduate research assistants, whereas his colleagues in history, philosophy, or Latin do their own filing, typing, and longhand note-taking. Scientific research at our great universities has become an industry—the "industry of discovery," Sumner Slichter called it—whereas the humanities remain handicrafts. Perhaps there is a university president who has told an esteemed professor, "Your work is splendid at a $50,000 level, but I cannot permit it at $500,000 a year," and thereby sacrificed a good man and a good program to maintain a better-balanced institution. But the more common solution is to segregate the professor's research establishment from the academic community, thereby maintaining both the real research industry and the nominal academic balance.

The boom in project research has generated much faculty criticism of university "commercialism" and administrators' "venality," direct or indirect pressure to obtain federal research funds, and the "abdication" to the government of responsibility for fostering research and even some aspects of graduate education in the sciences. Many science faculty strongly object to having their regular academic salary charged to federal project funds for that portion of their time which they devote to research, and also to the difficulty of getting university support for apparatus, graduate students, and research expenses (often because the university wishes to conserve available salary and research funds for departments with no opportunity for government aid). A recent All-University Faculty Conference at the University of California noted that "the heavy expenses of . . . [research by graduate students] are being borne increasingly in many departments, by extramural grants. To put the matter bluntly, the individual faculty member, rather than the University, provides the money needed for the supplies and equipment used by his students."[7]

Similar comments were made by many faculty on our questionnaire; most frequently, perhaps, by younger faculty at impoverished institutions and schools which have only recently embarked on major programs of graduate education, but also at some of the nation's richest and best-known universities. The following quotations are illustrative:

I am very uneasy about the projected transfer of the research budgets of universities to federal agencies. It is a dangerous principle that the financial responsibilities of a university apply principally to teaching. (*Associate professor, mathematics, private university, Group II.*)

Unfortunately, the American universities themselves do not assume any responsibility to sponsor research or provide new faciliites. For items worth as little as $200 the university asks the faculty members to get their own grants. (*Assistant professor, chemistry, public university, Group II.*)

I . . . regret and resent the attitude which places the burden of finding the funds to pay his salary and support his research upon the university teacher himself. (*Assistant professor, sociology, private university, Group I.*)

My major objection in relation to federal programs is the attitude generated in administrators that the individual staff member should finance his own research in terms of equipment, assistants, remodeling, etc., and incidentally supply the institution with overhead funds. The researcher thus spends too much time with paperwork and securing funds—work that the administrators should be doing—and the person without a federal grant, or one interested in teaching per se, is looked down upon by the administration and eventually forced out of the university into college teaching. (*Assistant professor, biology, public university, Group II.*)

Faculty replies to three questions indicate how widespread such views are. We asked respondents to "Assume that there are two men in your department of equal professional standing and teaching ability. Both are, also, equally able and productive when it comes to research. However, *Alpha* is active in an area sponsored by the government and has obtained a number of grants and contracts for his research work, including funds for the support of student assistants and the purchase of special equipment; *Beta* is in a field of research with no financial sponsorship from government or other sources. What is likely to be their relative standing in the eyes of: colleagues in the department? the cen-

[7] *Proceedings of the University of California Thirteenth All-University Faculty Conference,* University of California, April 1958, p. 50.

tral administration—deans and members of the president's office (as indicated by relative salary, promotion, and prestige)?" The response is detailed in Table 14-4 and summarized below.

TABLE 14-4.   *Opinion on the Relative Standing of Faculty With and Without Government Research Funds*

Of two faculty members with equal research and teaching ability, Alpha has government research funds, Beta does not. What is likely to be their relative standing in the eyes of: colleagues in the department? the central administration?[a]

Field and Institution Group	Percent of Faculty Replying That					
	Colleagues Will Esteem			Administration Will Favor		
	Alpha More	Beta More	Both Equally	Alpha More	Beta More	Both Equally
Total						
Group I	43%	5%	52%	72%	1%	27%
Group II	45	6	49	76	1	22
Group III	37	3	60	56	1	42
Sciences						
Group I	46	3	51	70	—[b]	29
Group II	45	3	52	73	2	25
Group III	34	2	64	59	2	39
Social Sciences						
Group I	47	3	50	75	1	24
Group II	42	7	51	78	1	21
Group III	44	3	54	53	2	45
Humanities						
Group I	35	9	57	71	3	26
Group II	49	9	43	79	2	19
Group III	36	4	60	56	—	44

[a] See text for exact wording of question.
[b] Less than 0.5 percent.

1. Very few persons suggested that *Beta* would be held in higher esteem by his colleagues and almost none, that he would come off better with "the central administration."

2. Most replied that both men would be held in equal esteem by their colleagues, but that *Alpha* would make out better with the administration.

3. The minority who stated that the administration would reward both men equally was decidedly larger at colleges than at universities,

and slightly larger at Group I than Group II universities. In short, confidence that the administration will deal equitably with a faculty member in terms of the quality of his work rather than the amount of money he raises was strongest in the close-knit college community least involved in federal programs, and weakest at universities in Group II, which lack the resources and stature of those in Group I.

Although the predominant opinion of faculty (in response to our question ". . . what is your view on the over-all issue of the role of the federal government in higher education?") was that federal programs are "necessary and desirable in the national interest, regardless of the financial condition of colleges and universities"—only 1 percent suggesting that they "are unnecessary and should be discontinued"—it was the scientists more frequently than the humanists or social scientists who stated that these programs "are unfortunately necessary, but it would be best for the nation if colleges and universities could do without them." (See Appendix A, Table A-20.) This finding is precisely what we would *not* have predicted; it is, however, explicable in terms of the greater pressure operating on scientists to "make good" and prove themselves by obtaining federal funds, and, presumably, their wish to escape from pesky regulations and from the need to answer or apply to others— even to the most free and best-administered agencies.

SUMMARY

Three quarters of the university scientists, somewhat less than half of the social scientists, and less than a fifth of the university humanists had ever applied for government research funds. Although the prevailing opinion of faculty was that federal agencies are both fair and efficient in handling research applications, more charged the government with inefficiency than with unfairness.

Federal programs have led to a rise in the size of academic administrative staffs, and to complaints that, in their thirst for money, universities have become too "business-minded." While there is substance to this criticism, at least at some schools, the indications are that administrative staffs have not yet reached the optimum size or efficiency needed to discharge their responsibilities.

Friction between university administrators and faculty may develop

204 EFFECTS OF FEDERAL PROGRAMS ON HIGHER EDUCATION

from efforts by administrators to "overcontrol"; to limit work and consulting in fields that are too applied or commercial and, hence, not academically respectable; and to withhold support for faculty research, in order to maximize income from the government and apply the institution's resources to other worthy purposes. Unfortunately, most faculty at our institutions believed that, of two colleagues with equal ability, their administration would favor the one with government research funds over the one without.

CHAPTER 15

Federal Payment of Academic Year Salaries

No CURRENT ISSUE is so "hot" on university campuses as whether faculty salaries should or should not be charged to federal research projects for the time devoted to the project. The other great battle between faculty and "administration," the overhead question, is evidently being won by the administrators, although various government agencies, university departments, and strongly placed individuals (on campus and in Washington) still refuse to concede the victory. The odds are that "administration" will win this battle too.[1]

THE TREND TO PUT SALARIES
ON RESEARCH BUDGETS

The present extent of the practice has been reviewed in Chapter 8 (and see Table 8-2). In 1960-61, one fourth of Group I scientists had part of their regular academic year salary paid by the federal government. If all twelve Group I universities had requested such payments and all

---

[1] One well-informed reader of this manuscript remarked that the division between "faculty" and "administration" viewpoints on the issue "is somewhat less clear-cut than you suggest. . . . On the one hand, . . . , many administrators fear the bind that they would be in if a professor holding tenure would have a claim on state or private funds with the failure of a federal support program to continue. On the other hand, the pressures which spread the practice on the campus very often originate from among the faculty themselves, with the administration merely allowing the proposals to go through rather than actively shaping a policy on it at all."

205

government agencies had made them, some three fifths of these scientists would have had, on average, a third of their academic year salary paid by the government. This represents a lot of money—if the average academic year salary of the scientists involved was $9,500, the sum for all scientists in these Group I departments would be at least $2.7 million a year. A recent study has, in fact, found that some $15 million of the academic year salaries of teaching faculty at forty-eight major institutions was derived from separately budgeted research funds.[2] More than one hard-pressed university president has instructed his aides to make every effort to induce faculty applying for research funds to include the appropriate portion of their salaries in the budget submissions.[3]

Such a request is, of course, completely proper. Not only have the principal executive agencies responsible for establishing policies for federal research programs at universities endorsed it as permissible, but they have begun to advocate it positively, as in the recent recommendation of the President's Science Advisory Committee that "universities should strengthen their faculties for both research and graduate teaching by accepting and using Federal as well as non-Federal support for faculty salaries."[4]

Nevertheless, there is still no uniform federal policy on the matter. The applied research agencies of the Department of Defense have been among the most liberal in reimbursing faculty salaries and even allowing supplemental payments in some cases, as a result of their relatively abundant funds and their practice of salary reimbursement in industrial contracting; one official estimated that about 75 percent of all Defense contracts with universities contain some payment for academic year salaries. Basic research agencies in the department, however, have been

[2] The total volume of separately budgeted research at these forty-eight institutions was about $300 million, excluding expenditures at off-campus research centers. The figure of $15 million for academic year salaries budgeted to research projects includes the time that teaching faculty devoted to research or research administration. The study, conducted by the National Federation of College and University Business Officers Associations, was reported by Nelson A. Wahlstrom, executive director, in a letter dated April 10, 1962.

[3] One university official is quoted as stating, "If an investigator does not include a request for payment to the university for a part of his salary, an administrator inserts the request or the proposal does not leave the university." See Fred R. Cagle, *Federal Research Projects and the Southern University* (Southern Regional Education Board, Atlanta, 1962), p. 47.

[4] *Scientific Progress, the Universities, and the Federal Government,* Statement by the President's Science Advisory Committee (The White House, Nov. 15, 1960), p. 29.

more reluctant to pay faculty salaries as a matter of course, preferring, whenever possible, to negotiate cost-sharing arrangements.

The Atomic Energy Commission has paid the prorated salaries of faculty attached to major university-operated centers like the Lawrence and Ames laboratories, but has practiced cost-sharing in its smaller basic research awards. In the latter, the university is invited to submit a budget detailing the full cost of the contemplated research, including faculty salaries, and then to specify what portion of the total it wants from the Commission.

Under the contracts and grants of the National Aeronautics and Space Administration, universities are not only permitted but expected to receive money for the time faculty devote to research. However, NASA's predecessor organization, the National Advisory Committee for Aeronautics, had sought some cost participation by universities in its far smaller program of fixed-price research contracts. Both the National Institutes of Health and the National Science Foundation, which now reimburse universities for faculty salaries, had also formerly discouraged the practice.

There has, then, been a trend toward the payment by science agencies of a larger portion of the academic year salary of principal investigators. Both civilian and military basic research agencies with a philosophy of "supporting" basic research had long resisted a policy of paying the full (direct or indirect) costs, preferring various forms of cost particiation on the grounds that educational institutions had an interest in basic research, benefited from it in many ways, and, after all, *asked* for the money—it was not thrust upon them. Fundamentally, their philosophy was akin to that of the private foundations, which seek evidence of genuine institutional interest in a project, and a financial contribution is good evidence. But, as their budgets expanded and relations with educational institutions assumed a continuing, long-term nature, the basic research agencies have gradually adopted, in this matter, the philosophy of the applied research agencies, which have traditionally "purchased" research and development on a full cost-reimbursement basis.

THE ROLE OF NSF

The National Science Foundation has played an important role in this development. Half a dozen years ago, a high-level committee established by the National Science Board found it impossible to reach agreement on the issue of academic year salaries for tenure personnel. The recommendation which finally emerged in 1958 really said nothing at all, or, rather, by approving both the policy of paying tenured salaries and the policy of not paying them, hardly contributed to a clarification of the problem:

> On balance, the Foundation believes the establishment and maintenance of salary schedules to be a responsibility of the installation, including the determination as to sources of available funds from which salaries are to be financed. With respect to individual research undertakings, the institution and the Federal agency should be free to determine mutually the composition of the project budget, including the extent to which full or part salaries are to be funded from such a budget. Some institutions and some agencies, particularly where the research being supported is basic or fundamental in character, may as a matter of policy limit support to nontenured staff and summer salaries of tenure staff.[5]

The Foundation's booklet, *Grants for Scientific Research,* issued in January 1960 as a guide to investigators submitting research proposals, was somewhat more explicit about discouraging payments to tenured personnel, stating that "the Foundation, as a general policy, does not encourage the subsidization of tenure faculty salaries during the academic year by means of grant funds." However, the policy remained ambiguous, since the very next passage said "it is entirely appropriate to request funds for the purpose of defraying some portion or all of the academic year salary of such an investigator to the extent that he is to be relieved of his regular institution teaching or other obligations in order to engage in the research."

Shortly thereafter, the National Science Board came out forthright for reimbursing in-year academic salaries, and, in June 1960, the Foundation issued the following straightforward amendment to its grant brochure:

> As a general policy, the Foundation recognizes that salaries of tenured and nontenured faculty members and other personnel associated directly with the research constitute appropriate direct costs, in proportion to the time to be spent on the research. Funds may be requested accordingly.

One well-informed official contended that nothing had really happened with this declaration except that the Foundation, which had previously been prepared to reimburse up to 50 percent of academic year

---

[5] National Science Foundation, *Government-University Relationships in Federally Sponsored Scientific Research and Development* (1958), p. 26.

salaries (where a man was relieved of half his teaching load in order to conduct research), would henceforth reimburse more than 50 percent. This contention is strangely substantiated by statistics showing that in fiscal year 1954, 32.5 percent of principal investigators had part of their academic year salary reimbursed by the Foundation, while in fiscal year 1960 (which was, however, too early to judge the effect of the Board's policy) this was true of only 27 percent. However, although we respect the official's judgment, we do not agree with it, for it puts too much emphasis on the technical aspect of the new policy and not enough on the general principle that was at stake, and it discounts the great influence of NSF among pure scientists and the government agencies who must deal with them. In fact, the decision of the National Science Board has helped to swing the balance of government-university relations away from cost-sharing and toward an assumption by the government of the more complete costs of university research.

From the viewpoint of scientists in liberal arts faculties, however, the Board's decision was not and is not entirely welcome. Indeed, in March 1960, the NSF Advisory Panel for Chemistry, in a signal demonstration of the intractable independence of some consultants, unanimously recommended that no portion of the academic year salaries of regular university staff should be subsidized in the Foundation's chemistry program. When NSF staff and advisory panels cut a grant below the amount requested, as they frequently do, the salary item is often a factor in their decision; and when, in turn, an investigator receives the reduced award, he is likely, as his first step toward reconstituting his original budget, to *not* tax the grant for the requisite portion of his salary.[6]

FACTORS AFFECTING
INSTITUTION AND DEPARTMENT POLICY

The issue of faculty salaries is acute at institutions with a large research volume and a relatively low pay scale. Some public institutions (particularly in poorer states) stand to gain less than private institutions

[6] "If an applicant requests the full costs of his research, including reimbursement of salary, the program director, supported by an advisory committee composed of university faculty members, may merely inform him that only a part of the funds requested may be granted. No reference is made to line items in the proposed budget—the decision of allocating the funds is left to the university (this usually means the investigator). The result is the deletion of those items in the budget, such as salary reimbursement, not under the direct control of the investigator. And NSF policy is defeated." (Cagle, *op. cit.,* p. 87.)

from billing the federal government for the research portion of faculty salaries, if their state appropriation is then reduced by the amount received from the government. Certain private institutions with large endowments have been slow to respond to the opportunity which beckons, although they *are* now beginning to do so and their policy will probably move cautiously in the same direction that needier institutions have more hastily gone.

The institutions whose reach exceeds their grasp, or (in a few famous cases) whose grasp exceeds their means, have lobbied strongly for a full-cost federal policy and tried hard to benefit from it. One such university, caught in a financial crisis as a result of a commendable effort to improve its quality, urgently besought its faculty to include the research part of their salaries in proposals to federal agencies; however, in this and another recent case, the strategem had little immediate success, owing to faculty recalcitrance and the lengthy cycle involved before all projects come up for renewal or renegotiation.

Many faculty object to receiving any part of their salary from the government, regarding this as "soft money" (i.e., withdrawable). True, government programs have expanded steadily and become an apparently permanent feature of the national landscape. But, under the project system, they are still discontinuous and subject to repeated application, renewal, and possible rejection; to secure funds continually, a scientist must remain not only productive but *au courant*. It is particularly difficult for small departments with staff of average ability to have sufficient confidence in the continuity of project funds to plan upon them for funding any important fraction of faculty salaries. Larger departments with men of national stature are better placed to do so. In an effort to ease this problem, some institutions have established special interdepartmental reserves, to give a degree of stability to the salary of faculty beyond the span of each research project.

A department may also fear that, once it has substituted government funds for part of its budget previously drawn from university sources, the sum will be diverted to other uses (such as the subsidization of salaries, graduate students, or research in the humanities) and no longer recoverable by the department. In short, by using government funds to pay part of their own salaries, physicists, for example, are being asked to help, not physics, but Greek or history, which requires a degree of nobility not yet attained by all physicists. To counter this problem, many universities have promised their science departments that they may use for departmental purposes any additional funds brought in by federal contributions to faculty salaries, but the nagging feeling persists that sooner or later there will be *some* diversion, or some reduction in budget increases the department might otherwise have reasonably expected from university sources.

The Line of Tenure

Then there is the line of tenure, which, as we noted, was so hard to cross in the National Science Foundation's policy deliberations on faculty salaries. A tenured professor has reached a position of enviable security. It may well be that tenure is a moral and not a legal obligation, and that a professor's salary may not, in fact, be drawn from protected endowments but from more volatile alumni gifts or student fees which vary with changing enrollments in different fields; and that, in any event, there is no final security in endowment, which is as subject to market forces as government appropriations are to international events and the political process. Nevertheless, tenure is not merely an obligation: it is an expression of confidence, an indication that the university esteems a man enough to want him permanently on its staff; and this will normally elicit a sense of identification with, and of loyalty and responsibility to the institution which can hardly be expected from junior or research staff. For some men, that loyalty is jeopardized when they receive part of their salary from the federal government. It is a singularly unfortunate consequence of the present project system that it often thus impairs loyalty to an institution, and even leads university administrators to promote disloyalty to themselves.

As a point of fact, at many institutions tenured faculty have part of their academic year salary drawn from federal funds less frequently than nontenured faculty. Thus, in 1959-60, the proportion of medical school faculty receiving some of their salary from federal sources was 25.5 percent; by rank the proportion was as follows: professors, 12.6 percent; associate professors, 23.9 percent; assistant professors, 32.2 percent; instructors, 30.3 percent.[7] We expected that our survey would document a similar situation at the twenty-four universities examined.

[7] *Journal of the American Medical Association,* Nov. 12, 1960, p. 183.

However, the proportion of university scientists and social scientists who received part of their 1960-61 academic year salary from federal sources turned out to be almost as large in the two upper ranks (associate and full professor) as in the two lower (instructor and assistant professor). But decidedly more faculty in the lower ranks received a larger *fraction* of their salary from the government (Table 15-1).

TABLE 15-1. *Proportion of Faculty Receiving Part of Their Academic Year Salary from Federal Funds, By Rank, 1960-61*

Field and Institution Group	Percent Receiving Part of Salary from Federal Funds[a]					
	Less than Half of Salary		Half or More of Salary		Total	
	A	B	A	B	A	B
Scientists						
Group I	16%	10%	9%	14%	24%	24%
Group II	10	5	4	11	14	16
Social Scientists						
Group I	8	9	4	7	12	16
Group II	7	6	8	10	15	16

[a] A: professors and associate professors; B: assistant professors and instructors.

An interesting way to foster the security of tenured faculty while obtaining their research salary from the government is being tried at one institution. Some of the money thus received is set aside in a reserve endowment to protect tenure salaries should the government income cease.

The Line of Age

The perceptible difference in viewpoint between older and younger staff is partly attributable to their different experience and conception of the university's responsibility for research. The young man accustomed to government fellowships, research stipends, and dependency allowances as a graduate student finds little amiss in federal support of his salary thereafter. The older man was paid by the university to do research before the government entered the scene. He had always regarded research and teaching as inseparable functions of the great university. Now a visible effort is being made to separate them and assign to the government the full costs of the research portion.[8] At the rich institution, this seems like an abdication of a traditional responsibility; at the poor institution, a failure to assume it.

The Reduction of Faculty Research Funds

Faculty opposition to salary charges against project funds, like faculty opposition to large overhead rates, has, also, a very simple basis: it reduces the amount of money available for student support, equipment, summer salaries, and other purposes. It is a widespread misconception that, because the government puts many hundred millions of dollars a year into research and development at universities and colleges, the amount going into a particular item like the investigator's salary in a particular grant or contract is inconsequential and does not affect the size of the award, which will be determined rather by the merit of the proposal and the investigator. Project money is not allocated from a large pot with 850 million silver dollars, nor from a single agency budget, but from a relatively small sum ranging from a few hundred thousand dollars or less to perhaps $5 million, assigned by an agency head to a particular scientific field or program. Within this program, a difference of $5-10,000 in a specific budget item has a significant effect on the number of proposals that can be supported. As a rule, the program director and his scientific advisers would like to support as many good proposals as possible, and to support the best proposals for as long as possible. Furthermore, scientific advisers are usually faculty members serving as consultants, who, like so many faculty, resent the diversion of "their" money to other purposes. And so, after fighting on his campus

[8] There is a striking inconsistency in the position of universities on the separability of research and teaching. In their arguments on the problem of how the full indirect costs of research should be calculated, they have contended that research and teaching are, in principle and in practice, inseparable (and hence that a common base including the indirect costs of both should be the point of departure for allocating the indirect costs of one). In their arguments for the reimbursement of direct costs, they contend that the two *are* separable. A reconciliation of these contradictory positions is easier in the realm of economics than of logic.

against the inclusion of academic salaries in the budget submission, he continues to fight in Washington for the reduction of the grant or contract by an amount at least equal to the salary requested.

The addition of academic year salaries as a direct project cost also, of course, increases the amount of overhead payable by the government to the institution, whether that overhead is calculated as a fixed proportion of the total direct costs (as by NSF and NIH) or as a proportion of the total direct salaries which is negotiated once a year for each institution (as in Defense Department contracts). This serves as another incentive to institutional administrators to request it, and another disincentive to the faculty member, since it further reduces (or he fears it will reduce) the amount he is likely to net for his own use.

PAY CHECKS AND TIME CHECKS

Putting part of a professor's salary on a government project has raised aggravating administrative problems of defining the nature of his full-time obligation to the university, and of measuring the portion of that time devoted to the project.

The Problem of Defining "Full-Time"

In the 1930's, "full-time" might mean 15 to 18 hours or more of classroom teaching, heavy additional administrative and student advisory duties, and summer teaching as well; in the affluent 1960's, for highly prized scholars at wealthy institutions, it can mean no teaching at all or teaching one 3-hour course for one semester or two quarters. The range of normal teaching responsibilities among faculty at the thirty-six institutions studied was from 0 to over 16 classroom hours.

Now, if a faculty member is paid to teach 0 or 3 hours—and, while the former figure is reserved for research professors and some of the most distinguished American scientists, the latter is more common at some of our greatest universities—what is his "full-time" obligation to the university and what part of that should be charged to the government? If he is paid to work 40 hours a week, and all but 3 hours goes into research, the government might (in principle—*not* in practice) be charged for 37 hours; if, though 3 hours may have in fact been the rule for full professors in a particular department for more years than can be remembered, the figure of 6, 9, or 12 hours is still accepted as the putative "full-time" load, then the government could be charged half, two thirds, or three quarters of the professor's salary. The formula for reimbursement rests ultimately on a conception of full-time obligation which is never strictly defined, and the academic instinct rebels vehemently against defining it.[9]

In practice, things are worked out, not by formula, but by judgment: first, the judgment of the principal investigator and his department chairman and dean as to how much of his salary it is reasonable to ask the government to reimburse; and second, the judgment of the program director in Washington as to whether the request is indeed reasonable, which will rest upon stated or unstated agency practice, further inquiry into the circumstances of the particular case, the general distribution of such requests in his program, and what his budget can bear. And, although there is some abuse and probably a growing disposition to ask for relatively larger proportionate reimbursement than had formerly been requested for the same amount of research, by and large universities have been conservative in their requests.

Not only is a "full-time" obligation undefined in any rigorous terms, but it also runs counter to one (not the only) long-standing conception of academic employment as essentially a *part-time* obligation under the terms of which a professor should be free to obtain additional income for intellectual and professional services rendered in his "spare time."

> Reference to teaching as a "part-time" profession has frequently been acknowledged. . . . It was, for example, made by Committee T of the American Association of University Professors. Their report was published in 1930 (at the time when faculty salaries were approaching the highest values reached at any time for real personal income) and included the statement that: "From the financial point of view, we are beginning to admit part of the situation in the oft-repeated phrase that teaching is

[9] " 'Full-time' is difficult to define. It implies controlling interest, loyalty, and first responsibility. In the academic world it means far more than an 'X-hour week in the shop.' It is believed preferable to leave the term loosely defined as above, depending upon a principle rather than a formula." *Policies and Procedures: A statement for the information and guidance of members of the staff of the Massachusetts Institute of Technology* (MIT, September 1961), p. 6.

only a part-time profession. Not only is teaching a part-time profession, but only a part of that part-time is really devoted to actual teaching."[10]

More than one university has found it convenient to subscribe to this conception of "part-time" or even, as one Air Force official noted, hourly employment: "X University says, 'No, we aren't paying the man $9,000 a year; he's only teaching Y hours, and we pay him in fact, $20 an hour.' I tell you there are five different meanings which can be given to $9,000 a year." It is a frequent practice on the clinical side at medical schools to permit outside earnings up to 100 percent of a "base salary" which, for a full professor, may run to $15,000 or more. This arrangement really assumes that the professor will devote roughly half his time to teaching and half to clinical practice. If, instead, he devotes his time to research, does his research income *supplement* his "base salary" or *substitute* for clinical fees?

There is no single ideal solution of these problems which is also practical, but many exigent solutions which are logically contradictory.

Time Records

Difficulties have arisen between universities and the Department of Defense with regard to the maintenance of records accounting for the time which faculty and other professional staff assign to government projects. Profit and nonprofit research organizations customarily keep such records to allocate the time of professional staff among various projects and many universities have also kept them, with that element of unreality that attaches to so many statistics about the activities of professional men. One student reproduces several forms that are in use to account for the time of professional personnel engaged on sponsored research and paid on an hourly, weekly, semimonthly, or monthly basis.[11] The figures come out very neatly, to be sure, whether reported

[10] Herbert E. Longenecker, *University Faculty Compensation Policies and Practices in the United States* (University of Illinois Press, 1956), p. 17. The quotation from Committee T is cited from the *Bulletin of the American Association of University Professors,* Vol. 16 (March 1930), p. 208. The Longenecker study should be read by anyone seeking to puzzle out alternative solutions to the problems of faculty reimbursement on and off government projects; it shows that the essential issues involved are generic to academic employment and long antedate the rise of federal research programs.

[11] See Comegys Russell de Burlo, Jr., *Administrative Problems of Sponsored Research Programs in Small Colleges and Small Universities,* doctoral dissertation,

as a percentage of total time, or as an absolute number of hours, because the system really works backwards from an initial understanding between the investigator and the agency that, let us say, 50 percent or a nominal 20 hours out of a nominal "full-time" week of 40 hours, or a total of X dollars, will be budgeted to the project. The whole exercise is an elaborate game, time-consuming but harmless so long as it is recognized that no self-respecting professional man will be clocked in and out like a factory worker.

Problems arise when government auditors take the figures literally (rather than as a sign of honest effort) and undertake the painstaking, futile, and insulting task of checking up on them; or when they refuse to allow an upward adjustment in time allocated during one period (such as Christmas) to compensate for time not allocated during another period (such as examination week), so that the total reimbursement will equal the sum agreed upon for the year. Or they may arise when an investigator continues to draw his salary from a project although patently no longer working on it. In one such instance, the investigator did this for two years while off in Europe on work that had no relation at all to the project.

The Armed Services Procurement Regulation requires that "current and reasonable estimates of time spent" may be substituted for exact time records. This should provide sufficient latitude to reconcile the reasonable requirement of government auditors that public funds are being used for the purposes for which they are appropriated and the reasonable need of academic men not to be hamstrung and held to account for every hour of every day. Any sensible scientist will instruct his—or the departmental—secretary to complete the required forms; any sensible auditor will accept this certification; and any sensible dean will see, quietly and without paperwork, that there are no abuses.

Unfortunately, not all auditors and scientists are reasonable. Thus, a considerable and (to an outside observer) quite unnecessary hassle recently developed between the Department of Defense, in the person of the three military audit agencies, and many universities about maintaining time records of professional personnel assigned to research contracts. Although the particular problem varied slightly on different campuses, the general issue revolved about the government's request that universities

Graduate School of Business Administration, Harvard University, March 1960, pp. 239-250.

not only estimate in advance the time a professor would assign to a project but indicate thereafter how he actually did spend the time. Most universities refused to do this.[12] Or, to be more precise, they refused to accede to the audit agencies' requirement that estimates after-the-fact be recorded on a daily, weekly, or semimonthly basis, and to their ruling that recollections of periods exceeding half a month or estimates made in advance were not acceptable time records. Only four of fifty institutions replying to an inquiry on the subject, made early in 1961 by Western Reserve University, had agreed to the requirement and were then maintaining semimonthly after-the-fact time records.

The audit agencies appeared to be unreasonable in not accepting retrospective records for a period longer than two weeks, and the universities in not providing them.[13] But no mathematical formula will solve a problem of this sort where the parties evidently sympathize with each other so little. The episode is instructive about the differences between the mentality of the academic man and that of the government auditors and contracting officers administering cost contracts. Undoubtedly much can and should be done to promote an understanding by each group of the responsibilities of the other, and procedures should and can be worked out to reduce paperwork requirements and yet provide those papers which seem an irreducible requirement of modern life (the academic man should know—he produces enough papers of his own!). We will return subsequently to the question of contracts versus grants. But it is a mistake to ascribe all the difficulty to the "cost-accounting" or the "military" mind. Problems of this sort recur periodically, if less frequently, with the granting agencies NSF and NIH, and, in the final analysis, are probably inherent in the government's relations with educational institutions. If educational institutions are going to use public funds allocated by the present research project system to pay faculty salaries, then they must be prepared to account in some way for these funds.

[12] Willis B. Foster of the Office of the Director of Defense Research and Engineering has said that "some universities insist on using budget estimates as a 'current and reasonable' estimate of the time spent . . . and we'd even be willing to accept these if [they] . . . gave evidence of having some sort of control system . . . a confirmation report . . . to detect differences between budget estimates and what took place, in fact." (Address to the American Society for Engineering Education, University of Kentucky, June 29, 1961.)

[13] The issue was subsequently compromised with the acceptance by representatives of the military audit agencies and university business officers of retrospective

CONCLUSION

The distance that higher education, or science education, has gone toward federal subsidization of faculty salaries is astonishing. It is hard to believe that a dozen years ago a committee at the Massachusetts Institute of Technology, which has been in the vanguard of so many innovations in federal-university relations, condemned the practice of providing *summer* salaries on federal research projects—

> This we believe to be an exceedingly unwise policy, and it is one that MIT has endeavored to avoid. It is a policy that tends to inflate the salary scale in some departments, giving rise to serious inequities and the promise of future discord when contract work is unavailable. Above all, it emphasizes the motive of financial gain rather than the intrinsic worth of a project in an educational institution. . . .[14]

or that, in 1952, the Director of the National Science Foundation stated that it is "a serious thing" for the government to pay the salaries of tenured faculty, "because after all the permanent officers of an institution are the board of directors educationally and it may very well be questionable for the government to be paying their salaries directly or indirectly."[15]

Within a given federal budget for research and development at universities, if more money is allocated to one purpose such as faculty salaries, clearly, less will be available for other purposes such as graduate students, research associates, and equipment. But universities don't look at it that way, assuming rather that federal research appropriations will continue to rise; and each institution, of course, hopes to maximize its *own* immediate income.

Our conclusion will not be popular in many university quarters, but we believe that universities are making a mistake when, in effect, they put their faculty on the federal payroll. (The mistake might be remedied if the present practice were only a way station to some broader form of

---

time records on a monthly basis. This provision was incorporated in Joint Letter No. 41A, issued by the audit agencies in November 1961.

[14] *Report of the Committee on Educational Survey,* Massachusetts Institute of Technology (December 1949), p. 62.

[15] Alan T. Waterman, in *Journal of Proceedings and Addresses,* Association of Graduate Schools in the American Association of Universities, Princeton, 1952, p. 123.

federal aid to educational institutions.) To be sure, those schools which first capitalize on a new government cost policy will get a bigger initial piece of the pie. Immediately, they stand to gain; but over the long run, it may be feared, they stand to lose two important assets: the ability to pay their faculty from independent sources of income, and, thereby, their ability to say "no" to the government. And the ability to say "no" is as fair a test of virtue in a university as in a woman.

CHAPTER 16

Overhead and Cost-Sharing

SURELY THE ADMINISTRATIVE ISSUE of "overhead" or "indirect costs" is the most tirelessly debated of the ample repertoire of issues composed by government and university administrators. If we do not discuss the matter at length here, it is because there is little new to say about it. The subject has been treated by an interminable number of government and university spokesmen, the issues are clear, the alternative courses are clear, and the only thing which is not clear is which course, if any, will allow everyone concerned to live happily ever after.

INTERRELATION OF
INDIRECT AND DIRECT COSTS

"Overhead" refers to those costs of administering, housing, and otherwise serving a project that can not readily or reasonably be identified as direct costs and itemized in the project budget or cost vouchers. For example, personnel (professional, technical, secretarial, and clerical), equipment (permanent or consumable), and travel are common direct costs. Housing the project (where no rent is paid) in a building with other functions, maintaining this and other buildings, grounds, and access roads; administering the university or a number of projects; and operating the library are common indirect costs. Many costs can be regarded as either direct or indirect, depending upon institutional accounting practice, the nature of a project, and the degree to which

221

sufficient use will be made of a specific service to warrant breaking it out and treating it as a direct cost. Because the same costs can, in principle and practice, be either "direct" or "indirect," and because indirect costs are calculated as a percent of direct (either of total direct or of direct salaries), no meaningful discussion of an agency's policy on indirect costs can overlook its policy on direct costs as well.

It should be stressed that the relative size of two institutions' overhead rates (e.g., 25 and 48 percent of total direct costs or, let us say, 37 and 63 percent of direct salaries and wages) is not necessarily an indication of their relative administrative efficiency but merely of their method of bookkeeping.[1] Some institutions distribute costs extensively, seeking economies by making each department or project pay directly for its own services; others, which seek economies by centralizing services, tend to have higher overhead rates. The treatment of fringe benefits alone, as either a direct or a indirect cost, has a substantial effect on the overhead rate.

One important guiding principle is that government contracts and grants not be treated discriminatorily: i.e., that the distinction between direct and indirect charges be made uniformly, consistent with normal institutional practice. But, as government funds constitute so large and continuing a source of income, there is a tendency for institutions to (uniformly) adopt those accounting practices that best serve their interests in dealing with the government. Further, in negotiating with the government, institutions enjoy certain advantages which they lack with private foundations or industry: they are not merely bargaining with a second party—after all, it is also *their* government. Should a decision go against them at the level of government program director and university professor, or government auditor and university business officer, the university president can take the matter up directly with the agency head,

[1] Even so experienced an administrator as Ernest Allen, NIH associate director for Research Grants, can fall into the common error of judging overhead rates in absolute terms rather than as percentages that are meaningful only when one knows the direct charges to which they are applied. Thus a recent hearing of the House Committee on Government Operations demonstrated that NIH had paid 15 percent overhead on a grant to a profit-making organization whose true overhead rate had subsequently been found by audit to be 6.6 percent. "I would never have dreamed there would be a profit-making institution with a 6.6 percent indirect cost rate," Allen remarked. "It is almost unbelievable to me that this is the proper rate. . . ." See *The Administration of Grants by the National Institutes of Health,* Hearings before a Subcommittee of the House Committee on Government Operations, 87th Cong., 2d sess. (March 1962), p. 55.

an appropriate congressman, or a well-placed friend on an agency advisory committee.

We don't suggest that there is any impropriety in this kind of appeal, or that it is used for trivial purposes. But as university representatives are free citizens, they are not beholden to anyone and least of all to the administrative channels civil servants must obey. They may use whatever avenue best advances their cause. And, over the long pull, they can participate fully in political efforts to change any policy with which they disagree, and it must be said that, since the war, they have been fairly successful at doing this.[2]

Universities have succeeded in broadening the range of items accepted as direct costs, and in moving toward the full reimbursement of indirect costs incurred in government projects. The recognition and subsequent liberalization of the formulas for reimbursing first summer and, then, academic year salaries; of personnel benefits like sabbatical leave; the retention of property purchased on cost contracts, title of which had previously lodged with the government; recognition of journal page costs for the publication of research finding; and raising the formula for reimbursing indirect costs of research grants are examples that come readily to mind. Requests for reimbursement of the tuition charges of research assistants and of the costs of administering the program of student loans under the National Defense Education Act are only two signs that the end is not in sight. It is not likely to come until a plateau is reached in the mounting federal expenditures at universities.

It is interesting to compare the costs recognized in government research grants with those in the long-established small grants program of the American Philosophical Society:

> Grants are not made toward the payment of salaries of members of the staff of an educational or scientific institution. . . .
>
> Grants are not made for:
>
> a. salaries, fellowships, or scholarships;
> b. the expenses of publication;

---

[2] Cf. Don K. Price, *Government and Science* (New York University Press, 1954): "In routine procedural matters the [government] contracting or accounting officer may annoy the business manager of a university in endless petty details and make his decisions stick. But on the really important issues the head of a university laboratory, or the president of the university, can appeal to echelons high enough in the government structure—and with much more authority and influence than any subordinate civil servant would have—to win his point" (p. 91).

    c. usual or permanent equipment of the institution involved but may be for special apparatus needed in the proposed research, such apparatus to be returned to the Society when the project for which it was purchased has been completed;

    d. expenses in connection with the preparation of a doctoral dissertation.

Support of a long continuing project is not undertaken, except in its initial stage.[3]

The policies of the National Science Foundation are diametrically opposed on every one of these points.

We have, then, a situation in which government research programs have been recognizing a widening area of direct costs and paying either the full or an increasing proportion of the indirect costs. What is the fuss all about?

The fuss is about two things:

1. How to arrive at a method of defining accurately and equitably just what constitute full indirect costs.

2. Whether, in principle, the government *should* pay the full indirect (*and* direct) costs of all its research programs at educational institutions.

The two problems are interrelated, because there is no simple and acceptable method of determining full indirect costs at an institution with a large volume of government projects. The yearly auditing of each university's books and the protracted negotiations between government auditors and university representatives that have been necessary to establish an overhead rate for each institution have led to much ill feeling, and push the universities into more businesslike and less academic administrative practices (which, in turn, usually drive up overhead costs). Some university business officers declared that they would prefer a flat overhead rate not subject to audit on *all* their government work even if this represented something less than the full audited rate. (They are more apt to say this in private, however, than on the public record, for they and their presidents are lobbying for full cost reimbursement.)

A flat overhead rate applied uniformly to all institutions must come out to something less than full indirect cost for many universities, since a uniform rate which met the full overhead of universities with a high rate would constitute more than full overhead at many other institutions.

---

[3] American Philosophical Society, *Year Book 1959* (Philadelphia, 1960), pp. 199-200.

In fact, even the present flat rate of 20 percent of direct costs in NSF grants undoubtedly comes to more than full overhead at *some* institutions.[4] In contrast to the position which seeks a high uniform rate with simplified administrative procedures established as standard government policy, university spokesman anxious to secure full overhead reimbursement on all government research projects argue that there is little difference in the administrative costs of government grants (carrying a flat rate below the university's full audited rate) and government cost contracts (paying the audited rate). They regard the flat overhead rate as an invidious feature of grants, since it obliges the university to divert scarce unrestricted funds from other educational purposes to meet the residual indirect costs of these grants.

For the foregoing reasons, a satisfactory government policy seeking full overhead reimbursement should (1) permit an institution to choose either an individually audited rate or a uniform flat rate set around or slightly below the average audited rate of most large institutions, and (2)

[4] The 15 percent of total direct costs which NSF established as its original overhead policy in October 1951 was based upon an analysis of the audited overhead rate of forty-three institutions receiving basic research contracts from the Office of Naval Research. The average full overhead at these universities, calculated on the then operative Mills formula, came to 29.8 percent of total direct costs, but that rate applied uniformly would have paid *more* than full overhead to twenty-three of the forty-three institutions; even the 15 percent formula paid more than full overhead to three of the forty-three.

More recently, an NSF study found that the average full overhead rate of ninety-three major institutions in fiscal year 1960 was 28.2 percent of direct costs (computed on the basis of Bureau of the Budget Circular A-21, the latest government dictum), weighted in accordance with the volume of federal R&D expenditures at each institution. However, if the government had uniformly paid an overhead rate of 28.2 percent, forty-seven of the ninety-three would have received more than their full overhead costs; indeed, present NSF overhead payments of 20 percent constituted more than full overhead for eight institutions. See National Science Foundation, "Indirect Costs of Research and Development in Colleges and Universities, Fiscal Year 1960," *Reviews of Data on Research & Development*, No. 32 (March 1962), p. 3 (plus unpublished information supplied by the NSF Office of Economic and Statistical Studies).

Dr. James Shannon, director of the National Institutes of Health, told the House Government Operations Committee that the NIH overhead rate of 15 percent of direct costs "is . . . *substantially below* what has been shown to obtain in each of the individual institutions that have been audited" (our italics), although later in the day he noted that, in two cases out of twenty, the institutions' rate was found to be "just a trace below" 15 percent. See *The Administration of Grants by the National Institutes of Health*, House Hearings . . . (March 1962), pp. 54 and 87.

permit the government to negotiate an individual rate in cases where the flat rate is notably higher than the audited rate. This was the policy recommended by the National Science Foundation to the Bureau of the Budget in June 1955, which has, however, not yet (August 1962) been implemented by the Bureau or, indeed, by the Foundation itself.[5]

But, to return to the two continuing problems.

HOW SHOULD FULL INDIRECT COSTS BE COMPUTED?

Until recently, the accepted method of calculating full indirect costs was the so-called "Blue Book" or "Mills formula" (named after Gail Mills, the comptroller of Princeton University) incorporated in the Armed Services Procurement Regulation. In September 1958 the Bureau of the Budget promulgated a new set of principles, "Circular A-21," and a revised version was issued in January 1961. The new basis, initiated more or less unilaterally by the government (particularly the military audit agencies), was at first strongly opposed by educational institutions, which objected above all to the allocation of operating and maintenance expenses on the basis of space utilized, respectively, for teaching and research, on the grounds that this distinction was impractical and incompatible with their indivisible teaching and research function. Although it is still too early to come to a final conclusion, the new formula may actually serve to raise overhead allowances, and university opposition has correspondingly slackened. There are still a number of changes the universities would like to see in A-21, including a larger use allowance for buildings and equipment and a fuller reimbursement of library costs.

A fundamental difficulty in the present method of auditing is that, in conformity with a January 1956 ruling by the Comptroller General, indirect costs must be determined retrospectively, based upon the records of actual costs incurred and may not be set prospectively, based upon the costs incurred during the previous year, as had long been the practice. Under the present retrospective method, it may take two years or more to establish an audited rate. In the spring of 1961, for example, an

[5] The Foundation's recommendation is reported in National Science Foundation, *Government-University Relationships in Federally Sponsored Scientific Research and Development* (1958), pp. 42-44.

audited rate had been determined at many universities in our study only for academic year 1958-59 and, at one school, for 1957-58. Either a reserve must be set aside until the final rate is determined, or the institution may overspend and find itself with smaller receipts from the government than it had anticipated; and no project director can know exactly how much money he has to spend in any given year. There is, indeed, little that can be said for the Comptroller General's ruling other than that it was required by his interpretation of the law prohibiting cost-plus-a-percentage-of-cost contracts; and legislation is in process to correct the situation.[6]

No set of rules is so specfic as to preclude differences in individual interpretation: and there has been considerable variation in the interpretation of auditing rules among the three military services (which, together with the Atomic Energy Commission, do most of the detailed auditing of university research accounts that precedes the determination of overhead rates) and among their regional offices. When accountants whose main experience is in auditing industrial contracts are assigned to university accounts in their region, unhappy consequences may often be anticipated. Much good would result from the formation of a corps of civil servants within each science agency to specialize in auditing and administering research at educational institutions and build up, over the years, experience with and sympathy for the problems of higher education. Agencies which have been most successful in dealing with educational institutions tend to be those with special statutory authority and staff confined to this function; those—like the Army Ordnance districts and the Air Force procurement agencies—which have been much criticized for their "hardware" approach to research contracting, tend to have other primary responsibilities and staff whose principal duty is industrial contracting.

SHOULD THE GOVERNMENT PAY THE FULL COSTS?

Is some cost-sharing in the best interest of both the government and the educational institutions, or should the government reimburse the full indirect (and direct) costs of all institutional research?

[6] H.R. 6984, adopted by the House of Representatives in April 1962, would permit government agencies "to pay for reimbursable indirect costs in contracts with colleges and universities for research and development on the basis of pre-

For many years, the operating distinction in federal programs lay between "purchased" and "supported" research. "Purchased" research, in which an agency contracted for research helpful to the fulfillment of its mission, paid full direct and indirect costs; "supported" research, in which an agency provided some funds to help a professor do work that *he* initiated, usually paid much but not all of the costs: the salary of the professor and some overhead were the main costs which the government would not pay, as a matter of policy. Typical programs of "purchased" research included the large applied research programs of the military services and the Atomic Energy Commission, generally conducted on cost contracts; typical programs in "support" of research included the research grants of the National Science Foundation and the National Institutes of Health and the (usually small) research contracts of the Office of Naval Research, the Office of Ordnance Research, the Office of Scientific Research, and the Atomic Energy Commission.

The cost-sharing of "support" programs resulted, in part, from their low budgets; in part, from a philosophy inherited from the private philanthropic foundations; and in part from their more liberal administrative practices which somewhat compensated for their low cost policies, such as advance payments, less paperwork, and the award of property to the institution. However, there has been increased pressure to have "support" programs eliminate cost-sharing as their budgets have risen (in 1961, NSF and NIH alone provided an estimated 46 percent of all federal R&D funds at educational institutions, excluding research centers, compared to 11 percent in 1952), and as basic research has come to be regarded less as an activity to satisfy the idle curiosity of the academician and more as an activity to strengthen the nation.

Fuller payment of indirect and direct costs has been opposed by the Bureau of the Budget, university scientists, and key congressional committees in an effort to keep administrative costs down, encourage cost participation by educational institutions, and put the maximum amount of federal money "directly" into research. In a famous instance in 1951, a request by university business officers that the overhead in NIH grants be raised above the 8 percent figure then prevailing was unanimously rejected by the eighty scientist members of the Advisory Councils; and in

determined fixed-percentage rates without the necessity for an adjustment based on a postaudit." See *Payment of the Costs of Research and Development at Universities,* House Report No. 1485, Committee on Government Operations (March 1962), p. 1.

1962, an irate university administrator insisted to us that NSF could have adopted a full overhead policy at any time in recent years and did not, not because of opposition from the Bureau of the Budget, but because "it is a scientist-ridden agency."

Faculty can hardly fail to regard overhead as a reduction in "their" research money, so long as it is calculated as a portion of the direct costs of each project. A revised system of funding only direct costs in individual agency budgets and of paying the indirect costs of all government programs—or, at least, all the projects of a single agency—in a lump sum to each institution might circumvent this problem. The effect would be to eliminate overhead as an item in individual project budgets (and, hence, as a matter of immediate concern to faculty and to agency program directors) and establish it as a new government-wide—or agency-wide—function.

No doubt there would be technical difficulties in implementing this suggestion, such as the difficulty of allocating fairly to different agency budgets that portion of an institution's overhead which can reasonably be ascribed to the type of work each agency sponsors, and the problem of synchronizing overhead payments with the payments of varying kinds of direct costs. But these difficulties are not intrinsically different from those which arise and are resolved under the present system.[7] The main advantage of the suggestion is tactical—the removal of faculty from involvement in the matter of indirect costs, which would no longer appear as an item in their budget or, therefore, figure in their plans. (No doubt faculty would and should remain concerned with the broad issues represented by alternative overhead policies for their institution and their government.) And, without the continual intrusion of faculty into an area in which they have no special competence (but now have both a real interest and real power), it should prove easier for university and government accountants and administrators to resolve the technical difficulties which will persist.

DISCUSSION

There is no doubt that universities have a good case for full cost reimbursement, and that has been the general direction of government policy despite a number of setbacks. The case is one of financial need,

[7] For example: (1) Should Agency X accept, in its contract at University Y, the audited institutional rate negotiated by Army auditors, when X's program will

and of a weakening of educational functions and of university-sponsored research through the siphoning off of institutional funds to pay the unmet costs of federally-financed research.

Yet, in the long run, we doubt the wisdom of a full cost policy for *all* federally sponsored programs. The issues involved in paying tenured faculty from government project funds have already been discussed. This is expedient and it is financially helpful; but is it preferable, in principle, to paying faculty from independent income? Overhead poses a similar question.

Proponents of a full overhead and full cost policy argue that this will eliminate the drain of institutional funds into the unreimbursed costs of federal programs, thereby increasing the sums available for other activities. Many acknowledge that federal control may follow federal aid, but reason that it is safer to have the government pay the full costs of *some* institutional activities than some costs of *all* activities, on the assumption that federal influence can be encapsulated and confined to federally financed activities. Their logic would be more persuasive if they did not also seek to extend federal aid to more institutional activities. They are inclined to dismiss the distinction between "purchased" and "supported" research as untenable in practice and a relic of the days when federal research expenditures were far lower and taxed institutional resources far less. If basic research is important enough to the nation to warrant the current scale of federal financing, they declare, it is important enough for the government to pay its full costs.

We agree neither with these arguments nor with the conclusion that the government should pay the full costs of all federally financed research. That such a policy might reduce the drain of institutional funds into the sciences is possible but by no means assured. Large-scale scientific research generates powerful demands for institutional funds in the sciences for other purposes than research—for example, for fellowships, classroom and laboratory space, faculty salaries, and public service—which cannot reasonably be covered by any research appropriations. Strong science departments not only absorb all the government money they can get but compete strongly with humanities departments for

---

incur relatively less indirect costs? Or (2) should ONR contract A which gives a mathematician half of his salary and a whole box of chalk pay the same overhead as contract B which is mainly for an electron microscope or contract C that makes heavy use of the institution's library, purchasing department, and utilities?

institutional funds. In short, the problem of maintaining a balance between scientific and nonscientific disciplines will persist under a full cost policy. Although the immediate financial burden of federal research programs may be eased by such a policy, it is quite possible that the ultimate burden and the ultimate disciplinary imbalance will be greater, since there will be less ground to resist the expansion of federal research and the concomitant expansion of science departments. It is debatable if an institution is more imbalanced by large medical research grants which do not pay full cost or by large military research contracts which do. As noted in Chapter 6, the problem of balance is serious and difficult, but it must be faced directly, by regulating the volume of sponsored research, the number of teaching and research staff, and the budgets in different departments.

We do not want to open up here the large question of federal control (to be discussed in Chapter 19), which is dismissed by so many as nonexistent when it represents an influence of which they approve. The notion that the undesirable influence of a powerful and hostile government would politely be confined to those institutional activities directly financed by it does not merit extended examination. In any event, recognition that political control may follow financial aid does not inhibit some educators from lobbying for further aid. Thus, Lee DuBridge, president of the California Institute of Technology, has combined present advocacy of salary payments for the time which faculty devote to sponsored research with past warnings of their dire consequences:

> Keeping in mind the antics of just one Congressional Committee relative to just one government-employed scientist recently, let us ask what would be happening *today* [1949] if all the professors of all our colleges and universities . . . were paid in whole or in part by Federal tax money. What a witch hunt might be in progress right now! Academic freedom is not something which is destroyed only by concentration camps and firing lines. It can be withered to a shadow merely by the threat of economic insecurity, of unearned disgrace, of unsupported public attacks.[8]

[8] DuBridge, Address to the Mid-Century Convocation at the Massachusetts Institute of Technology, in John E. Burchard, ed., *Mid-Century, The Social Implications of Scientific Progress* (Technology Press, 1950), p. 396. Burchard's footnote on the congressional committee states, "Referring, one imagines, to the Director of the National Bureau of Standards, Edward U. Condon, and the Committee on Un-American Activities, although not necessarily, for other less dramatic cases could be cited."

In formulating an equitable cost policy, we believe, the distinction between "purchased" and "supported" research remains of value and, far from being discarded, should be restated, clarified, and strengthened.[9] *Purchased* research programs are closely monitored by agency staff; findings are therefore available to the agency before publication, and publication may be subject to government review; research is restricted to subjects known or deemed to be relevant to the agency's mission; and the work is usually financed by cost contracts that are fully audited. *Supported* research is not closely monitored by agency staff; findings are not necessarily available to the agency in advance of publication; the subject of research is as broad as the domain of science sanctioned by the Congress and advisory committees of scientists; and the work is usually financed by grants or fixed-price contracts. These practical operating procedures are as useful in distinguishing "purchased" and "support" programs as is the conventional distinction about where the research ideas originate—in Washington or on campus.[10]

Two additional principles are relevant:

1. *"Problems of Government-university relationships in the Federal support of research at colleges and universities should be explicitly and completely dissociated from the budgetary needs and crises of the institutions and from the general issue of Federal aid to higher education. In the consideration and administration of these relationships there should be no implication that Federal sponsorship of research is a convenient*

[9] A good statement of the two types of programs is given in National Science Foundation, *Government-University Relationships in Federally Sponsored Scientific Research and Development* (1958), pp. 9-11. Support programs are characterized as "programs in which university scientists are financed to conduct research of their own choice—generally, but not invariably, basic research with no immediately foreseeable utility"; purchased programs, as "programs in which the government departments, on their own initiative, contract with universities for applied research necessary to the development of products, systems, and processes, as well as for fundamental research related to the practical mission of the department." (Original capitalized and italicized.) See also Alice Rivlin, *The Role of the Federal Government in Financing Higher Education* (Brookings Institution, 1961), pp. 40-44, and Charles Kidd, *American Universities and Federal Research* (Harvard University Press, 1959), pp. 5-9.

[10] The ideas of "purchased" research programs are supposed to come from agency staff; those of "support" programs, from university scientists. However, ideas cannot be so neatly compartmentalized and "purchased" programs owe a great deal to the productive thinking of university faculty, just as many ideas in "support" programs originate in suggestions of government staff or the stimulus of government experience.

subterfuge for Federal financial aid to institutions of higher learning."[11] Neglect of this principle has been responsible for a certain wastefulness and administrative sloppiness in some federal research programs, notably those of NIH, which have quite properly been criticized by the House Committee on Government Operations.[12]

2. Universities have a vital interest in encouraging and supporting academic research with a little money as well as a lot of words; indeed, any university which does not, cannot be regarded as a genuine institution of advanced learning.

What cost policies follow from the foregoing considerations?

There is no serious division of opinion over the government's policy of paying the full cost of *purchased* research. Division arises only with respect to the payment of full cost and, particularly, full overhead, in programs of research *support.* Accordingly, the remainder of this discussion will be confined to the latter programs.

Every effort should, we believe, be made to encourage continued institutional participation in the direct and indirect costs of federally supported research, and agencies should at all times retain the right that is reserved by industry, foundations, and private donors to negotiate individual cost-sharing arrangements. The lump-sum awards of the Atomic Energy Commission offer a model that might well be more widely adopted, whereby the total costs of each project are set forth as the basis of discussion, but the government and the institution then proceed

[11] National Science Foundation, *Government-University Relationships* . . . (1958), p. 21. (Italics in original.)

[12] See the four reports and hearings of the House Committee on Government Operations dealing with the National Institutes of Health, dated April and August 1961 and March and June 1962. As further evidence, the following remarks of Philip Handler may be cited: ". . . our medical schools lean heavily on the use of so-called research funds to accomplish their prime function of medical education. This is morally indefensible and legally sanctioned, thanks especially to the wisdom of the so-called bureaucrats who administer the federal programs in support of medical research. . . .

"As a case in point, again looking at our department, a recent cost analysis indicated that in the past year something over 60 percent of the total funds used to pay for the instruction of first-year medical students in our institution was actually derived from funds which had arrived in the institution in support of research. When this activity is multiplied on a national scale, it amounts to an enormous contribution to the total cost of medical education." See "Symposium on Medical Education," II, *Journal of the American Medical Association,* June 3, 1961, pp. 92-93.

through negotiation to arrive at a sum representing the government's contribution toward the costs of the work. That contribution might range from 100 percent to 50 percent or less in different projects and programs.

At the same time, one must be realistic about how much cost-sharing is reasonable in massive research programs, without large measures of aid to bolster the financial strength of institutions. Broadly speaking, the degree of cost-sharing should be proportionate to the resources of both the institution and the agency. Affluent federal programs like those of NASA or NIH should not impose extensive cost-sharing on impoverished institutions any more than well-endowed institutions should require payment of full costs by penurious programs of the TVA, the Office of Education, or the Children's Bureau.

In view of the enormous range in federal programs and in the appropriations of different agencies, in the nature of federally financed research and in the scale of institutional involvement and resources, no arbitrary overhead rate should be set for all federal transactions at all educational institutions. The uniform rate of 20 percent of direct costs fixed by the 87th Congress for DOD and NIH research grants is grossly inequitable, since that rate may constitute more than the full indirect costs at some institutions and only half or less than half of the indirect costs at others. If the Congress wishes to enjoin cost-sharing in overhead, it would be fairer to adopt a formula like "75 percent [or 50 or 90 percent] of the *individually audited institutional* rate." The need for a quickly determinable institutional rate for use at schools whose volume of research does not justify the expense of a detailed audit has been repeatedly attested, and its feasibility has been established by a recent NSF study.[13]

CONCLUSION

Without presuming to dispose briefly of a problem that has plagued government-university relationships for nearly twenty years, resolution of the overhead issue may be sought through greater flexibility rather

[13] See National Science Foundation, "Indirect Costs of Research and Development in Colleges and Universities, Fiscal Year 1960," *Reviews of Data on Research and Development*, No. 32 (March 1962), p. 2. The receipt of $250,000 in direct costs was the cutoff point for use of the abbreviated method set forth in the Bureau of the Budget Circular A-21.

than greater rigidity in federal awards in support of research. In principle, cost-sharing by educational institutions should be encouraged; in practice, the degree of sharing should generally be reduced as the volume of agency research and of institutional participation rises. The acceptance of individually audited institutional rates rather than arbitrary government-wide rates would constitute a more equitable basis for determining the degree of cost participation in particular institutions and programs.

CHAPTER 17

The Need for Better Information

THE BIG SCHOOLS are favored, not simply because they are good, but to a certain extent because they are "in the know." Any serious effort to disperse project funds more broadly or to foster full and fair competition to insure that the best qualified persons do indeed receive these funds should include a better system of information on present programs, policies, and staff.

It should be said at the outset that the fullest information will *not* transform the present institutional distribution of funds. The visible reluctance of federal administrators to publish lively and useful information about their programs (in striking contrast to their readiness to publish repetitive statistics, bibliographies, and project listings) probably reflects this very feeling, plus the wish to avoid unwanted pressures and to enhance their freedom to administer their programs as they think best. But these reasons are just not good enough. The public has a right to know the policies of public agencies, and faculty at every institution have a right to know what only some faculty at some schools know quickly.

What kind of information is needed?

INFORMATION ON
AGENCY ORGANIZATION AND STAFF

President Pusey of Harvard has stated, "We in the universities are very seriously in need of a map showing the many sources within the Federal Government from which moneys for many purposes—principally the Government's purposes (which are not necessarily those of education)—flow into institutions of higher learning."[1] And a memorandum prepared for several midwest universities refers to "the difficulty of knowing where to submit proposals because of excessive compartmentalization of government agencies." Such views, expressed by representatives of great private and public universities, are echoed by spokesmen for smaller institutions.

The last directory of federal science agencies was issued by the National Science Foundation in 1956.[2] Although a revised edition is in preparation, this collection of nameless organization charts, useful as it may be for certain purposes, is not what is called for here. The current telephone directories of the principal science agencies (which generally indicate major organizational units as well as agency staff), distributed regularly to the libraries of educational institutions, would be a more useful and less expensive way to supply the needed information about initial points of contact. To be sure, anyone can send a general letter of inquiry to the head of any agency and (after due delay) receive some kind of formal reply, but this is hardly the best way to get a pointed and prompt reply to the kind of questions a professor with an idea wants answered. Will the agency seriously entertain the idea? In which program does the idea fall, and who runs it? What are the real chances of getting money for it this (or next) year? Roughly how much money might be available? What sort of people are likely to review the proposal? How long will it be before a decision is reached? Exactly what details should go into the proposal? The answers will determine whether it is reasonable to put in several weeks or just two hours drafting a proposal, or whether the professor should bother with it at all. They can be obtained in a brief telephone conversation with an honest program director, or skirted in a formal letter, announcement, or lecture by the same man. And a professor who is a friend of the program director or who is influential at a major university is likely to get the former treatment, the unknown man at a minor institution, the latter.

Faculty Acquaintance with Agency Staff

We asked faculty, "At which agency(s) do you know a staff member well enough to ring him up and get his formal advice on an idea you

[1] *The President's Report, 1959-1960,* Harvard University, p. 12.
[2] National Science Foundation, *Organization of the Federal Government for Scientific Activities* (1956).

TABLE 17-1. *Faculty Acquaintance with Federal Agency Staff*

"At which agency(s) do you know a staff member well enough to ring him up and get his informal advice on an idea you have?"

Field and Institution Group	Percent of Faculty Indicating										Number of Respondents
	One or More Agencies[a]	NSF	PHS	Navy	AF	Army	AEC	OE	State	ICA	
Total											
Group I	46%	26%	13%	12%	9%	7%	9%	6%	6%	2%	1,794
Group II	37	18	13	8	6	6	5	4	2	1	1,084
Group III	24	13	6	3	1	2	2	2	4	2	518
Sciences											
Group I	58	40	16	20	14	10	19	1	1	—[b]	804
Group II	54	33	18	13	9	10	12	2	1	1	445
Group III	40	32	11	4	2	4	6	1	1	1	170
Social Sciences											
Group I	53	26	22	10	9	7	1	12	10	8	487
Group II	41	16	18	10	8	6	1	7	3	2	297
Group III	33	6	8	4	2	2	–	4	7	7	122
Humanities											
Group I	18	4	1	1	1	2	1	8	8	1	503
Group II	13	1	1	1	—[b]	—[b]	1	6	4	–	342
Group III	8	1	—[b]	1	–	—[b]	—[b]	2	4	–	226

[a] Including other agencies than those listed at right.
[b] Less than 0.5 percent.

have?" In the case of most agencies, but not all, the replies indicated a decline in the proportion of faculty who knew a staff member, moving from Group I to Group II universities and from Group II universities to the colleges in Group III (see Table 17-1). This was to be expected, but the agency exceptions are interesting and merit study.

Thus, National Science Foundation staff were known to as many scientists in Group III colleges as in Group II universities, and staff of both the Public Health Service and the Army were as well known in Group II as in Group I institutions. Staff of the State Department and of the International Cooperation Administration were relatively better known to social scientists in Group III colleges than to those in Group II universities, while Navy and Air Force staff were as well known to social scientists (psychologists?) in Group II as in Group I universities. Such acquaintance, of course, not only helps in the initiation of proposals, but reflects the relative degree of dispersion of present agency programs. National Science Foundation staff were known to far more faculty in the departments canvassed than were the staff of any other agency. In part this has resulted from the Foundation's practice of employing faculty on leave from educational institutions, its broadly dispersed programs of science education, and its delegation of substantial responsibility to program directors; but the staff of some other agencies would no doubt have scored better if faculty at schools of medicine, engineering, and agriculture had been included in our survey.

INFORMATION ON PROGRAMS AND POLICIES

There is probably no one alive who is familiar with every significant federal program and policy of interest to the faculty at a single major university. The modification of programs, budgets, and policies is endless.

The Usefulness of Timely Information

A marked advantage accrues to the professor who gets in "on the ground floor" of a new program or policy. These are often administered with particular care to convince previous opponents (inside or outside the agency) that the departure was justified, and to establish a position of strength from which more venturesome work may subsequently be undertaken. This is the time when investigators are hand picked; they are likely to be as eminent and uncontroversial men as can be interested in the program, and personal visits will often be made to explain precisely what points should and should not go into the proposal. In one case preliminary proposals were already in the drawer of an experienced administrator before the agency head had authorized the new program. These had been solicited from key people and were followed up later by visits to make sure that certain points of political and administrative sensitivity were satisfactorily dealt with. Inquiries from unwanted scholars merely received written replies.

Sometimes, of course, proposals are invited—even though there is little likelihood of their being successful—to establish a large demand which serves, in turn, to strengthen the case for enlarging a program's budget. This may be all very well if a professor is told the true facts and submits a mock proposal as part of the strategy to increase support for a particular discipline. But another man will be the fall guy and put in an inordinate time preparing a futile proposal. Once bitten, twice shy; we know of cases where such a professor has refused to submit further proposals, despite every encouragement and a good chance of support.

The ground rules of a program that has operated for a number of years tend to become better known and more formalized, so that less advantage goes to the insider. But things are never completely static, and even in well-established programs it is helpful to know about changes in staff and the membership of advisory committees, in policy, and in the many points of judgment and emphasis that never do get put down fully on paper. Above all, it is important to know what is currently possible and what will soon be done in a particular program, and which of a maze of possible programs is most worth the investment of a man's time and energy. The varied episodes cited below illustrate the usefulness of such information.

1. The first five grants in NSF's formal program of "Anthropological and Related Sciences," awarded in fiscal year 1955, were confined to the politically "safe" areas of archeology and physical anthropology. The initial ventures into social anthropology, the following year, were tied to "fields of convergence" with the natural sciences, the formula then necessary to sell the social sciences, and applicants for straight ethno-

graphic field-work were discouraged. In fiscal year 1957, however, a few small grants were made for ethnographic work. By fiscal year 1960, forty-nine grants were awarded in "Anthropological Sciences" alone ("Sociological Sciences" having been hived off into a separate program) including the first award to a foreign university, made to an eminent foreign anthropologist who had been advised a short time before that he could not expect aid from this program! Today, most of empirical anthropology is open for support; but it required keen judgment, good information, and good advice to know just when just what proposal would be entertained.

2. A department chairman in quite another field complained that, to his knowledge,

> . . . the National Science Foundation has changed policies on certain matters without adequately calling this to our attention. Specifically, several years ago our request for funds to help purchase Varians nuclear magnetic resonance equipment was turned down on the argument that the . . . Foundation was not buying equipment per se. The argument was that some one professor would have to have requested the money as a supplement of part of an over-all research program that was being requested. A year or two later, in talking with a . . . Foundation representative, he indicated that that policy had been changed and, yet, we were not specifically informed and, of course, the National Science Foundation records indicated that we had a real interest and concern in this matter.

3. One university, following the letter of the law as specified in an NIH grant, put no teaching space in its biological sciences research facility. Other institutions more experienced with the spirit of the law and of NIH administration have not hesitated to incorporate a limited amount of teaching space in such facilities.

4. The psychology department at one state university conducted little research until a new chairman arrived on the scene, a man who "knew the ropes" in Washington. Within a few years, and with substantially the same staff as before, the department had an active research program going. Of course, the practical encouragement of the new chairman and his readiness to reduce teaching loads helped. But his knowledge of what could be done and of how to go about doing it were vital. In the same department, a professor who familiarized himself with the details of federal and private fellowship programs had astonishing success in increasing the number of undergraduates who won national fellowships. Evidently, there was no startling increase in student caliber;

TABLE 17-2. *Faculty Interest in Various Agencies*

"*Which agency's research programs or policies would you like to know more about?*"

Field and Institution Group	Percent of Faculty Indicating										Number of Respondents
	One or More Agencies[a]	NSF	PHS	Navy	AF	Army	AEC	OE	State	ICA	
Total											
Group I	57%	22%	13%	15%	14%	12%	10%	22%	19%	15%	1,794
Group II	62	23	15	15	14	12	11	25	18	17	1,084
Group III	60	17	12	12	13	10	11	28	24	18	518
Sciences											
Group I	54	23	14	20	20	16	18	10	7	10	804
Group II	64	26	21	23	18	17	19	14	6	12	445
Group III	62	22	18	21	19	16	28	15	6	11	170
Social Sciences											
Group I	69	29	20	17	14	13	5	30	28	26	487
Group II	72	35	21	17	18	16	9	30	26	31	297
Group III	75	30	21	11	20	14	4	34	30	29	122
Humanities											
Group I	51	11	5	5	4	4	2	36	28	14	503
Group II	50	8	2	3	4	3	1	35	26	12	342
Group III	51	6	3	5	4	4	1	35	34	18	226

[a] Including other agencies than those listed at right.

there was simply one man who took an interest in the students and helped them through the maze of papers posted on bulletin boards. A similar achievement should be credited to the graduate dean of another university who was familiar with the program of a private agency and raised the number of its awards at his institution above that of far more eminent institutions.

Faculty Knowledge of and Interest in Various Agencies

Even among scientists at Group I universities, less than a fourth felt adequately informed about the current research programs and policies of all agencies in areas of professional interest to them (the proportion fell to 15 percent among scientists at Group II universities, 10-11 percent among university social scientists, and 8 percent among university humanists). Most university scientists and social scientists indicated that they felt adequately informed about some agencies in which they were interested but not others, whereas most humanists were well informed about no agency.

Faculty replies to our question about which agency's research programs or policies they would like to know more about can be interpreted in several ways. From the straightforward tabulation in Table 17-2, one notes among humanists and social scientists a considerable degree of interest in the Office of Education, resulting from the initiation of the National Defense Education Act.[3] These groups were also notably interested in the State Department and, social scientists, in the International Cooperation Administration, the National Science Foundation, and, to a lesser extent the Public Health Service. The agencies cited most frequently by scientists include NSF and PHS, the three armed services, and the AEC. (The AEC was cited by Group III scientists more often than any other agency, probably because of its program of grants for the purchase of equipment to aid in the teaching of atomic physics, and the opportunities it affords college faculty to undertake research at national laboratories during the summer.)

Judged by the relative number who want to learn more about any agency, social scientists are somewhat more inquisitive than scientists and humanists; they still have more time uncommitted than have

[3] However, several humanists were under the impression that the NDEA was administered by the Department of Defense!

scientists, and more opportunities are opening up for them than for humanists. The degree of faculty interest in a particular agency tends to vary by department rather than by type of institution; there is, in fact, a remarkable consistency in the degree of interest exhibited in each agency by faculty in the same field at our three groups of institutions.

An interesting kind of analysis that we will leave the reader to complete is a comparison of the proportion of faculty who know an agency staff member with the proportion who would like to know more about that agency's programs or policies. Table 17-3 cites some examples

TABLE 17-3. *Faculty Acquaintance with Agency Staff and Interest in Agency Programs*

Agency and Faculty	Percent of the Faculty Who[a]	
	A	B
NSF —Scientists	40%	23%
PHS —Scientists	16	14
Navy—Scientists	20	20
AF —Scientists	14	20
Army—Scientists	10	16
OE —Social Scientists	12	30
OE —Humanists	8	36
ICA —Social Scientists	8	26
ICA —Humanists	1	14

[a] A: know a member of the agency staff well enough to ring him up and get his informal advice on an idea; B: would like to know more about the agency's programs or policies.

drawn from faculty at Group I universities. Without carrying too far the dangerous line of reasoning from selected statistics, these data suggest that opportunities to get informal advice from agency staff are unexcelled at NSF and roughly in balance with their interest in the programs at PHS and the Navy among scientists at Group I universities— i.e., among some of these agencies' major clientele. The lack of informal channels to Air Force and Army staff, *relative to the wish for information,* and the more striking imbalance at the Office of Education and ICA can hardly be unrelated to frequent faculty criticism of the administration of these programs. Informality both establishes and reflects rapport; it is not only a good way to dispense information, but a method of good administration.

INFORMATION ON PROPOSALS

The proposal in *n.* copies is obligatory in most programs that do not award money on the basis of some formula. The key decisions may already have been made or be based on facts that do not appear in the proposal (such as the eminence of a scholar), but action cannot be taken until the proposal is in hand. A successful proposal may be poorer (judged anonymously) than some which were unsuccessful; it may also be so surprisingly good as to lead to an award, even though that was the last thing the administrator had expected when he politely invited it. Proposals may be deliberately judged on a double standard (despite contrary opinion, staff of granting agencies often lean over backwards to give *some* money to a man at a small institution if they can find anything original or meritorious in his proposal), or there can be free, fair, and equal competition for funds determined solely on the evidence presented in proposals. In any—and virtually every—event, the proposal is essential. It is the mark of application; protection to the administrator against the suspicion of arbitrariness; a way to get an appraisal of one idea by different scholars and to compare the relative merits of two ideas. It is a sign of administrative due process.

For all of its significance, proposal writing remains an arcane art. Agency instructions give little guidance on the really important points. To the best of our knowledge, there is still no treatise, no graduate or correspondence course, no paperback entitled *How to Write Successful Proposals.*

To be sure, some artless souls succeed despite the utmost clumsiness. They are inexcusably gauche, and the only thing in their favor is that they are brilliant and well known. And in certain fields with much money and few men, it scarcely matters whether one is brilliant or simply alive. But in the average contract and grant program; in new programs; in programs with a large demand for relatively limited funds; in submissions from institutions and departments of ordinary quality, from young and relatively unknown men, from older scholars who have recently done work that is slipshod or undistinguished, from distinguished scholars known to be overcommitted—in short, in a great many cases—the proposal assumes a key importance.

One biologist at a private college had made quite a study of proposals, collecting for this purpose a number of successful examples from his friends. He concluded that the abstract is of special importance; the budget should be prepared carefully, be internally consistent, and contain a justification of unusual items. A draft should be circulated to colleagues for comment, and, wherever possible, the idea should be discussed in advance with someone at the agency.

Knowledge of agency practice is clearly helpful in preparing the budget and may make a substantial difference in the amount of money received, but the key element in a research proposal, of course, is not the budget or the style but the content: what one intends to do and how one intends to go about it. Certain problems and approaches are popular, and it helps to know what they are and, above all, to anticipate the area which will next be popular. The clean experimental design likely to produce *some* result is often more successful than a more original but less rigorous and less *projectable* suggestion. In applied work, it is vital to know the agency's ultimate goal, and helpful to know about related work it is supporting.

Once the proposal has been submitted, the professor wants to know when he can expect a decision, and often, when the decision is delayed, if the proposal has at least cleared preliminary hurdles so that he can estimate his chances and the extent to which he should proceed with his plans and reasonably discourage potential research assistants from making other commitments. At this stage, phone calls and letters of inquiry are common, and a friend or official visiting Washington may be asked to check with the agency to find out how things are going and, hopefully, speed up action.

The moment at which honest information is particularly helpful and particularly difficult to get is when a proposal is rejected. What a professor wants to know are the real criteria used in evaluation and the real reason for rejection, so that he can determine if he was treated fairly, how he can prepare a better proposal in the future, and whether he should bother to do so. But the agency cannot very easily say, in effect, either: "You and your idea are just not good enough" or "Professor Y, who reviewed your proposal, did not like it, although Professor X did." Accordingly, there is much reference to budgetary limitations, the competition of other excellent proposals, or other points which are true but not the decisive truth.

As formal letters of declination tell so little, a good deal can be learned about agency policy by examining the membership of key advisory committees and the lists of persons and departments who have recently received awards. The de facto criteria of established programs can often be deduced in this way; as a matter of policy, information of this sort should be maintained by every agency on a current basis and should be published or otherwise made publicly available. By and large, the granting agencies have a better record in this respect than the contracting agencies, which must more frequently cope with the delicate issue of competition among rival profit-making and nonprofit groups.

It is important for an agency to publicly and clearly define as fully as possible the criteria upon which awards are made, and to announce publicly any important changes in these criteria. The Office of Education has been criticized for its failure to do this in the allocation of graduate fellowships under the National Defense Education Act. The shifts of policy in the distribution of these awards have puzzled many department chairmen. Initially, in the opinion of many chairmen, the program leaned too far away from quality in an effort to stress the congressional objective of geographic dispersion; subsequently, it moved perceptibly in the other direction. The result was to create confusion about the underlying criteria of the awards. In an evident effort to deal with this criticism, the Office took the unusual step, in January 1961, of circulating a brief memorandum to all institutions which had submitted proposals for graduate fellowship, explaining the most common reasons for the rejection of proposals. In defense of the Office, it should be said that the task of satisfying both the Congress and the entire academic community in the public award of a limited number of fellowships is extraordinarily difficult, and the awards have, of course, been enthusiastically received by successful departments.

CONCLUSION

Let us conclude this discussion by suggesting what, concretely, can be done to improve the flow of information on government programs.

The institutional officer responsible for coordinating the administrative aspects of research proposals is a useful source of information on every campus; occasionally he distributes a newsletter informing faculty of new program developments. The American Council on Education recently recommended that each president appoint an officer to keep him informed about government programs. On a national basis, the formation of the National Council of University Research Administrators, the National Federation of College and University Business Officers Associations and the new Council of Graduate Schools in the United States will no doubt help to keep institutions abreast of important developments, and the central role of the American Council on Education in these matters could be strengthened. The receipt by the Council in July 1962 of $2.5 million from the Ford and Carnegie foundations for general strengthening of its program, and its concomitant reorganization and increase in staff suggest that this development is now likely.

On the government's side, we have already suggested several simple measures that would prove useful: the circulation of organizational and telephone directories with up-to-date designation of staff, and the prompt publication of contract and grant awards, and also the membership of advisory committees. The commercial publication of such elementary information at unduly high prices points to a demand that is simply not being met.[4]

How far beyond these measures each agency should go and what central government-wide services should be provided is a matter of judgment. The National Science Foundation might well establish a small staff to serve as a guide and point of first contact for information about all science agencies, and the Office of Education might fulfill the same function for programs of concern to humanists and to higher education in general. These agencies might also publish a regular bulletin

[4] For example, one publication on the National Aeronautics and Space Administration, priced at $25, offers little more than a review of the agency program, the phone numbers of principal staff, and a list of recent contracts. Two services which report periodically more substantial information on government contracts and regulations cost $75 and $130 a year.

The reader may be interested to examine the bemusing correspondence in 1961 between Navy officials and Congressman John Moss about the restricted status of unclassified Department of Defense telephone directories. Navy Secretary John Connally stated: "There are obvious reasons for restricting the distribution of these directories, of which the primary ones are the cost of production and the indiscriminate use of the information contained therein by salesmen and business houses which seek to solicit employees of the Department of Defense." See *Availibility of Information from Federal Departments and Agencies, Eleventh Report by the Committee on Government Operations*, House Report No. 1257, 87th Cong., 1st sess. (September 1961), pp. 77-82.

in which the more significant new programs and policies could be reported. The monthly publication of the Office, *Higher Education,* could be expanded to serve this purpose, but the Foundation has no comparable publication. It goes without saying that all agencies should be as explicit as possible about their program objectives and criteria; the booklets issued as a guide to proposals could generally be improved in this respect. Finally, there is no substitute for travel by agency staff, for personal discussion and conferences, and attendance at professional meetings, as a means of conveying information frankly, fully, and informally. Nothing is more damaging to the interests of their own constituencies than the frequent curtailing by Congress of agency travel budgets, for where travel economies are necessary, they hit first the more distant states which are more likely to be out of touch with developments in Washington.[5]

[5] A careful study of the relative effect of distance and the amount of agency travel funds upon the volume and nature of research awards to schools of comparable quality would be of some interest. Of course, the availability of institutional travel funds and of agency regional offices must also be taken into account.

CHAPTER 18

The Project System

THE PROJECT SYSTEM is often said to be the root of all evils in the administration of federal research programs. Although there is much truth in the charge, the wisest course is not to discard, but to retain, improve, and augment the present pattern. Let us discuss the matter more fully.

COMMON CRITICISMS

The underlying administrative design of the project system is clearly more suited to applied than to basic research. After all, in applied research there is a goal, definable in advance, and a system in which that goal is stated and funds allocated by contracts permitting changes in cost and in time depending upon subsequent experience makes a lot of sense. In the proposal stage, it also permits the competitive evaluation of alternative approaches, and the choice of whichever one seems most economic or most likely to succeed, or the support of different promising approaches by different scientists.

There is, however, a fundamental incompatibility between the search for unpredictable scientific knowledge and the requirement that the secrets of nature be disclosed in advance to government administrators, that the methods, the costs, and the time of discovery be itemized and subject to prior review. Nature does not obediently deposit her secrets at our feet upon payment of a requisite fee. Could Archimedes, anticipating the moment of inspiration, have applied to his government for

250

one bath, three quarters full of water? Galileo, with a clearer purpose in mind, could presumably have asked for his weights and a timepiece. Before 1906, it is doubtful if Einstein would have got a penny. He had a job, and what would he have needed, or how could he have justified an application for funds simply to think? After he became famous, no doubt, he would have had no difficulty getting money, but it would have been largely wasted, or paid in grateful tribute, as Finland supported Sibelius until his death long after he wrote his last symphony. Michelson and Morley, on the other hand, should have had no trouble getting money for their proposal to measure the speed of light.

Even these few classic cases suggest that the project system is suited to the experimentalist but not the theoretician, to the empirical procedure which can be sketched out in advance, not to the idea which cannot be forecast or commanded.

A long list of additional, well-founded criticisms can be leveled against the system, which have been detailed in numerous reports by agency and university representatives and individual scholars, and were repeated again by many faculty responding to our questionnaire.[1] As, however, we believe that none of these criticisms alone nor all of them

[1] E.g., *Administration for Research,* Vol. 3 of *Science and Public Policy,* The President's Scientific Research Board (1947), pp. 180-194; Interdepartmental Committee on Scientific Research and Development, *Report on Grants and Research Contracts* (1950); Report of the Surgeon General's Committee on Medical School Grants and Finances, Public Health Service (1951) particularly *Part I,* pp. 17-30, and *Part III,* pp. 29-46; Department of Defense, Research and Development Board, *A Review of Current Problems in Contractual Procedures Affecting Relationships Between the Department of Defense and Educational Institutions* (1952); National Science Foundation, *Government-University Relationships in Federally Sponsored Scientific Research and Development* (1958); American Council on Education, *Sponsored Research Policy of Colleges and Universities,* A Report of the Committee on Institutional Research Policy (1954); Charles V. Kidd, *American Universities and Federal Research* (Harvard University Press, 1959), particularly Chap. 6, "Terms and Conditions"; (Annual) *Proceedings of the National Conference on the Administration of Research;* Comegys Russell de Burlo, Jr., *Administrative Problems of Sponsored Research Programs in Small Colleges and Small Universities,* doctoral dissertation, Graduate School of Business Administration, Harvard University, 1960; Daniel O. Price, *University Research Administration Policies,* and Fred R. Cagle, *Federal Research Projects and the Southern University* (both published by the Southern Regional Education Board, Atlanta, 1962); and innumerable articles in the general professional and/or education journal of many scientific professions as well as reports by science agency committees and staff which, although not generally classified, are often relatively inaccessible because reproduced poorly and in few copies.

together justify abandonment of the system but rather indicate how it should be improved, altered, and supplemented, we will follow each criticism with a reply.

Time-Consuming

It is said that too much of the time of faculty goes into the preparation of proposals, and too much of the time of eminent scientists, into reviewing them. Bentley Glass and Warren Weaver, among others, have bemoaned the amount of our best scientists' time which is consumed on advisory panels and in reading the stacks of proposals and staff material that must be considered before and after each panel meeting.[2] Leo Szilard, delightfully considering the problem of how to retard scientific progress, can suggest no better way than the project system:

> Research workers in need of funds could apply for grants, if they could make out a convincing case. Have ten committees, each composed of twelve scientists, appointed to pass on these applications. Take the most active scientists out of the laboratory and make them members of these committees. And the very best men in the field should be appointed as chairman.[3]

Surely, the solution of this problem is to reduce the detail required of applicants in proposals, especially from men of established reputation, and to lengthen the term of awards so that fewer proposals are required.

[2] Glass, "The Academic Scientist: 1940-1960," *Bulletin of the American Association of University Professors,* Vol. 46 (June 1960), p. 152: "The drawback of this fair, but elaborate, system lies in its demand upon the academic scientist of an ever-increasing proportion of his one priceless and most strictly limited commodity, his time."

Weaver, "A Great Age for Science," in *Goals for Americans,* The Report of the President's Commission on National Goals (Prentice-Hall, for the American Assembly, 1960), p. 115: ". . . the April 1, 1960 booklet entitled 'Members of Advisory Councils, Study Sections, and Committees of the National Institutes of Health' required 127 pages merely to list, in various arrangements, the scientists who furnish thought and time in connection with the allocation of the large funds provided by Congress to NIH. . . . The paper material sent to each member [of the National Advisory Cancer Council] . . . forms a pile which is literally from fifteen to twenty inches high per meeting. To give conscientious attention to this material requires roughly a week of work preliminary to each meeting. Are we developing decision procedures for the allocation of federal funds for research that are so complicated and time-consuming that we are lowering the effectiveness of our use of our best scientists?"

[3] Szilard, *The Voice of the Dolphins* (Simon and Schuster, 1961), p. 100.

We are less concerned about the time of eminent panelists. No one can dictate the time of eminent men, and those who prefer their laboratories to Washington presumably remain in them. The eminent scientist who devotes his time to administration and policy formation performs an important public service for which he deserves and receives various rewards. His time can be economized in some ways, of which greater delegation of responsibility to staff is most important, but in the final analysis, administration and influence, like research, take time, and each man must decide for himself how much time he wants to spend being inquisitive, and how much being influential.[4]

Excessive Records and Reports

We are in complete agreement with the criticism that excessive records, reports, and publications are required in the present pattern of research administration. In part, this criticism is directed at requirements associated with contracts rather than grants, which will be discussed subsequently, and in part at the project system. (In part, also, at the American academic system of "Publish or perish"; in part at American society, with its plethora of communication media, most of which communicate very little; and, ultimately, at the simultaneous explosion of population, literacy, education, and science.) The project system is responsible only insofar as some show of success is helpful to an agency in increasing its appropriations, and to the scientist in winning another award.

It would be admirable if brevity could be substituted for length; if each profession would establish a journal for the (very brief) report of wrong ideas and unsuccessful experiments (there would be no shortage of contributions); and if early achievement could substitute for later performance. But, sooner or later, each scholar must justify his present promise with present performance and society's investment in him with some return to society. Basic research agencies do recognize publication in professional journals as an acceptable fulfillment of project performance, and have recently adopted the dubious policy of subsidizing

[4] It may be noted that, in contrast to other scientists' ready grasp of power, Einstein declined to participate in the primal meetings of the Advisory Committee on Uranium appointed by President Roosevelt in 1939. See Richard G. Hewlett and Oscar E. Anderson, Jr., *The New World, 1939/1946* (Pennsylvania State University Press, 1962), pp. 20, 23.

the costs of publication in their grants (whereupon some journals instantly instituted page charges for publication).[5]

Safety, Not Boldness, Is Encouraged

The project system, it is said, fosters "safe" ideas on which at least some results can be produced and popular ideas known to be in vogue with members of advisory panels, rather than bold and original ideas that may not pan out and may even make a bad impression on superiors and project reviewers. Roman Smoluchowski observes:

> Many individuals responsible for the distribution of considerable sums of money for research are seriously concerned about the lack of courage and imagination in research proposals. There seems to be a widespread feeling that the competition for research money is so keen that the proposed research has to have a very good chance of success because only in this way can a flow of publications and reports be assured which in turn "guarantees" a renewal of the contract. In this vicious circle "safe" and "reasonable" research, which is often unimaginative, is favored at the expense of pioneering ideas. Whether this conservatism in research is a separate malady or whether it reflects a more general trouble with our present-day society is difficult to assess. The problem certainly does not lie with the agencies which dispense research money or with reviewers of papers and proposals who themselves are worried about the flood of uninspired though "satisfactory" research.[6]

[5] Some government administrators have questioned the adjective "dubious." We question the policy because it: (1) Pays government funds in advance of publication and, therefore, even when publication does not occur. (2) Creates a double standard, since the government but not an individual scholar is taxed for the costs of publication; thus, the Conference of Biological Editors has stated that journal charges "should not be payable by the author personally, but by his institution or the funds that support his research." (*Science,* March 31, 1961, p. 1003.) (3) Employs the project system as a politically convenient means to support journals of both high and low quality. The issue of government aid to scientific journals of varying quality should be faced openly and decided on its merits.

[6] Smoluchowski, "Basic Research in Semiconductors," in *Proceedings of a Conference on Academic and Industrial Basic Research* (National Science Foundation, 1961), p. 38. Cf. the summary of discussion at the conference: "The present atmosphere of intense competition for jobs, for prestige, and for research grants places too much emphasis on the achievement of quick and fairly certain results at the expense of the slower and more valuable maturing of the scientist. The younger men have become concerned with making their reputations as quickly as possible; to do this they are forced to choose problems they are sure will yield

However, science agencies and panelists can scarcely be absolved of responsibility. The simplest way for them to get bold proposals is to invite them, and to reject safe ones. Word will get around quickly enough—and if the volume of applications falls off while scientists are recovering their wits, so much the better. To acknowledge that "safe" proposals are being supported in volume is to indict, not the project system, but its frequent misuse to support higher education and poorer science.

Expressing concern with the problem, the President's Science Advisory Committee recently suggested a valuable solution:

> Somehow diverse proposals of extraordinary novelty and import must be generated. . . . Perhaps new programs can be established within the National Science Foundation which are primarily concerned with novelty and diversity. . . . The climate and the means should be created whereby ideas which are challenging and sound but unconventional and different can be hospitably considered and encouraged.[7]

Empire-Building

Research projects are often used to build up "teams" to whom work is delegated, and to support not research but equipment, staff, and students. These are not only dangers, but realities on many campuses and there is no easy way to cope with them. Regrettably but inescapably, large projects are often dictated not by scientific but by personal or institutional considerations—that is, the project is devised not because it is the only way to explore an idea of high scientific priority that makes the best use of a scientist's talents, but because a professor and an institution have become responsible for the support of a large research staff and their families, money is available in Washington, and money facilitates salary increases and fosters a sense of importance and achievement.

Several policies could reduce the propensity of many investigators to

---

publishable results in a short time, rather than the more difficult problems with uncertain results. Some of the participants in this Conference felt that the research of younger men is becoming more superficial and even trivial, although in the past it was the younger men who made the deepest and most stirring contributions to science" (p. 75).

[7] *Strengthening American Science*, A Report of the President's Science Advisory Committee (The White House, December 1958), p. 27.

inflate proposals beyond the scale genuinely required by the nature and importance of their ideas, and others can readily be developed. The principal investigator should be required to devote a significant amount of time to any project for which he receives funds, which would require a change from "most" to "all" in the following policy as stated by the National Science Foundation:

> The Foundation expects that the principal investigator will be responsible for direct supervision of the work and, in most instances, will participate in the conduct of the research regardless of whether he is to receive compensation from the grant funds.[8]

If relatively more money went directly into the support of senior fellowships, training grants, and the support of graduate students, and less into the indirect support of personnel via research projects, research empires would be correspondingly reduced. And, in general, it appears to be rational policy to give money directly for the purpose for which it is ultimately intended—if for student support, then training grants and fellowships; if for equipment, then for equipment grants; if for research, then solely for research. Fortunately, after nearly two decades of research programs at a constantly rising level, this seems to be one direction of federal policy. However, it must also be acknowledged that the vast sums appropriated by Congress for research in special fields such as defense, health, and space virtually impose a degree of lavishness on agency staff if they are not to drown in the torrent of money or meet the even more horrible fate of turning some back to the Treasury at the end of the fiscal year. In short, empires are needed not only on campus but also in Washington, and so long as that remains true, we must expect them to persist.

One thing the government has not learned and apparently has little interest in learning how to do well, and that is to give small grants and contracts quickly. Again and again, faculty commented on this point: "I think most individual project grants in the sciences, including my own, are too large. . . . There seems to be, at present, no adequate provision for small, $100 to $1,000 size grants." "More stress should be placed on *small* personally directed efforts; less on large projects. Research production per dollar correlates about −.80 with size of grant." "I think that it would be useful to have federal funds available in small amounts ($500 to $2,500) for sheerly independent, individual, *scholarly* research and as 'pilot' grants."

[8] National Science Foundation, *Grants for Scientific Research* (1960), p. 5.

Similar points were made in a study conducted by the National Institutes of Health some years ago, which remarked upon the difficulties facing the scientist who needs a little money quickly to pursue a "hot lead" before he can substantiate an idea with experimental evidence or even prepare a detailed proposal. (And, it was added, "The scientist is often reluctant to disclose his idea to competitors on grant committees until after he has had an opportunity to establish some sort of prior claim through publication.")

A program of small grants could be set up in several ways. Authority could be delegated to staff with instructions to act rapidly under policy guidelines set by the agency and its advisors; or responsibility could be transferred to professional societies or a special agency staffed specifically for the purpose. The wisdom of lump grants direct to institutions for local allocation is doubtful unless some way can be found to introduce a quality control into the choice of eligible institutions and faculty. But as the need for small sums is stressed by so many faculty, as they are said to be more productive dollar-for-dollar than large sums, and it is, on the face of it, preposterous to be able to dispense large sums but not small ones, the government might at least try a one-time experiment of lump awards solely for this purpose. A worthwhile experiment at a few representative institutions could be conducted for several hundred thousand dollars; a national experiment, for $5 million or less.

The signal status and evident success of the institutes for advanced study at Princeton and Palo Alto point to another direction that science agencies might take to discourage the unnnecessary proliferation of empires and foster individual sovereignty and originality. These Institutes have brought eminent men together with no equipment or staff, and no responsibility other than to think. Understandably, this has precipitated something of a crisis for some Fellows. Important ideas are not generated simply by putting intelligent men in a congenial place. (In contrast to the saying that "It is the little things that keep us from doing the big things" it might be said that we often pursue the little things because they can demonstrably be done.) But the Institutes have also had their outstanding triumphs, and their mere existence has done something to enhance the status of the independent intellectual. One rationale of many government programs is to maintain contact with the latest scientific thinking, and another is to stimulate and improve the quality of that thinking. It would seem that government support for the existing Institutes and the judicious sponsorship of a few additional institutes in untouched scientific and geographic areas would be a most direct and economical way to achieve these ends.[9]

"Cliques" of Panelists

The charge is often made, particularly by departments with relatively little in federal research funds, that the project system is run by a "clique" of panelists at a few eminent universities. The refrain "clique" recurred independently in the comments of many faculty.

> Federal support during the past fifteen years has set up a chain reaction continually increasing the concentration of high quality staff, students and equipment at a few schools. It is extremely difficult for those universities that are not "members of the club" to get much more than token support for expanding their facilities. (*Physicist, Group II.*)

> Somehow or other I feel that the granting agencies have too many members drawn from faculties of big-name institutions. Great cliques seem to be in operation, composed of members of the granting agencies and the big universities. Of course, it is obvious that were the big research grants terminated by the agencies, many science departments in the universities would collapse. This is one reason for the "lobbying" done by these educational institutions. (*Biologist, Group II.*)

> We have a need, but the problem of getting into the grants clique as awarded in my field is a hard one. With a heavy teaching load and administrative responsibilities one is not able to publish at a fast enough rate to get sprung into orbit. (*Mathematician, Group I.*)

> It appeared from an announcement subsequently received that about one-third of the 18 grants given went to institutions or areas connected with members of the advisory review committee. (*Sociologist, Group II.*)

We cannot say if these critics or the many defenders of the objectivity of advisory panels are right. The suspicion that there is something to the charge of "clique" is not dissipated by the record of one small program in which a panelist from a second-rank institution received aid for several years and the program director subsequently accepted an appointment at the same institution. Familiarity with such

[9] Members of the Princeton institute have received considerable sums from federal agencies for their work in pure physics and mathematics and applied mathematics, and many short-term members have been supported by federal fellowships.

cases suggests, however, explanations simpler and more natural than collusion. Science agency staff are, for the most part, able, conscientious, and honest men, and the new staff member who comes to Washington with the cynical expectation of uncovering improper personal influence will soon be disabused.

But staff are not omnipotent or omnipresent; they have much say in the choice of panelists, and their choice inevitably reflects their background and that of their advisers; they cannot visit every school or know everyone (although they travel widely, and know a great many people). And so a pattern of preference, of visit, of confidence, of application, and of award to certain schools can often be discerned in research programs.

A sophisticated and unprejudiced study of the workings of the panel system would be the best way to evaluate the "clique" criticism, and, if it is sound, to learn how to correct it. Such a study should include not only an examination of the present institutional affiliation of panelists, and awardees, but also the institutions at which they and staff did their graduate and undergraduate work, their fields of specialization, and the criteria and methods of appointing panel members, and whether these are aimed solely at eminence or also at professional and institutional representativness (and a placid disposition).[10]

---

[10] The difference in the goal and, therefore, in the composition of advisory committees is manifest in a comparison of the affiliation of members of the President's Science Advisory Committee and the National Science Board in fiscal year 1961:

	PSAC	NSB
Different Institutions	13	23
Members	18	24
Professors	7	7
Deans, Laboratory Directors	5	—
Presidents, Vice Presidents, Board Chairmen	6	17
Affiliated with Institution in		
Northeast	13	8
Midwest	1	7
South	1	6
Mountain States	—	1
Far West	3	2
Public Institutions	3	7
Private Institutions	15	17

The only major study of this sort known to us is an excellent, lengthy analysis prepared by the staff of one agency for internal use, which reached the conclusion that while no impropriety was present in the awards of one program which had been challenged by a powerful professional association, it would be wise to establish another program and another panel to satisfy the association. The House Committee on Government Operations has more briefly examined the composition of NIH panels and called attention "to the close relationship between the institutional affiliation of scientific advisers and the distribution of grants."[11]

The related question of the potential—some would say, inherent—conflict of interest between the obligations of scientists as government advisers and as representatives of their profession and institution is too difficult and important to be dealt with briefly and without special study. Back in 1951, James Earl Russell suggested that the use of advisory boards of institutional representatives to allocate public funds "seems to protect the institutions from government control, but to remove protection of the interests of the government." "Thus," he proceeded with singular inaccuracy, "it is not likely to be widely adopted."[12] A scientist and administrator with long and high-level experience with many such boards and panels that have been established during the last decade to advise on the allocation of funds and the formulation of policy writes:

> . . . scientific competence does not guarantee objectivity in judgment where personal interests are involved. . . . Having science advisers say what they want for their particular fields is a little like appointing milk-hungry cats [to] advise on how a dairy should be operated. One wishes that there were no question about the nobility of motive of advisory committees or panels; that they could be trusted to be single-minded in the endeavor to use government funds most prudently, where they would accomplish most for research and education in the sciences. Unfortunately and sadly I must admit that I have seen much evidence of self-serving, and of small concern for the intellectual advancement of those who haven't emerged as big names.

The question has been considered recently but hardly disposed of by the President, the President's Science Advisory Committee, the Attorney General, and an investigating subcommittee of the House Armed

[11] *Health Research and Training*, Second Report by the House Committee on Government Operations, 87th Cong., 1st sess. (April 1961), p. 29.

[12] Russell, *Federal Activities in Higher Education After the Second World War* (King's Crown Press, Columbia University, 1951), p. 49.

Services Committee. The memorandum, *Preventing Conflicts of Interest on the Part of Advisers and Consultants to the Government,* sent by President Kennedy in February 1962 to the heads of executive departments and agencies appears to be more of a palliative than a solution; but, in the nature of the problem, it is unlikely that any clean-cut solution can be found to the dilemma of the public and private interest drawing upon the same unique expertise.

Additional Criticisms

Additional criticisms of the project system could be multiplied: the difficulties encountered by interdisciplinary proposals or those falling outside the framework of a particular program or review panel; the slowness of decision; the short term of so many awards; the excessive emphasis on applied research or, many may be surprised to learn, on basic research—a criticism directed mainly at the National Science Foundation by natural scientists with practical interests, and by social scientists with interests in current social and policy problems; the special difficulty of evaluating the proposals of young men of unknown ability; abuses such as the routine submission by eminent scientists of the same proposal, year after year, the submission under an eminent name of the ideas of a man of lesser standing, and even the submission of proposals for work which has already been completed and, at times, paid for by another agency; and so on. But perhaps enough has been said to indicate what is wrong with the system, and it is time to say what is right.

WHAT IS RIGHT ABOUT THE PROJECT SYSTEM

Three things, above all, are right with the system, and so very right as to outweigh its demerits and call for its retention regardless of what additional measures may be adopted to strengthen science and higher education: (1) the designation in both applied and basic research of specific tasks which are in the national interest; (2) the essential quality control introduced by professional evaluation; and (3) the retention of power over the use of money where it belongs—in the hands of the men who need it, and for whom it is appropriated.

Implements the National Interest

That many scholars want to study what they please is clear enough. It is one function of a good university to give good scholars the time to do precisely this, in exchange for some teaching duties. Why it should be the function of the government is not at all clear. (It may be desirable for the government to give general aid to educational institutions, or even aid designed to right the imbalance it has created at universities between the sciences and the humanities; but that is another matter.) The argument is made that, by a kind of natural law of scholarship equivalent to the laws of the market place, whatever a scholar wants to do is ultimately in the national interest, and the argument has gradually proved persuasive to Congress in its support of basic research in the natural sciences. But even here, carte blanche is not given; under the project system, the government does not write a blank check to every or any scientist to do everything or anything that he wants, but requires periodic evaluation of his work by men well qualified to do so. And this is quite reasonable and right.

Criteria of Quality Are Maintained

It is difficult to devise a better system for allocating research funds among scientists than the professional standards introduced by the leading men in each field who serve as proposal reviewers and policy advisors. (Indeed, the most legitimate complaint against applied research projects is not that they are applied, but that the government employees who set the objectives and monitor the work are not as well qualified in their profession as they should be.) The difficulties and dangers of this system have been cited—the time demands on leading scientists are the main difficulty; conservatism and adherence to fashion, the main dangers—but what would be better? To substitute the judgment of one man for the judgment of many might occasionally be an improvement if he is the right man (the sort needed, perhaps, is the editor type, accustomed to appraising a wide range of work), and, of course, great influence is wielded by program and agency directors; but the dangers of picking the wrong man and the limitations of any one man are obvious. To turn money over to departments or institutions without prior evaluation of *which* departments and *which* institutions is to substitute either the best qualified local professional judgment for the best qualified national professional judgment (and, statistically, the former is not likely to be right as often) or to introduce local academic-political considerations into scientific awards.

Scientists Make the Scientific Decisions

That the present project system retains control over the distribution of research funds in the hands of active scientists rather than non- (or ex-) scientist deans and academic administrators is generally recognized, and is, in general, all to the good. A 1951 study of the Public Health Service observed "There is inherent in the project system some transfer of the power of decision from the medical school to the groups which decide which projects are to be supported. . . . Most deans . . . prefer that the institution itself allocate research funds among investigators."[13] The Public Health Service concluded that this was no valid ground to change the basis of support from the project system to a system of block grants. President Lee DuBridge of the California Institute of Technology has recently attacked the power of advisory committees of scientists not only for opposing block grants, full overhead reimbursement, and payment of faculty salaries from project funds, but also for suppressing "daring ideas" (a cutting thrust—but are university presidents more daring?):

> As a long-time faculty member myself, I can pray fervently that both I and my faculty may be delivered from dictatorship by government faculty committees. Give me a good smart administrator to deal with and I can dispense with faculty advisory committees, except when they deal with purely scientific affairs, and not with administrative or fiscal matters. Scientists, when they get into government, are their own worst enemies. When they have control over activities of their colleagues, through the administration of research grants, they become autocrats of the most difficult kind.[14]

[13] The Surgeon General's Committee on Medical School Grants and Finances, *Part I, Conclusions and Recommendations* (Public Health Service, 1951), p. 26.
[14] DuBridge, "Basic Research and the Private University," in Dael Wolfle, ed., *Symposium on Basic Research* (American Association for the Advancement of Science, 1959), p. 114.

As the scale and variety of federal aid to science has risen, the logic of increasing the authority of central university administration has undoubtedly become more persuasive, and there has been a visible shift in the balance of power of academic scientists and academic administrators in government councils. With regard to all of the measures to which DuBridge refers—block grants, overhead, and faculty salaries—federal policy has moved slowly in the direction which academic administrators advocate and scientists resist. Scientists have good, if gradually losing, arguments on their side on these administrative issues, but on the scientific issues they can hardly be faulted.

It will be a sad day for the nation as well as the nation's science when the power to allocate funds within each field (within the levels and policies set by the nonscientific Congress and the nonscientific as well as the scientific Executive) is removed from the hands of the only persons qualified to evaluate the content of the work. (No one would quarrel with this statement if "the power to allocate funds" referred solely to the scientific criteria of research. The dilemma of science administration is that purely scientific criteria seldom suffice to determine key policies;[15] nor is there a purely administrative realm which does not ultimately impinge on the proper domain of science.) The project system has established a highly successful working relationship between the government's needs for long- and short-term research and the academic scientist's abilities and interests. That relationship should not be disturbed by the intrusion of unnecessary middlemen either on campus or in Washington.

CONTRACTS VERSUS GRANTS

The use of contracts instead of grants is often assailed—more often by faculty than by administrative officers—as the source of needless red tape, paper work, and controls inappropriate to academic research. To encourage the use of grants in the basic research programs of other federal agencies, the National Science Foundation recommended in 1958 "that, where such authority does not now exist, legislation be

---

[15] This point is discussed with insight and sophistication in the context of nuclear weapons policy by Robert Gilpin in *American Scientists and Nuclear Weapons Policy* (Princeton University Press, 1962).

sought to authorize Federal agencies, where appropriate, to support scientific research, including facilities and equipment, by means of grants as well as contracts."[16] This recommendation was subsequently adopted by the Congress in Public Law 85-934 (September 1958), which authorized each agency with authority to contract for basic scientific research at nonprofit institutions to also make grants for the same purpose, and to vest in the institution title to equipment purchased with grant or contract funds.

The principal agencies affected were the Department of Defense, the National Aeronautics and Space Administration, and the Atomic Energy Commission, the first two of which have since adopted the use of grants as well as contracts, although the extension of grants in the Defense Department has been slowed by the problem of determining the overhead policy which should apply. In April 1962 the President's Committee on Government Contracting for Research and Development, which included among its members the principal officers of the foregoing agencies, added its recommendation that the use of grants be encouraged in federally financed basic research at the universities.[17]

NASA as a new agency with a booming budget, has paid fully audited overhead on grants (although the House of Representatives in August 1962 sought to hold this to 25 percent of direct costs) and is planning a major extension of its grants program at universities to facilities and training as well as research. The AEC has had no special problem with the overhead issue in its unique system of lump-sum, cost-sharing awards, since neither overhead nor any other item of cost is separately identified in the award. The issue has, however, been critical at DOD, which, subject to close scrutiny of its accounting procedures by Congress and the General Accounting Office, was reluctant to embark immediately on a full overhead policy in its grants programs when neither

[16] National Science Foundation, *Government-University Relationships in Federally Sponsored Scientific Research and Development* (1958), p. 33.

[17] "Government agencies use both grants and contracts in financing research at universities, but in our judgment the grant has proved to be a simpler and more desirable device for Federal financing of fundamental research, where it is in the interest of the Government not to exercise close control over the objectives and direction of research. Since all relevant Government agencies are now empowered to use grants instead of contracts in supporting basic research, the wider use of this authority should be encouraged." *Report to the President on Government Contracting for Research and Development* (The White House, April 1962), p. 37.

NSF nor NIH had been permitted to do so (by the Bureau of the Budget and the Congress, respectively).

Accounts vary, but apparently some programs of both the Army and the Air Force initially offered research grants at less than full overhead; after they were rejected by a number of schools, both services came round to paying full audited overhead. The Office of Naval Research, which managed the pioneer postwar basic research program so well with the use of contracts that it became the administrative model not only for the basic research programs subsequently established by the Army and Air Force but also for NSF, has lagged in the introduction of grants and had previously been rather unconvinced of the need for granting authority. In fiscal year 1960, the volume of Defense grants was only $9 million, but in 1961 it rose to $26 million and in 1962 to $40 million. In the DOD appropriation bill for fiscal year 1963, the Senate yielded to the insistence of the House for some restriction, and Congress set a ceiling of 20 percent of direct costs as the overhead payable in the grants of both DOD and NIH. This represented a reduction in overhead for DOD but an increase for the far larger volume of NIH grants.

To the faculty member the philosophy of the grant, with its inherent freedom, is usually preferable to that of a contract, with its commitment to perform and deliver, when all he can rationally pledge is his best effort. The exact sum of money and the period for which it is available are known in advance, including the portion to be subtracted for overhead, and no further approval must be sought from the agency prior to its expenditure. Reporting and record-keeping requirements are minimal. Equipment purchased is the property of the institution and may even be transferred with the investigator should he move to another institution. The investigator is specifically authorized by the grant to make such changes in the disposition of the budget as may serve to advance the research, and even to change the objective and nature of the work should the original plan no longer appear scientifically fruitful. Thus, NSF policy (the first paragraph of which is copied almost verbatim in the Department of Defense instructions on the administration of basic research grants) specifies:

> The Foundation believes that the principal investigator, operating within the established policies of the grantee institution . . . is best qualified to determine the manner in which the grant funds may be used most effec-

tively to accomplish the proposed research. Therefore, once the grant has been made, the grantee may use the funds for the proposed research without strict adherence to the original budget estimates. However, the Foundation should be kept informed of contemplated major deviations from the budget estimates and the reasons therefor.

The Foundation also believes that the principal investigator, operating within the established policies of the grantee institution, should always feel free to pursue interesting and important leads which may arise during the conduct of the research. Therefore, the principal investigator may discontinue or materially modify unpromising lines of inquiry, without fear of jeopardizing the continuance of support for the remainder of the grant period, when it appears that the inquiry as originally envisaged will no longer be fruitful from a scientific standpoint.[18]

In short, with a grant, the investigator is master of his own ship.

However, many administrative and business officers are not so enamored of the grant instrument, and often prefer a well-written, liberally administered contract. The business officer points out that he has to keep virtually the same records on expenditures under grants as under contracts, and that "many provisions of the contract form have gradually been incorporated into the grant agreement particularly with the advent of large scale financing programs of such groups as the Public Health Service. . . . Such provisions deal with the right of termination, periodic reports, . . . audit, etc."[19]

One business officer asserted that there is not "three quarters of one percent difference in the cost of administration of what they [the government] call a grant and a contract." Accordingly, business officers of institutions with a major volume of federal research generally look askance at the less-than-full overhead rate of government grants and have strongly resisted the offer by military programs, in their new research grants, of the NSF flat overhead rate of 20 percent of total costs. Most business officers have insisted either on receiving the full audited overhead rate in military grants, or on retaining the contract form in lieu of the proffered grant. With the authority that federal contracting officers now have to award to educational institutions equipment purchased under a contract, the principal financial advantage of the grant remains the advance payment of funds, and even this can be arranged in major military contracts. Against this, the cost contract offers an

[18] National Science Foundation, *Grants for Scientific Research* (1960), p. 12.
[19] Comegys Russell de Burlo, Jr., *op. cit.,* p. 52.

ease of extension and flexibility with regard to total costs that is not merely an advantage but a virtual necessity in types of research where costs can not be exactly forecast, whereas the grant instrument sets a fixed sum and a time limit beyond which a new application must be made for additional funds. Fixed-price contracts involve neither an audit nor the requirement that unexpended funds be returned; cost contracts permit the government to reimburse uninsured liabilities incurred by an institution, to audit subcontracts, and to furnish equipment and materials. None of the foregoing advantages is provided by grants.[20]

In theory, the grant is designed to support but not to monitor research. In practice, the law requires some monitoring of all grants; the granting agencies have successfully dispensed large sums with a minimum of red tape, but Congress and the General Accounting Office have recently brought pressure on the National Institutes of Health to tighten various controls in their grants.[21] In theory, the cost contract is designed to purchase scientific services. In practice, it has been used as successfully as the grant to support basic research (as the Office of Naval Research has demonstrated), or with much friction, red tape, and undesirable controls (as in some Army and Air Force programs).

The root of success or failure in the administration of agency research programs at educational institutions does not lie with the legal instrument used to effect the transfer of funds, but with the experience of

[20] These and other advantages have been pointed out by Raymond J. Woodrow, director of the Princeton Office of Research Administration, in a memorandum on *Government Grants Versus Contracts* (December 1960).

[21] The GAO has been critical of excess advance payments in NIH grants, the lack of controls and of records in the purchase of equipment, inadequate audit procedures, and the absence of guidelines for charging faculty salaries to research grants or of confirmation that the time charged was actually devoted to the research; the House Committee on Government Operations has severely criticized NIH grants management—the lack of staff review of the financial requirements of proposed projects, the lack of control over foreign travel, the failure to ascertain that investigators actually worked the amount of time for which their salaries were charged to the grant, the failure to establish guidelines for grantees' use of public funds, and so forth. See the two reports of the Comptroller General to the Congress, *Review of Research, Training and Fellowship Grant-in-Aid Programs Administered by the National Institutes of Health . . .* (November 1959) and *Survey of Policies Followed by Selected Medical Schools in Charging Faculty Salaries to Research and Training Grants Awarded by National Institutes of Health . . .* (November 1961), and the two reports of the Committee on Government Operations cited earlier, *Health Research and Training . . .* , House Report No. 321 (April 1961), and *Administration of Grants by the National Institutes of Health,* House Report No. 1958 (June 1962).

administrative officers, their understanding of academic institutions, and the statutory and administrative regulations under which they must operate.

Vannevar Bush, in his 1945 report to the President, pointed out:

Since research does not fall within the category of normal commercial or procurement operations which are easily covered by the usual contractual relations, it is essential that certain statutory and regulatory fiscal requirements be waived in the case of research contractors. For example, the National Research [subsequently, Science] Foundation should be authorized by legislation to make, modify, or amend contracts of all kinds with or without legal consideration, and without performance bonds. Similarly, advance payments should be allowed . . . when required. Finally, the normal vouchering requirements of the General Accounting Office with cost contracts should be relaxed for research contractors. Adherence to the usual procedures in the case of research contracts will impair the efficiency of research operations and will needlessly increase the cost of the work to the Government. Without the broad authority along these lines which was contained in the First War Powers Act and its implementing Executive Orders, together with the special relaxation of vouchering requirements granted by the General Accounting Office, the Office of Scientific Research and Development would have been gravely handicapped in carrying on research on military matters during this war.[22]

The forecast of impaired efficiency and needless costs has been borne out by postwar experience. The administration of contract research has, in general, been liberalized and improved in recent years, but would still benefit markedly by the enactment of a statute codifying what is best in the present relations between federal agencies and nonprofit institutions, and exempting research from needless controls governing the procurement of goods and services from private industry.[23] The formation of a special staff of contracting officers and auditors to deal solely with educational institutions would also improve the administration of military research programs.

[22] Bush, *Science—The Endless Frontier* (Office of Scientific Research and Development, 1945; reprinted, National Science Foundation, 1960), p. 39.
[23] Hollis P. Allen's 1950 study for the Hoover Commission, *The Federal Government and Education* (McGraw-Hill, 1950), likewise concluded (pp. 267, 274): "There is great need for simplification in the procedures governing the negotiation of contracts with Federal agencies, the terms of such contracts, the reporting of work . . . , and the accounting procedures that govern reimbursement. . . .
"The crying need . . . is the simplification of the contract itself."

AMPLIFYING AND SUPPLEMENTING
THE PROJECT SYSTEM

The project system is best designed for the administration of a quality program of applied or basic research. Some of its present drawbacks stem from its success: there are simply too many proposals being written, too many reviewed, and too many being awarded. A system which is highly selective, informal, and reasonably efficient with 400 proposals and 100 awards becomes overburdened, more bureaucratic, and lowers its standards with 20,000 proposals and 13,000 awards. Increasing the size and duration of awards staves off the day of reckoning, but sooner or later some simplification, some reorganization must ensue. "If you're going to have a program of this size, you've got to get out of the retail business and into the wholesale business," a staff member at NIH remarked, and the comptroller of a Group I institution complained that the government should find another way "to buy research than buying it by the inch."

Just as research in the hard sciences has opened the door to research in the softer sciences, so support of project research has led gradually to support of departmental research in broad scientific areas and interdisciplinary fields, to the use of research funds first for training graduate students and then for direct training grants, to awards for the construction of research facilities, and finally to general institutional grants in aid of research in the sciences by NSF and NIH.

Broader Forms of Support

A 1958 NSF report outlined seven forms of support for basic research ranging from the particular to the general. The first three cited were the "narrowly defined," "moderately defined," and "broadly defined" project, the last specifying merely "the general area of science . . . to be explored" and "a general indication of the new knowledge or understandings expected to be gained." In fourth place was the award to an individual. Fifth and sixth places were assigned, respectively, to narrowly and broadly defined departmental awards, and the seventh, to the award of funds to an institution "for general support of its research activities—usually for an activity in one or another large area of science—medicine, agriculture, etc." These were described as gradations in the *existing* forms of federal support.[24]

Many of these broader forms of support may still come as news to institutions with, at most, a few small research grants. For, as usual, it is the eminent universities and institutes of technology which pioneer in new types of support, and, containing the heaviest concentration of both federal money and scientific talent, present the greatest incentives for administrative innovation. A policy innovation (often termed an "experiment," partly for honest reasons and partly as protection should political opposition develop) introduced at one or two impeccably chosen institutions may not be widely advertised. By the time it is formalized in an official agency statement, several years may elapse, the battle has been won, forward contingents already occupy new positions and staff are scouting farther ahead.

Among the significant departures from the standard project system are research grants or programs geared to a particular program, department, laboratory, research institute, professional school or institution.

The first two have been the easiest to establish in urgent fields of science, because their relation to agency missions in these fields has been clear, and they carry the least taint of general support to education. Without making too much of the distinction between "departmental" and "program" awards, it may be said that, in the former, the field of support is synonymous with a department; whereas in the latter, the organizational unit can lie either within one department or embrace several departments and disciplines.

Examples of the former are broad research grants and contracts worked out by several federal agencies with leading departments of mathematics or psychology; some of the NIH research training grants might be regarded as either departmental or program awards. It would be interesting to know the actual use that is made of the many million dollars awarded in training grants—how these funds are allocated between faculty, students, equipment, other direct costs, and overhead—and how this allocation differs from the distribution of research funds. Training grant programs have boomed in volume and variety, without any clear public understanding of the policies which govern their initiation or the allocation of grants to individual departments and institutions,

[24] National Science Foundation, *Government-University Relationships in Federally Sponsored Scientific Research and Development* (1958), pp. 34-35.

and how these criteria may differ from those governing broad research grants.

Various federal science programs have awarded large grants or contracts for reseach in areas like aging, cancer, low temperature physics, or nuclear sciences; for the construction and support of clinical and private research centers; or for the operation of existing laboratories varying in scale from a small facility such as the Inter-University High Altitude Laboratory in Colorado through more substantial installations like the Yerkes Laboratory of Primate Biology in Florida, the Marine Biological Laboratory at Woods Hole, or MIT's Research Laboratory of Electronics. Both granting and contracting agencies have been going in for arrangements of this sort increasingly in recent years. Their common feature is that an investigator need not submit individual project proposals to Washington: the funding of research is handled on a package basis by a single large grant or contract negotiated periodically with the agency by the laboratory director; within that commitment to undertake work in a broad area, projects can be discussed and decided informally by the investigator and the laboratory director.

Institutional Research Grants

The most far-reaching departures from the project system are the new institutional research grants of the National Science Foundation and the National Institutes of Health.

NSF's institutional grants surprised some of its friends who knew the strength of its devotion to the project system as the mainstay of quality and protector against politics in research programs. This was announced in June 1960 as "an experimental program" to strengthen institutional "research and research-training activities" in the sciences. The notice sent to eligible institutions stated:

> The purpose of these institutional grants is to strengthen the general research functions and programs of the institution in the mathematical, physical, biological, social, and engineering sciences, by supporting the development and maintenance of a sound, well-balanced program of basic research, research training, and related scientific activities, without specifying the precise research and related activities to be undertaken with the grant funds. Such grants, for example, could be used for the employment of research staff, purchase of research supplies, or other appropriate measures to strengthen basic research and related scientific activities.

However, the institutional grant should be used to supplement, rather than replace, institutional funds already budgeted for such scientific activities.

The amount to be awarded initially was 5 percent of the total research grants made to the institution by NSF during the previous year, with a ceiling of $50,000. Some $1.5 million was actually awarded to 248 institutions under this program in 1961; 141 institutions received $2,000 or less, while 10 received the maximum amount ($37,500, as the base period for the first awards was nine months).[25]

The base to be used in calculating awards had been the subject of some discussion in the government; the Bureau of the Budget was persuasive in its view that the base should be restricted to NSF's own awards, on the grounds that this would serve to disperse funds more broadly than would a base of total government research expenditures. However, this argument is demonstrably false, as all federal agencies expend research funds at more institutions than does NSF alone. A graduated formula assigning, for example, 10 percent for the first $100,000 of research money received by an institution from the federal government, 5 percent for amounts from $100,000 to $199,999, and so on, would better promote dispersion. The formula for institutional grants in 1962 took a step in this direction by awarding 100 percent of NSF basic research grants up to $5,000 plus 5 percent of grants in excess of $5,000, with a maximum award of $50,000 to any institution. Under this formula, $3.7 million was distributed to 302 institutions; 17 institutions received the maximum of $50,000; only 8 received $2,000 or less, and 37, $5,000 or less; the preponderant grant was in the $5,000-$10,000 range, awards of that order going to 171 institutions.[26]

Thus, despite many years of concern about the political impossibility and scientific undesirability of general institutional grants based on a formula, the Foundation finally acted on its existing statutory authority. The Public Health Service, however, felt the need for prior congressional authorization. This was received in September 1960 under Public Law 86-798, which authorized PHS to award:

> . . . grants-in-aid to public or nonprofit universities, hospitals, laboratories, and other institutions for the general support of their research and research

[25] National Science Foundation, *Eleventh Annual Report for the Fiscal Year Ended June 30, 1961* (1962), p. 69.
[26] From National Science Foundation press release, July 6, 1962.

training programs . . . not to exceed 15 per centum, as the Surgeon General may determine, of the amounts provided for grants for research projects for any fiscal year through the appropriations for the National Institutes of Health. . . .

The Act authorizes grants to *universities* and *institutions*. However, because of the political dangers of general aid to institutions and a division of responsibility with the National Science Foundation, the National Institutes of Health have initially geared their program of block grants to the level of medical and other professional *schools* in the health field.

The formula governing the first set of grants in fiscal year 1962 allotted to each school a minimum of $25,000 "plus an amount proportional to the level of its research activity as reflected by the value of its Federal and non-Federal grants, contracts, and gifts. In order to encourage the schools to seek non-Federal research support funds, the sum awarded in respect to non-Federal funds is proportionately twice as large as the sum awarded in respect of Federal funds."[27]   In 1962, $20 million or 6 percent of NIH research support funds was distributed

[27] *Departments of Labor and Health, Education, and Welfare Appropriations for 1963,* Hearings Before a Subcommittee of the House Committee on Appropriations, 87th Cong., 2d sess., *Part 3,* Statement of Dr. James A. Shannon, director of NIH (Feb. 7, 1962), pp. 796-797. The specific formula utilized was as follows (the provisional terms having been subsequently adopted):

"1. Each eligible institution will receive a basic amount, to insure that it will have a minimum financial base for a research and research training program. During fiscal year 1962 this amount will be $25,000.

"2. The second factor in the formula is based upon the total health-related research expenditures of the recipient institution in its latest complete fiscal year, up to a maximum of $2 million, sponsored by Federal research grants and contracts (excluding grants, contracts, and awards for education, training, and construction). The preliminary computation of the formula will utilize figures representing 5 percent of the first $1 million of such expenditures, and 3 percent of the amount between $1 and $2 million.

"3. The third factor is based upon the total health-related research expenditures of the recipient institution in its latest complete fiscal year, up to a maximum of $2 million, sponsored by non-Federal grants, contracts and gifts restricted for research (excluding grants, contracts, and awards for education, training, and construction). The preliminary computation of the formula will utilize figures representing 10 percent of the first $1 million of such expenditures, and 6 percent of the amount between $1 and $2 million.

"4. The sum of the amounts produced by application of the above factors will, if necessary, be increased or decreased by whatever uniform percentage is required to adjust the total amount of the awards to the total funds available for General Research support grants.

"5. For each recipient institution, an amount equal to 15 percent of the grant will be added to the grant for support of the indirect costs of research and research training." (*Ibid.,* Part 3, pp. 958-959.)

under this program to 153 schools of medicine, dentistry, public health, and osteopathy at 95 institutions. With 15 percent indirect costs added to the sums computed by formula, grants to individual institutions ranged thus: $28,750 to Fairleigh Dickinson University, $926,093 to the University of California, $606,560 to Columbia University, and $589,265 to Harvard.[28] Since NIH is considering extending the program in 1963 to schools of veterinary medicine, pharmacy, and nursing (as well as hospitals and other nonprofit institutions) and graduate departments of biological and other health-related sciences may be included thereafter, and since the volume of funds distributed in this manner is still well below the present statutory ceiling of 15 percent of total NIH research grants, it is evident that the day of the million-dollar institutional block grant is not far off.

The remarks of Lowell T. Coggeshall, vice-president of the University of Chicago, before the House Committee considering the legislation on PHS block grants are of interest for the delicate line of argument required to both endorse the project system and yet condemn and seek to rectify some of its effects:

> (1) Medical schools have encountered difficulty, quite frankly, in retaining a substantial measure of control over the content, emphasis, and direction of their research and training activities. (2) Lacking any significant amount of unrestricted moneys for the support of research which we can administer as we see fit, many schools attempted to expand research in areas where funds were readily available, while other problems of a less dramatic nature but no less scientific significance have been given lesser priority. (3) Strong departments with outstanding researchers have attracted grant support and grown stronger. Weak departments have had greater difficulty in obtaining support for their research activities which could give them the necessary impetus for improvement. (4) I do not mean to imply, however, that such restrictions upon research funds have caused schools to develop problems which they did not want. Rather the problem is our inability to finance and develop equally important research activities which may be of less interest to Federal agencies but which the dean, faculty, and research staff know are needed to give balance and direction to their medical research and their research training programs.[29]

Faculty Opposition to Block Grants

The hostility of so many of the best scientists, who are admirably satisfied with their individual grants and contracts, to the newer and

[28] *Ibid.*, pp. 964-967.
[29] *Journal of Medical Education*, May 1961, p. 516-517.

broader forms of support is wondrous to behold. In one case, NIH asked the president of an eminent institution if he would accept a large and extremely broad experimental block grant for research in "health sciences." However, the offer was declined after a faculty committee appointed to advise the president concluded that the institution could not rationally allocate the funds among the extraordinarily diverse kinds of work that could be subsumed under "health sciences," ranging from sanitary engineering and topology through acoustics and biophysics to genetics, anthropology, and communication theory. The committee recommended, however, acceptance of block grants for research in more narrowly defined areas. Large sums proffered by the Advanced Research Projects Agency for interdisciplinary research have been spurned by some departments which feared that acceptance would reduce their independence of *other* departments and their control of their own research funds. At one university, the chairman of a geology department of such high standing that it would be reasonably sure of favorable action on a request for a departmental research grant was unable to persuade his colleagues to agree to such an arrangement. The only point of agreement he found was possible willingness to share some secretarial services. The chairman concluded that his colleagues' opposition to a block grant reflected not merely a wish to control their own funds and, thereby, the direction of their research, but a feeling that the winning of a grant in open competition with the rest of their profession was a cherished mark of worth. Charles Kidd trenchantly observes that:

> . . . the broader the definition of research, the higher is the point in the academic hierarchy at which research funds are controlled. As a rule, the higher a person stands in the academic hierarchy, the more acute is his sense of the problem of sustaining balance among the major functions of the university, the less does he view research as a self-contained function. . . .
>
> . . . The prime feature of the existing system which serves as a barrier to the distribution of federal research funds by formula, and to pressures from congressmen to help institutions in their states, is emphasis upon the project and upon the individual scientist. The more the current system moves toward block grants to universities with increasing emphasis upon the educational as well as the research function, the greater the pressure and, indeed, the logic of shifting the criterion of distribution to a formula measuring the total financial needs of universities.[30]

[30] Charles V. Kidd, *op. cit.*, pp. 110, 112.

General Institutional Aid?

As expenditures on scientific research and education have risen, and federal programs have multiplied in variety and breadth, calls for general federal aid to higher education are heard from powerful spokesmen for the sciences. The President's Science Advisory Committee states—and the italics are the Committee's:

> *Whether the quantity and quality of basic research and graduate education in the United States will be adequate or inadequate depends primarily upon the government of the United States. From this responsibility the Federal Government has no escape. Either it will find the policies— and the resources—which permit our universities to flourish and their duties to be adequately discharged—or no one will.*[31]

And the National Science Foundation declares:

> The situation appears to call for general aid to U.S. universities patterned somewhat after that provided universities in the United Kingdom by the University Grants Committee. In any event, the question arises of direct subsidy to educational institutions in order to increase the overall strength of their departments and to provide greater flexibility in their administration.[32]

In neither case is reference made to general aid for *science*; clearly the thinking of leading scientists has ventured beyond that point to an open espousal of some form of general federal aid to higher education as being in the best interests of science and the nation.

This position that leading scientists have taken is highly commendable, and it is evidently supported by the large majority of their colleagues, over two thirds of whom stated in our survey that they favor more federal aid for the humanities even at the cost of some reduction in federal aid to the sciences. The scientists have done well for themselves, and were their outlook simply selfish and parochial, they could, to be blunt about it, let the humanities go hang and in effect or in fact hive off from the rest of the institution. Important groups of scientists have done just that. But the core of men in the pure sciences has remained loyal to the notion of an integrated institution of higher learn-

[31] *Scientific Progress, The Universities, and the Federal Government,* Statement by the President's Science Advisory Committee (The White House, Nov. 15, 1960), pp. 10-11.

[32] National Science Foundation, *Annual Report, 1960* (1961), p. 16.

ing, and, if broader forms of federal aid to the humanities and to higher education eventuate, they will have done much to bring them about.

We are not as sanguine as many about the feasibility of managing such general federal aid without the deadening overlay of red tape and the periodic, uncontrollable intrusion of political forces. It is easier to speak of the independence from government control which British universities have achieved while receiving government funds through the University Grants Committee than to duplicate in this country the social, educational, and political institutions that make that Committee work; even in Britain, the change from private to government financing has been accompanied, reluctantly but ineluctably, by a change from private to public accountability and policy formation. The relative independence from political pressures which science programs have achieved has not been won without a constant struggle, has met with significant setbacks, and offers some lessons but no assurances for the future independence of either science programs or of broader forms of aid. If certain broader types of federal aid are necessary, and we believe they are, it is best to enter upon them alert to their inherent dangers. The best safeguard of an institution's independence remains its financial independence.

SUMMARY

The many valid criticisms of the project system do not justify its abandonment but rather point the way to its improvement and supplementation. Both discrete projects and broader forms of support are needed, and both contracts and grants should be retained as the legal instruments for transferring public funds to educational institutions and defining the ensuing faculty and institutional responsibilities.

The principal charges against the project system are that it is too time-consuming, requires excessive record-keeping and reporting, encourages "safe" rather than bold research, fosters private empires, and establishes "cliques" of favored institutions and scholars. Many of these criticisms are directed at characteristics of American science or American society rather than at the project system per se, but certain corrective measures are indicated to improve present administrative procedures. The essential principles of the project system remain sound and valuable: the designation of specific tasks; the evaluation of quality by the scientists best qualified to do so; and the control of scientific work by the scientists themselves.

Broader departmental, program, and institutional awards, which have been inaugurated in recent years, represent a welcome addition to the project pattern.

CHAPTER 19

Federal "Control"

NO DISCUSSION of institutional experience with the administration of federal programs would be complete without some mention of the issue of federal "control."

The danger of federal control is like the danger of a dragon waking. Many academicians believe it never will wake (it has slept so long); many, that it is not asleep but awake and quite tame; others that there is no dragon at all, but a drayhorse or a milch cow.

Whatever their image of the national government, the dominant sentiment of the academic community today unquestionably favors an expansion of federal aid to higher education. Although fears of federal control persist, they have not been so strong as to override the attractions of that aid or to lead many institutions to refuse it. Less than 2 percent of our faculty respondents subscribed to the view that "federal programs are unnecessary and should be discontinued"; over a third were prepared to say that "federal programs are unfortunately necessary, but it would be best for the nation if colleges and universities could do without them"; but the majority opted for the positive statement that "federal programs are necessary and desirable in the national interest, regardless of the financial condition of colleges and universities."

GENERAL INSTITUTIONAL ACCEPTANCE
OF FEDERAL AID

The presidents of some church-affiliated colleges have expressed concern about the forgiveness feature of the federal student loan program on the grounds that this is not the way to build self-reliance, but will lead students to expect "handouts" from the government. At least one institution is not participating in the program because of its officers' conviction that the terms constitute too much of a subsidy for students. For similar reasons, the Southern Assembly recently warned that a large program of federal scholarship for undergraduates "might be detrimental to the maximum development of individual responsibility."[1] The feeling that the present generation of students, and particularly graduate students, has things "too soft" because of federal money and does not value higher education for its own sake but merely as a means to earn higher salaries is, of course, frequently encountered. Few voicing this opinion suggest that government loans and fellowships be discontinued; but the feeling is undoubtedly a strong factor in congressional opposition to the enactment of a national scholarship program for undergraduate students (which was, until recently, opposed and is now unenthusiastically supported by The Association of State Universities and Land-Grant Colleges and The State Universities Association[2]).

The line between disapproval and approval of federal aid on these grounds is often drawn between loans and outright grants on the tenuous logic that a loan is not "aid" whereas a grant is.[3] The Association of American Colleges, for example, opposed the College Housing Loan Program for some years and, as late as 1960, refused to endorse the

---

[1] The Sixth Southern Assembly, *Final Report, The Federal Government and Higher Education* (Bioloxi, Miss., January 1961; mimeographed).

[2] "Scholarship and loan programs, broadly based and institutionally administered, are needed and serve valuable objectives in insuring the availability of higher education to many students. They are not, however, an adequate substitute for educational opportunity available at low cost to individuals of wide-ranging ability, interests and financial means.

"Any Federally financed program of scholarship grants should be institutionally administered and should be designed so as to reach needy students of wide-ranging ability. . . . Highest priority should be given to institutional aid which would have the effect of reducing costs to all students." (*Recommendations on Desirable National Action Affecting Higher Education* by The Association of State Universities and Land-Grant Colleges and The State Universities Association, January 1962, p. 14.)

[3] "The College Housing Loan Program rests on two debatable propositions. . . . The first is that, since the program is for assistance in the construction of non-academic facilities, it should not be considered as a program in aid of education, but rather as a housing program. The second is that a loan is not an aid to education—and hence religion [i.e., church-controlled institutions]—whereas a grant is." See Homer D. Babbidge, Jr., and Robert M. Rosenzweig, *The Federal Interest in Higher Education* (McGraw-Hill, 1962), p. 140.

282 EFFECTS OF FEDERAL PROGRAMS ON HIGHER EDUCATION

principle of federal grants for academic buildings.[4] The trustees of one institution in our study refused, a few years ago, to sanction even government loans for dormitory construction, believing that the money should be raised commercially. They later changed their minds after the president had convinced them that, in the experience of other schools, the loans had been administered without dictation, and that it was not fair to tax students (via tuition) the additional $10,000 a year interest that would have to be paid on a $1 million private loan.

Another board of trustees, who remain opposed to federal *grants,* also accepted a loan for the construction of dormitories after obtaining a letter from the Housing and Home Finance Agency assuring them that the loan could be paid off at any time. They sought this assurance as protection against any objectionable regulations, but their experience with the administration of the loan has been satisfactory to date. The change in attitude by the two boards was accompanied, in both cases, by a change in the presidency of the institution and the appointment of some younger trustees upon the death or retirement of older men who had been more firmly opposed to federal aid of any sort.

While loans for income-producing dormitories, cafeterias, and student centers have proved acceptable to most institutions, public and private institutions have not been able to agree on the desirability of a loan program for sorely needed non-income producing teaching facilities. By and large, such loans are more acceptable to private institutions, which can more readily cover the charges from endowment income and student fees, than to public institutions, which prefer direct grants since they strive to keep student fees low and may be barred by state law from loans for non-income producing purposes.

Loans and, particularly, grants to church-related institutions have also been opposed on the grounds of violating the First Amendment to the Constitution: "Congress shall make no law respecting an establishment of religion. . . ." The major organizations representing both

[4] The Association "had met in Boston in January, 1960, and considered a resolution from its Legislative Committee, authorizing that Committee to support 'the most suitable form' of Federal aid to assist the Nation's colleges in meeting their physical-facilities needs. The resolution was adopted, but only after assurances had been demanded and given that 'the Association would not be committed, without further reference to the membership, to any proposal involving outright grants.' The membership did not feel it could endorse such an 'open-end' authorization, because it was unable to resolve itself on the question of 'the separation of Church and State.' " (*Ibid.,* p. 105.)

private and public institutions of higher education have united in supporting legislation to provide loans *and* grants for the construction of "academic" facilities at public *and* private universities and colleges (excluding, thereby, facilities for sectarian religious instruction); but opposition to loans and/or grants to private institutions have been voiced by powerful spokesmen for public secondary and elementary education.[5]

The United States Commission on Civil Rights recommended in 1960 that "the Federal Government . . . take such measures as may be required to assure that funds under the various programs of Federal assistance to higher education are disbursed only to such publicly controlled institutions of higher education as do not discriminate on grounds of race, color, religion, or national origin." The chairman and two other members of the Commission also proposed that federal funds not be disbursed to any *private* institution of higher education "which discriminates on grounds of race, religion, or national origin." The recommendation followed a careful study which concluded that a variety of present federal programs in aid of scientific research, education, and educational housing "have the effect of supporting racial segregation, and continue the educational deprivation of those excluded from [segregated institutions]."[6]

Some faculty and more officials of Southern institutions visited shortly after the publication of the Commission's report expressed concern lest federal programs be used to impose integration upon institutions not desiring it, and, in the case of certain private institutions, required by

---

[5] The associations of higher educational institutions whose officers united in February 1962 in support of pending legislation to make loans *and* grants available to public *and* private institutions were the American Council on Education, the American Association of Junior Colleges, the Association of American Colleges, the Association of State Colleges and Universities, the Association of State Universities and Land-Grant Colleges, and the State Universities Association; the associations of public secondary and elementary education which, in June 1962, opposed either grants or both grants and loans for the construction of facilities at private institutions of higher education were the American Association of School Administrators, the American Vocational Association, the Council of Chief State School Officers, the National Congress of Parents and Teachers, the National School Boards Association, and the National Education Association. See *Higher Education and National Affairs* (American Council on Education), Feb. 26, 1962, p. 4, and July 2, 1962, p. 2.

[6] United States Commission on Civil Rights, *Equal Protection of the Laws in Public Higher Education, 1960* (1960), pp. 267, 273.

their founding charter to remain segregated.[7] The Sixth Southern Assembly, meeting in January 1961, urged that "the achievement of social reforms . . . be severed from the federal government's participation in higher education" and warned that "Federal support also designed to compel social change might terminate other support of equal or greater significance." Nevertheless, the Assembly's report is noteworthy for its mild tone on this emotionally charged issue, and over-all, the Assembly endorsed an expansion of federal programs—or, to be more exact, the present level of federal programs—"federal support cannot be substantially diminished without doing serious damage to the nation and its many major institutions of higher education," and recognized that "unless private, state, and local funds can be greatly expanded . . . the federal government will continue to increase its support."

Criticism of the International Cooperation Administration's management of its contracts with universities was perhaps more unrelieved than that directed against any other agency. At a meeting of university business officers at Notre Dame a few years ago, ICA was subjected to merciless and doubtless quite deserved criticism for failing to comprehend what a university is all about; substantially the same criticism was repeated during our interviews.[8] Yet how many universities have refused to participate in ICA programs until the requisite administrative reforms are made? (The Massachusetts Institute of Technology refused to undertake an ICA management program at the Vienna Technische Hochschule

[7] This concern received some confirmation in December 1961, when the Department of Health, Education, and Welfare "told universities chosen to participate in the training institutes for high school language teachers and guidance counselors that a new clause would be included in their contract with the Government which would require that there be no discrimination in admission to the institutes." A similar clause requiring candidates to be considered solely on the basis of their ability "without regard to race, creed, or color" will be made a condition of NSF awards for summer and academic year institutes effective in the summer of 1963 and the academic year 1963-64. (Address of HEW Secretary Abraham Ribicoff at the Gethsemane Baptist Church, Washington, D.C., June 14, 1962, and oral information from the Office of the General Counsel, NSF, July 1962.)

[8] Cf. *The University and World Affairs,* Report of the Committee on the University and World Affairs of the Ford Foundation (1960): "ICA does not make adequate and effective use of university resources at the operating level. Its day-to-day orientation is away from rather than towards the universities" (p. 54). Also the observation of McGeorge Bundy, Dean of Faculty of Arts and Sciences, Harvard University, that "the Point Four contracts are perhaps the weakest single program connecting the Federal government with American universities." (Letter, *The Reporter,* Sept. 1, 1960, p. 12.)

because, after careful study, it decided it could not do a first-rate job; but this was another, if highly commendable, ground of action.[9])

It is, in brief, easier to oppose federal programs in the abstract or on general principles than to refuse to participate in a specific program which—despite certain drawbacks, deficiencies, and controls—offers immediate advantages to an institution. Thus, a treasurer at a far-from-wealthy college was critical of the chorus of requests that the government pay the administrative costs of the student loan program, feeling that this, at least, the schools should do themselves. "We're helping students get through school—that's our *job*." He added, however, "Of course, if they give overhead here, I'll take it."

INDEPENDENCE MUST BE MANIFESTED

Nothing would lend so much conviction to the institutions' cause and do more to forestall harmful controls than a firm statement of institutional policy on specific provisions of federal programs, and a resolute implementation of that policy, carried, where necessary, to the point of refusing to participate in objectionable programs.

The foremost recent example of such action is the refusal by twenty-nine institutions to participate in the student loan program of the National Defense Education Act because of the disclaimer affidavit in Title X, Sec.(f) which provides:[10]

> No part of any funds appropriated or otherwise made available for expenditure under authority of this Act shall be used to make payments or loans to any individual unless such individual . . . has executed and filed with the Commissioner an affidavit that he does not believe in, and is not a member of and does not support any organization that believes in or teaches, the overthrow of the United States Government by force or violence or by any illegal or unconstitutional methods. . . .

[9] This story is recounted in Walter Adams and John A. Garraty, *Is the World Our Campus?* (Michigan State University Press, 1960), pp. 112-113.

[10] As of December 1961, twenty institutions had withdrawn from this program, an additional nine had never participated because of the disclaimer affidavit, and another two were expected to withdraw the following academic year. About eighty additional institutions which continued to participate in the program had publicly stated their disapproval of the affidavit. (Official statements on file at U.S. Office of Education; and see *American Association of University Professors Bulletin*, Vol. 46, December 1960, p. 413.)

Each institution must, of course, be responsible for formulating and implementing its own policy, but eminent institutions bear a broader responsibility, for if the strong yield on a point of principle, what can be expected of the weak? It is noteworthy that, although other schools had acted earlier, it was only after Harvard and Yale withdrew from the student loan program that the affidavit issue received national attention, Congress held hearings, and a bill was introduced to repeal the provision.

For reasons we do not completely understand, institutions have confined their nonparticipation in the affidavit provision of the Act to the student loan section, although affidavits are equally required and have been submitted by graduate fellows under Title IV, trainees in counseling and guidance institutes under Title V B, and language trainees under Title VI.[11] A similar affidavit had for many years been required of recipients of NSF fellowships without arousing institutional opposition, which has given rise to cynical suggestions that the well-endowed universities made a show of independence with respect to relatively unimportant student loan funds but not with respect to more important government fellowships. It has also been noted that significant opposition to the NDEA affidavit was not displayed until after its enactment.[12] The

[11] Among the reasons advanced are that graduate students are more mature than undergraduates and able to decide for themselves what they should do (but graduate students also receive loans under Title II of the Act); that the institutions need not use any of their own funds or take responsibility for administering the affidavit under sections other than Title II (a moot point); that similar affidavits are required of graduate fellows by NSF and NIH; and even that more graduate than undergraduate deans are scientists and hence accustomed to security investigations and disclaimers of disloyalty.

[12] "It was only several months after the [National Defense Education] Act was passed that most people in the academic community were even aware that the [affidavit] requirements existed—far too late, of course, to do anything but to sound injured and to agitate for repeal. It then turned out that essentially the same requirements were a part of other student-aid programs and had been for some time—eight years in the case of the National Science Foundation. An observer not involved in the issue might well sympathize with the irritation of some Congressmen that the higher-education community—eight years after the fact—had suddenly discovered that it was being injured." (Babbidge and Rosenzweig, op. cit., p. 203.) Sec. 16 (d) of the National Science Foundation Act of 1950 specifies: "No part of any funds appropriated or otherwise made available for expenditure by the Foundation under authority of this Act shall be used to make payments under any scholarship or fellowship to any individual unless such individual (1) has executed and filed with the Foundation an affidavit that he does not believe in, and is not a member of and does not support any organization that believes in or teaches, the overthrow of the United States Government by force or violence or by any illegal or unconstitutional methods. . . ."

foregoing record indicates the need for consistency and timeliness if the institutional response to legislative proposals is to be convincing and effective.

Some universities *have* refused to cooperate in maintaining time records of faculty conducting contract research for the Department of Defense; to undertake classified research on campus; to accept research grants from the Department of Defense carrying less than the full audited overhead rate; to submit their salary schedule to the government in connection with a research budget; and to accept major research awards from the Advanced Research Projects Agency and the National Institutes of Health set up along interdepartmental lines key professors disapproved of. Without getting into the merits of individual decisions, such resolute acts must be applauded—indeed, they should be commended to institutions as a periodic test of their independence. It is said that justice must not merely be done—it must be seen to be done. So independence must not merely be proclaimed, it must be visibly demonstrated.

EVER-PRESENT DANGERS

As these remarks may suggest, we are not inclined to dismiss the danger of federal control as a myth designed simply to serve the interests of local and sectional forces. It is and will remain a continuing danger to the independence of academic institutions, and must be guarded against more vigilantly as the role of the federal government in higher education grows.

The ultimate danger, political dictation of what should be taught and who should teach it, is generally conceded to have been remarkably absent during the great postwar expansion of federal programs. Further, faculty and students of the subject affirm that such efforts at political control as they have experienced tend to come from local rather than national sources. "Studies by staff of the Commission on Financing Higher Education indicate that 'political' threats to the land-grant institutions have come at the state and local level rather than from the Federal Government . . . partisan political pressures of the kind most often warned against in connection with federal aid to education have almost without exception occurred at the state and local level; federal grants have helped the colleges and state extension services to resist these pressures."[13]

This is the prevailing judgment; but not everyone concurs in it. Thus, one scientist and university president recounted his personal knowledge of short-sighted federal opposition which prevented important basic research at certain experimental stations; he suggested, further, that a sophisticated re-examination of the land-grant experience might reveal other such episodes that have commonly been glossed over. And the comment of a political scientist (given in reply to our questionnaire) merits serious consideration:

> . . . with state or private aid, we can at least escape from the resulting pressures for conformity from our benefactors, when they become intolerable, by going to some other college or university where the controls have not become proportionate to the subsidies. But when there is extensive federal aid (with the inevitable controls), then where do we escape? To Canada? State-supported education is defective both from the standpoint of its sufficiency and from the standpoint of the resulting suffocation of culture in the interest of the subsidizing elements. But at least, under the state-supported system, there is some competition, and educational institutions are torn between subservience to state interests and the prevention of mass flight of their faculties to other (and perhaps no better) institutions. But with total federal aid (which can be the ultimate end), institutions will have less need to offer favorable academic climates to their faculties, because faculties will have no other place to go. . . .

A more evident danger, which is the more difficult to withstand as the expansion of educational institutions and of our society normally takes the same course, is the growth of bureaucracy and its tendency to change universities from academic to impersonal or even business institutions. We have repeatedly noted the tendency of government programs to make increased administrative demands on academic institutions, obliging them to enlarge their administrative, accounting, and clerical staffs, and the amount of time which faculty devote to administration. A fifth of the time of full professors at Group I universities is now devoted to administration (although, as there is no difference in this respect between professors of science and of humanities, it is clear the government programs are not *all* they are administering). Often, as new government programs age, they are run less by men and more by rules, less by personal and more by formal communications, less by the indi-

[13] Richard G. Axt, *The Federal Government and Financing Higher Education* (Commission on Financing Higher Education, 1952), pp. 205, 207.

vidual examination of individual situations and more by general regulations. This is control not by dictation but by red tape, which can frustrate and devitalize much intellectual effort. To combat it we need able administrators whose objective is to fulfill major agency missions rather than minor agency regulations, the frequent rotation of academic and government personnel, the fostering of professional standards and environment in agencies serving the academic community (and in some academic institutions), and, where necessary, special legislation to free these agencies from yearly budgetary and reporting requirements inappropriate to their mission.

A serious danger is that the spontaneous and willing redirection of academic effort to areas of national interest will lead to the essential nationalization of our greatest universities. (More than one wag has renamed MIT the National Institute of Technology.) This is a danger to which President Eisenhower referred in his farewell address: "The prospect of domination of the nation's scholars by Federal employment, project allocations, and the power of money is ever present—and is gravely to be regarded." The danger is not so much of the government "buying up" our leading scholars or, to put it even more crassly, of the scholars "selling out" for money, but, rather, of the goals of universities being shaped by the needs of the nation rather than the needs of science, of scholarship, and of man. As one professor put it in commenting on several items in our questionnaire dealing with the "national interest":

> I grate against the idea of "national interest" in a university. There is one danger, as I see it, of Federal funds for education—the danger that higher education will become more and more "nationalized" rather than "universalized." After all, the word *university* implies universality—the study of the universe and all that is therein.

This danger is great because it is real and inescapable, and because it can be seriously argued that it not so much a danger to be avoided as a goal to be sought. Does not a noble conception of the national interest embrace the interest of man? What university could or should remain aloof in time of war? Is peace not now so perilous as to require the best efforts of the best minds in every field? But do scholars best serve the nation by forsaking their laboratory and their study for mechanical and political arts? Does not a bricklayer serve his nation well by laying bricks well, and a scholar by good scholarship? Each scholar and each institution has answered these questions in its own way.

The last danger to which we will refer is the danger of conformity and the suppression of unpopular ideas. The history of such suppression does not begin with our Republic, but, unfortunately, our Republic has at times extended the history. All readers will recall the climate of political suspicion in the early 1950's, which affected not only the agencies of government but of learning, in which the assumption of innocence and the due process of law requisite to establish guilt were abrogated. Charles V. Kidd has recorded "the shadowy procedure and elusive criteria" by which the Department of Health, Education, and Welfare, without a hearing or show of cause, denied grants for unclassified medical research to scientists when "fortuitious . . . information" led officials to question their loyalty. "The criterion was less often a threat to the security of the nation than a threat to the personal security of administrators at all levels or to the security of the programs of the executive branch against retaliatory action by Congress. . . . Those who made initial judgments and final decision were not inclined to endanger the nation, their budgets, or themselves by establishing lax standards of loyalty for medical research scientists."

Kidd is, in general, sanguine about federal aid to education: ". . . there are weighty reasons for believing that federal financing of higher education need not be followed by federal control. Fifteen years of financing of research with no federal control suggests that general aid could be provided without deadening uniformity, control of curricula, or federal selection of faculty." However, his general approval of federal aid leads one to ponder all the more the following sombre observations:

> The one occurrence that has shaken my conviction that general federal aid to higher education poses no inherent danger to the freedom of universities has been the imposition of security clearances for those engaged in federally financed unclassified research. This whole episode in our history, now happily past, is repugnant because it involved an essentially immoral abandonment of the values without which our form of government and indeed our society cannot survive. The dignity of man was submerged, for rationality and freedom were abandoned. The hard search for a workable balance between the rights of the individual and the needs of the state was temporarily abandoned. No margin was allowed for human fallibility and frailty. There was at the height of the fever little personal moral responsibility, tolerance, compassion, or wisdom. If general federal aid to higher education had been in force over the period 1951-1956, the freedom of American universities would have been seriously threatened.

To be fair, we should add Kidd's further observation:

> The significance of the great security-loyalty aberration was not, however, that federal aid to higher education inevitably means federal control through one route or another, but that no sector of our society can remain untouched by the great surges of fear, suspicion, hate, and anger that accompany war and the slow return of peace. Many universities, it should be remembered, were not overly vigilant in defending the values to which they are ostensibly dedicated when defense of wrongly accused faculty members endangered private gifts and state appropriations.[14]

Unfortunately, the peace that was known before Alamogordo is indeed slow to return and we may be banished from it forever like Adam from Eden.

It may not be widely appreciated how much, to faculty at isolated colleges who have little or nothing to do with most federal programs that impinge mainly on universities and graduate and professional schools, the image of the government is shaped, not by the National Science Foundation, the National Institutes of Health, or the U.S. Office of Education, but rather by the Internal Revenue Service and investigators from the Federal Bureau of Investigation who come to inquire about the beliefs and associations of former students and colleagues. The repeated, unannounced stranger on the small campus is soon spotted and identified to his colleagues by some hostile, sharp-eyed professor. In their survey of a nationally representative group of social science teachers at four-year colleges, Paul Lazarsfeld and Wagner Thielens found that, during 1954, an agent of the FBI had talked one or more times with 61 percent of the faculty (three or more times with 33 percent); and 41 percent of faculty had worked on a project or job in which government security clearance was necessary.[15]

That political pressure may still influence the administration of the best federal programs at educational institutions is indicated by the action of the National Science Foundation in June 1961 in revoking a fellowship to a graduate student at the University of Illinois who had satisfactorily met all the legal and administrative requirements, after Alan Waterman, the Foundation Director, had been grilled on the award at a hearing of the House Science and Astronautics Committee. The student, Edward

[14] Kidd, *American Universities and Federal Research* (Harvard University Press, 1959), pp. 119-122.

[15] Lazarsfeld and Thielens, *The Academic Mind* (The Free Press, 1958), pp. 401, 382.

Yellin, had been convicted of contempt of Congress, and his case was under appeal to the Supreme Court; but a member of the House Committee warned Waterman, "I give you notice that if the Supreme Court reverses the case, don't you give this Yellin a fellowship." The entire episode, including the only ground cited in the Foundation's telegram of revocation—"the possibility that you may not be able to pursue your studies without interruption"—can hardly give much comfort or assurance of protection from political pressure to the holder of any government fellowship or grant.[16]

SUMMARY

Their wish for greater federal aid has blinded many educators to the very real dangers: (1) that academic values and objectives will be surrendered to those of a business enterprise or the more important goals of the nation, and (2) that some form of political control will, indeed, follow federal aid. Not merely opposing, but the stronger step of refusing to participate in undesirable federal programs and policies is, at times, necessary to manifest and, thus, to maintain an institution's independence.

[16] In a letter to Dr. Waterman (July 12, 1961), the director of the American Civil Liberties Union pointed out that, even should the Supreme Court rule against Yellin, the time likely to elapse in hearing and rehearing the case "would in all probability be long enough to permit him to finish the academic year 1961-62. It would seem to us that for the Foundation to base the revocation . . . on the time factor is to prejudge what the Court's action, or actions, will be." In his reply (July 18), Waterman stated that the revocation was based on "the reasonable possibility" that Yellin "will not be able to devote full-time to his fellowship." He observed that NSF had, on other occasions, canceled fellowships after receiving word from the recipient that he would be unable to devote full-time to his studies but acknowledged that "we have never [before] had occasion unilaterally to revoke a Foundation fellowship." In view of the strong defense of the award made by Waterman during his appearance before the committee and the subsequent apparent reversal of the Foundation's position, we can only conclude that political pressure was the cause of the cancellation. One rumor at the time had it that the Foundation backed down at the instruction—or, shall we say, suggestion—of a presidential aide.

Conclusion

THIS INQUIRY COMMENCED with three questions:

1. What have been the effects of federal programs upon the quality of higher education, particularly at the undergraduate level?

2. To what extent can or should fuller use be made of institutions not heavily involved in present federal programs?

3. What has been the experience of institutions with the administration of current federal programs?

The text has elaborated the complexity of these questions, and the difficulties of giving simple answers to them. Nevertheless, our answers may be summarized as follows:

1. The direct effects of federal programs have been profound and beneficial in the sciences, noticeable but more imbalanced in the social sciences, and negligible in the humanities. Federal programs have *not* notably affected the relative proportion or quality of faculty or students going into the sciences, but *have* concentrated a large number of faculty and many of the best students at a few leading institutions. While improving the content of instruction by enlarging our knowledge in the sciences, their emphasis upon graduate research and education has depreciated the status of undergraduate teaching and reduced personal contact between senior faculty and lower classmen, especially at large universities. Nor has the quality of undergraduate science education been advanced by the deflection of the best graduate students from teaching assistantships to federal fellowships and research assistantships. The government (and vaster historical forces) has divided the liberal arts faculty into a contingent of relatively young scientists and social scientists with lighter teaching loads, higher income, substantial research

293

support, and other perquisites, and another contingent of older humanists, with heavier teaching loads, lower incomes, and little research support.

2. The heavy concentration of federal research and development funds at a few major installations should be continued; but a greater effort is warranted to extend other programs of scientific research and education to more institutions below the doctoral level which do not now participate extensively in them. The desirability of dispersing more broadly among doctoral level institutions funds now heavily concentrated at a few leading universities must be determined by the degree to which this advances the objectives of individual programs. High priority should be given to strengthening scientific research and education at leading state universities.

3. Government programs have developed along two administrative lines: the project system, in which funds are controlled by individual faculty for designated purposes; and various forms of aid for broader purposes, in which funds are controlled by alliances of faculty or by higher administrative officers. Both methods of support are needed: the project system is vital to the maintenance of high professional standards and the freedom of the individual investigator; broader forms of support are desirable to strengthen neglected scientific and educational areas. In both systems, it is important to emphasize criteria of quality and to resist pressures to distribute money on the basis of a mathematical formula.

To alleviate demands on their own unrestricted income, universities are requesting and receiving from the government increasing sums for the salaries of both junior and tenured faculty for that portion of their time which they devote to federally sponsored research; and they are also seeking reimbursement of the full indirect costs of this research in government grants as well as contracts. We fear that the former policy, especially, is short-sighted, for it reduces the institution's ability to say "No" to the government. Broader forms of aid in which faculty salaries are not tied to specific research undertakings would be preferable; but institutions must remain alert to the dangers of control inherent in any form of large-scale aid. These dangers are not merely past or prospective; they are always present.

APPENDIX A

Additional Tables

Table A-1. *New Faculty with Doctorates, 1959-61**

	New Faculty Hired in 1959-60 and 1960-61**							
	Total		Sciences		Social Sciences		Humanities	
Institutions	Number	Percent with Ph.D.	Number	Percent with Ph.D.	Number	Percent with Ph.D.	Number	Percent with Ph.D.
Group I***	424	59.7 %	197	73.6 %	80	41.2 %	91	38.5 %
Group II	286	43.0	89	50.6	38	63.2	81	16.0
Group III	107	40.2	49	42.9	17	41.2	40	32.5

* Source: National Education Association.
** Total includes fields other than the three reported here, and these three are here confined as
follows: Sciences, chemistry, physics, mathematics, and biological sciences; Social Sciences, economics,
psychology, and sociology; Humanities, English, history, and philosophy.
***.Two of our Group I universities did not report.

Table A-2. *Number of Group I and II Universities Ranked Among the Nation's Best, 1925 and 1957**

Field	Group I		Group II	
	1925	1957	1925	1957
Ranked Among Best 17 Graduate Schools				
All Fields	7	7	1	-
Physical Sciences	7	6	1	-
Biological Sciences	6	7	-	-
Social Sciences	7	7	2	-
Humanities	7	7	-	1
Ranked Among Top 10 Graduate Departments in				
Chemistry	5	4	-	-
Geology	5	5	-	-
Mathematics	4	5	-	-
Physics	3	6	-	-
Botany	4	4	-	-
Zoology	5	4	-	-
Economics	4	4	-	-
Political Science	5	4	1	-
Psychology	3	5	1	1
Sociology	3	2	1	1
Classics	5	4	-	-
English	4	4	1	-
German	3	5	-	-
History	6	5	1	-
Philosophy	4	4	-	-
Romance Languages	5	4	-	1

* Source: Rankings by university department chairmen reported by Raymond M. Hughes, A Study of the Graduate Schools of America (1925), and Hayward Keniston, Graduate Study and Research in the Arts and Sciences at the University of Pennsylvania (University of Pennsylvania Press, 1959). Institutes of technology were excluded by Keniston, although our Groups I and II each include one.

Table A-3. *Recent Shifts in Staff Quality*

"Comparing the present picture in this department with that a
few years ago--about 1955-56--I would say that the average quality
of the staff in the department has..."

| Field and Institution Group | Percent of Faculty Present at the Institution in 1955 or 1956 Replying | | | | Number |
	Improved	Stayed About the Same	Declined	Total[*]	
Total					
Group I	63 %	28 %	9 %	100 %	1,169
Group II	62	30	9	100	729
Group III	61	34	5	100	316
Sciences					
Group I	57	32	11	100	548
Group II	68	24	8	100	303
Group III	64	32	4	100	98
Social Sciences					
Group I	70	24	6	100	279
Group II	72	17	11	100	186
Group III	61	34	5	100	62
Humanities					
Group I	66	25	9	100	342
Group II	45	47	8	100	240
Group III	60	35	5	100	156

* Here and in subsequent tables detail may not add to totals
because of rounding.

Table A-4. *Number of Faculty, by Field, 1958-59 and 1954-55**

Field**	All Institutions,*** 1958-59 (estimated)		138 Universities, 1954-55	338 Colleges, 1954-55
	Number	Percent	Percent	Percent
Excluding Agriculture, Engineering, and Health Sciences				
Sciences	45,000	32 %	35 %	26 %
Social Sciences	33,500	23	26	23
Humanities	64,250	45	40	51
Total	142,750	100 %	100 %	100 %
Including Agriculture, Engineering, and Health Sciences				
Sciences	82,750	46 %	54 %	30 %
Social Sciences	33,500	19	18	22
Humanities	64,250	36	28	48
Total	180,500	100 %	100 %	100 %

* Source: National Education Association, Teacher Supply and Demand in Universities, Colleges, and Junior Colleges, 1957-58 and 1958-59 (1959), p. 51; ibid., Teacher Supply and Demand in Degree-Granting Institutions, 1954-55 (1955), p. 136.
** Sciences include biological and physical sciences and mathematics; Social Sciences: economics, geography, psychology, sociology, and, in these data, history; Humanities: English, fine arts, foreign languages, and philosophy.
*** Universities, colleges, and junior colleges.

Table A-5. *Trends in Scholastic Aptitude Test Scores at Thirteen Institutions*

Institution	Mean Verbal Score of Class Entering Fall			Mean Mathematical Score of Class Entering Fall		
	1960	1953	1947	1960	1953	1947
Group I						
1	650	572		728	654	
2	641	594		675	629	
3*	550		486	553		451
4*	501	455	431	510	431	399
Group II						
5	620	520	514	635	542	526
6***	570	435		534	414	
7*	497	420**		518	440**	
Group III						
8	681**	636**	642**	667**	620**	593**
9	641**	517**	527**	658**	519**	496**
10	638	583	588	670	626	602
11	626	620	600	628	600	
12	612	512	526	637	563	551
13	575	454		566	469	

Header note: Mean SAT Scores of Entering Class in College of Liberal Arts and Sciences

* State University.
** Median.
*** Women only.

Table A-6. *Proportion of Degrees Awarded in Sciences, Social Sciences, and Humanities During Recent Decades**

Years	Sciences	Social Sciences	Humanities
Bachelor's Degrees			
1916-20	31.8 %	10.4 %	57.8 %
1926-30	30.0	17.1	52.9
1936-40	29.5	22.7	47.8
1946-50	29.5	29.5	41.1
1951-53	27.8	28.7	43.5
1958-59	31.4	28.7	39.9
Doctor's Degrees			
1916-20	49.2 %	17.3 %	33.5 %
1926-30	53.5	19.1	27.5
1936-40	56.2	16.6	27.3
1946-50	54.1	18.3	27.6
1951-53	54.5	21.7	23.7
1958-59	54.3	23.4	22.3

* Sources: Dael Wolfle, America's Resources of Specialized Talent, The Report of the Commission on Human Resources and Advanced Training (Harper, 1954), pp. 294-295, 300-301; U.S. Office of Education, Earned Degrees Conferred 1958-59 (1961), pp. 31-35.

Table A-7. *Median Intelligence Score of Students in Various Liberal Arts Fields**

	College Graduates			Graduate Students	
Rank	Field	Score**	Rank	Field	Score**
1	Physics and Mathematics***	127	1	Psychology	132
2	Chemistry	125	2	Physics and Mathematics***	131
4	Psychology	123	3	Philosophy and "Other Humanities"	130
4	English	123	4.5	Chemistry	129
4	Languages	123	4.5	English	129
6	Economics	122	6.5	Languages	126
8	Biological Sciences	121	6.5	Biological Sciences	126
8	Earth Sciences	121	8	Economics	125
8	Fine Arts	121	10	Earth Sciences	124
10	History	120	10	History	124
11.5	Philosophy and "Other Humanities"	118	10	"Other Social Sciences"	124
11.5	"Other Social Sciences"	118	12	Fine Arts	121

* Source: Dael Wolfle, America's Resources of Specialized Talent, Report of the Commission on Human Resources and Advanced Training (Harper, 1954), pp. 317-322.

** 50th percentile on the Army General Classification Test.

*** These appear to be the main fields subsumed under Wolfle's "physical sciences," which also includes metallurgy.

Table A-8. *Recent Trends in Average Class Size*

Field and Institution Group	Percent of Faculty and Department Chairmen Indicating Increase in Average Class Size in Department Since 1955[*]					
	Faculty[**]			Department Chairmen		
	a	b	c	a	b	c
Total						
Group I	62 %	64 %	66 %	55 %	67 %	68 %
Group II	61	69	71	64	74	71
Group III	54	55	-	58	54	-
Sciences						
Group I	65	68	69	59	67	75
Group II	63	72	72	74	84	74
Group III	63	58	-	68	59	-
Social Sciences						
Group I	64	57	58	59	67	59
Group II	61	59	69	60	63	71
Group III	41	40	-	50	53	-
Humanities						
Group I	56	62	66	47	67	67
Group II	59	75	72	57	73	67
Group III	54	60	-	54	52	-

[*] Representing replies to the question: "What has happened to the average size of classes in your department in recent years--since 1955 or 1956? a. Freshman and sophomore classes, b. Junior and senior classes, c. Graduate classes." "Don't know" responses and cases in which classes of the designated level were not taught in the department have been excluded.

[**] Only faculty present at the institution in 1956 or 1955 are included.

Table A-9. *Estimated Number of Graduate Students Supported by Federal Agencies, 1960-61**

Agency	Estimated Number of Graduate Students Supported in Academic Year 1960-61		
	Total (1)	Sciences** (2)	Type of Stipend
1. Atomic Energy Commission	200	50	Fellowship
2. National Science Foundation	2,400	1,800	Fellowship
3. Office of Education	2,500	800	Fellowship
4. Public Health Service	1,000	600	Fellowship
5. Public Health Service	4,200	1,100	Traineeship
Subtotal	10,300	4,450	
6. All Research Agencies			
a. Low Estimate	18,600	9,300	Research Assistantship
b. High Estimate	35,000	22,750	Research Assistantship
c. Reasonable Mean	26,800	13,400	Research Assistantship
Total, lines 1-5 and 6c	37,100	17,850	

* Sources: Column 1, lines 1-5, Alice Rivlin, The Role of the Federal Government in Financing Higher Education, (Brookings Institution, 1961), pp. 62, 88; line 6b, U.S. Bureau of the Budget, Special Analysis of Federal Research and Development Programs in the 1961 Budget, (January 1960), p. 10; Column 2, derived by information and inference of which lines 2 and 3 are precise, 4 and 5 estimates, and 6 a-c broader estimates. Without going into excessive detail, lines 6a-6c, the most important and most unreliable figures, derive ultimately from estimates of the average total federal research and development dollars per research assistant.

** Biological and physical sciences including mathematics, but excluding agriculture, engineering, medical sciences, psychology, geography, social sciences, and humanities.

Table A-10. *Recent Shifts in Quality of Education*

"Comparing the present picture in this department with that a few years ago--about 1955-56--I would say that the over-all quality of the education this department is giving has..."

Field and Institution Group	Percent of Faculty Present at Institution in 1955 or 1956 Replying				Number
	Improved	Stayed About the Same	Declined	Total	
Total					
Group I	69 %	23 %	8 %	100 %	1,167
Group II	74	19	7	100	726
Group III	82	16	2	100	317
Sciences					
Group I	66	25	9	100	552
Group II	78	17	6	100	301
Group III	85	12	3	100	99
Social Sciences					
Group I	73	20	7	100	271
Group II	79	13	9	100	182
Group III	83	16	2	100	64
Humanities					
Group I	71	21	8	100	344
Group II	67	26	7	100	243
Group III	81	19	1	100	154

Table A-11. *Mean Academic Year Salaries in Humanities and Sciences at a Private University, 1960-61**

Rank	Mean Salary		Number	
	Humanities	Sciences	Humanities	Sciences
Professor	$14,289	$15,176	32	45
Associate Professor	9,506	9,482	11	32
Assistant Professor	7,423	7,577	25	26
Total, Three Ranks	$10,991	$11,489	68	103

* Humanities: classics, English, philosophy; Sciences: chemistry, mathematics, physics.

Table A-12. *Mean Academic Year Salaries by Field at Another Private University, 1959-60*

Field	Professor	Associate Professor	Assistant Professor	Instructor
Sciences	$14,300	$9,200	$6,700	$5,400
Social Sciences	12,500	9,000	6,700	5,400
Humanities	13,500	9,400	6,800	5,400

Table A-13. *Faculty Summer Research Stipends at a Private University, 1960*

Fields and Selected Departments	Percent of Faculty with Summer Research Stipends*	
	A	B
Sciences	67 %	59 %
Social Sciences	14	29
Humanities	0	4
Physics		71
Mathematics		70
Biology		58
Psychology		57
Chemistry		50
Geology		40
Economics		39
Oriental Studies		38
Political Science		28
History		9
Art		7
Classics		0
English		0
Modern Languages		0
Music		0
Philosophy		0

* A and B represent the results of two studies made at this institution. Column A includes the percent of all ranks of faculty receiving summer research salaries for two months; Column B the percent, rank of assistant professor and up, holding summer research appointments for at least one month.

Although the statistics include unusually abundant stipends from private sources for research in social sciences, over three fourths of all summer research stipends are estimated to come from federal funds.

Table A-14. *Concentration of Federal Funds at Educational Institutions, 1948, 1954, and 1958*

(dollar amounts in millions)

Concentration of Funds	Academic Year*					
	1947-48	100.0 %	1953-54	100.0 %	1957-58	100.0 %
Total Federal Income Reported**	$528.0	100.0 %	$419.5	100.0 %	$712.4	100.0 %
Veteran's Tuition and Fees	365.1	69.1	44.4	10.6	5.1	0.7
Land-Grant Institutions	43.2	8.2	50.6	12.0	83.9	11.8
Research and Development***	95.3	18.0	282.4	67.3	534.4	75.0
Other	24.5	4.6	42.2	10.1	89.0	12.5
Top 10 Institutions	118.5	22.4	203.5	48.5	368.9	51.8
Next 10 Institutions	49.2	9.3	40.4	9.6	68.8	9.7
All Other Institutions	360.2	68.3	175.6	41.9	274.7	38.5
Group I Universities	108.1		165.6		312.6	
Group II Universities	21.1		12.2		16.7	
Group III Colleges	2.7		.2		.2	

* Number of colleges and universities reporting: 1947-48, 1,741; 1953-54, 1,871; 1957-58, 1,940.
** Income for educational and general purposes received from the federal government, as reported to the U.S. Office of Education; excludes sums going directly to veterans and other students, and loans to institutions for college housing.
*** Income for research at land-grant agricultural experiment stations reported in line above.

Table A-15. *Mean Intelligence Score of Recent Ph.D.'s by Their Baccalaureate Institution**

	Mean Intelligence Score[**] by Institution and Group			Number of Cases		
	I	II	III	I	II	III
	70.8	70.9	72.2	56	43	39
	70.1	65.7	70.3	61	36	50
	70.0	64.8 p	70.3	109	8	7
	68.5	64.6	68.8	109	36	14
	66.5	64.6	68.3	131	17	10
	66.4	64.5 p	66.9	66	44	11
	65.4 p	64.2	66.4	27	24	16
	65.1 p	63.4 p	65.7	44	22	9
	64.8 p	63.0 p	64.6	117	15	5
	64.6 p	61.9	64.0	184	10	10
	64.4 p	61.5 p	62.8	123	44	9
	62.2 p	61.0 p		51	20	
				1,078	314	179
Institutional Median	65.9	64.4	66.9			
Mean	66.6	64.2	67.3			
Individual Mean	66.4	64.6	69.2			

* Source: National Academy of Sciences. Ph.D.'s received in 1958 and 1959; undergraduate attendance at these baccalaureate institutions was c.1946-51; the intelligence tests were administered in high school around 1947, 1946, or earlier years.
** Public institutions are indicated by "p."

Table A-16. *Mean Intelligence Score of Recent Ph.D.'s by Their Doctoral Institution* *

	Mean Intelligence Score** by Institution and Group		Number of Cases	
	I	II	I	II
	69.5	68.2	102	55
	69.2	67.4	166	37
	67.3 p	65.3	110	16
	66.9	64.6 p	171	45
	66.0	64.2 p	171	25
	65.2 p	64.2 p	287	43
	64.7 p	64.0	346	26
	64.7	64.0	147	37
	64.2	63.5 p	200	134
	63.5 p	61.4 p	81	29
	63.4 p	60.0	109	36
	60.8 p		108	
			1,998	483
Institutional				
Median	65.0	64.2		
Mean	65.5	64.3		
Individual Mean	65.4	64.3		

* Source: National Academy of Sciences. The doctoral institutions conferred the Ph.D.'s in 1958 and 1959; the intelligence tests were administered in high school around 1947, 1946, or earlier years.

** Public institutions are indicated by "p."

Table A-17. *Certain Characteristics of Wealthy and Poor Institutions**

Characteristics	Private Institutions		Public Institutions	
	High Endowment	Low Endowment	High Budget	Low Budget
Number of Institutions	30	30	30	30
Endowment per Student	$21,583	$180	$1,028	$28
Operating Budget per Student	$1,992	$478	$1,806	$431
Per Student Income from Contract Research and Services	$1,408	$134	$205	$13
Average Ability of Entering Students**	96th	87th	84th	80th
Number of Merit Scholars per 10,000 Students**	129	3	8	0.5
Percent of Faculty with Doctorate	65 %	36 %	45 %	40 %

* This table is summarized from Tables 2 and 4 in a paper by
Alexander W. Astin and John L. Holland, The Distribution of "Wealth"
in Higher Education (National Merit Scholarship Corporation, 1961);
their information was derived from Mary Irwin, ed., American Universities and Colleges (American Council on Education, 1960), except for
the two items with double asterisks. The first of these represents
the mean percentile score on the National Merit Scholarship Qualify-
ing Test of a sample of freshmen enrolling in Fall, 1959.

Table A-18. *Frequency of Faculty Application for Federal Research Awards**

Field and Number of Applications	Percent of Faculty Applying Various Numbers of Times in Group		
	I	II	III
All Fields			
Number of Applications			
0	48 %	53 %	71 %
1-2	25	24	21
3-5	15	16	6
6 or More	10	7	2
Total	100 %	100 %	100 %
Sciences			
Number of Applications			
0	25	26	43
1-2	30	31	37
3-5	25	27	15
6 or More	20	16	5
Total	100 %	100 %	100 %
Social Sciences			
Number of Applications			
0	52	56	79
1-2	30	25	15
3-5	12	16	5
6 or More	5	3	2
Total	100 %	100 %	100 %
Humanities			
Number of Applications			
0	81	84	88
1-2	15	14	12
3-5	3	2	0
6 or More	1	0	0
Total	100 %	100 %	100 %

* Representing replies to two questions: "Have you ever submitted an application to a federal agency for a research grant or contract?" "If yes, how many applications have you made? (If the same proposal went to two agencies, count it as two applications.)" For the numbers upon which these percentages are based, see Chapter 14, Table 14-1.

Table A-19. *Number of Federal Research Awards Received by Faculty, by Field*

Field and Institution Group	Percent of Applicants for Federal Research Grants and Contracts Receiving Various Numbers of Awards					Number of Applicants
	0	1-2	3-5	6 or More	Total	
Sciences						
Group I	8 %	45 %	26 %	22 %	100 %	612
Group II	12	46	28	14	100	324
Group III	18	55	20	7	100	96
Social Sciences						
Group I	19	52	20	8	100	237
Group II	23	54	18	5	100	130
Group III	19	55	19	6	100	31
Humanities						
Group I	23	71	3	3	100	95
Group II	43	52	5	0	100	63
Group III	45	55	0	0	100	31

Table A-20. *Faculty Opinion about the Government's Role in Higher Education**

Field and Institution Group	Percent of Faculty Replying That Federal Programs Are				Number
	Unnecessary	Unfortu- nately Necessary	Necessary and Desirable	Total	
	(1)	(2)	(3)		
Total					
Group I	1 %	35 %	64 %	100 %	1,788
Group II	1	38	61	100	1,088
Group III	1	38	60	100	516
Sciences					
Group I	1	41	58	100	803
Group II	1	46	52	100	441
Group III	2	53	45	100	169
Social Sciences					
Group I	1	23	76	100	482
Group II	1	26	73	100	291
Group III	0	25	75	100	120
Humanities					
Group I	1	35	63	100	503
Group II	2	37	61	100	356
Group III	2	34	64	100	227

* Representing answers to the question "Finally, what is your view on the over-all issue of the role of the federal government in higher education?

"(1) Federal programs are unnecessary and should be discontinued.

"(2) Federal programs are unfortunately necessary, but it would be best for the nation if colleges and universities could do without them.

"(3) Federal programs are necessary and desirable in the national interest, regardless of the financial condition of colleges and universities."

APPENDIX B

Desired and Actual Allocation of Faculty Time
to Teaching, Research and Administration, 1960-61

Table B-1. *Desired Allocation of Time to Various Activities, 1960-61: All Faculty Ranks* *

Field and Institution Group	Mean Time (percent)						Number
	Teaching and Preparation		Research	Administration	Other Academic Activity	Total	
	Undergraduate	Graduate					
	(1)	(2)	(3)	(4)	(5)		
Sciences							
Group I	19.1 %	22.9 %	52.1 %	4.3 %	1.6 %	100 %	805
Group II	22.3	24.7	45.9	4.4	2.7	100	434
Group III	55.5	7.1	31.0	3.4	3.0	100	173
Social Sciences							
Group I	19.3	25.8	48.0	4.4	2.5	100	478
Group II	24.4	27.1	38.9	5.4	4.3	100	290
Group III	45.6	14.0	31.1	5.9	3.4	100	121
Humanities							
Group I	29.3	26.5	37.3	4.7	2.2	100	500
Group II	35.3	25.3	33.4	3.4	2.6	100	357
Group III	55.3	9.7	29.2	2.4	3.3	100	230
Total							
Group I	22.0	24.7	46.9	4.4	2.0	100	1,783
Group II	27.1	25.5	39.9	4.3	3.1	100	1,081
Group III	53.1	9.9	30.2	3.5	3.2	100	524

* Including a few respondents of unknown rank. Tables B-1 through B-5 represent the mean response to the question: "If you were free to choose, how would you like to spend your working time? (Enter percent of time you would like to devote to each activity. Please see that percentages total 100%.)"

316

Table B-2. *Desired Allocation of Time to Various Activities, 1960-61: Professors*

Field and Institution Group	Teaching and Preparation		Research	Administration	Other Academic Activity	Total	Number
	Under-graduate	Graduate					
	(1)	(2)	(3)	(4)	(5)		
	Mean Time (percent)						
Sciences							
Group I	18.2 %	24.5 %	49.3 %	6.3 %	1.7 %	100 %	358
Group II	22.4	26.4	41.3	6.3	3.7	100	164
Group III	60.0	3.6	28.5	4.3	3.5	100	57
Social Sciences							
Group I	18.0	27.5	46.8	5.4	2.2	100	207
Group II	23.7	27.4	36.7	7.9	4.4	100	98
Group III	46.5	13.1	29.0	9.1	2.4	100	40
Humanities							
Group I	25.3	27.9	39.9	5.6	1.3	100	189
Group II	30.2	28.2	35.1	3.7	2.9	100	108
Group III	58.1	6.5	28.4	3.9	3.1	100	72
Total							
Group I	19.9	26.2	46.3	5.9	1.7	100	754
Group II	25.0	27.2	38.3	6.0	3.6	100	370
Group III	56.0	7.1	28.6	5.3	3.1	100	169

Table B-3. *Desired Allocation of Time to Various Activities, 1960-61: Associate Professors*

Field and Institution Group	Teaching and Preparation		Mean Time (percent)			Total	Number
	Under-graduate	Graduate	Research	Adminis-tration	Other Academic Activity		
	(1)	(2)	(3)	(4)	(5)		
Sciences							
Group I	20.1 %	23.2 %	51.5 %	3.1 %	2.0 %	100 %	161
Group II	22.7	25.1	46.0	4.1	2.1	100	133
Group III	54.8	7.0	29.4	5.2	3.5	100	41
Social Sciences							
Group I	21.3	26.0	46.4	3.2	3.0	100	103
Group II	25.0	27.3	40.1	4.6	3.0	100	84
Group III	47.9	11.9	32.2	5.7	2.3	100	32
Humanities							
Group I	31.5	25.9	35.3	5.0	2.3	100	103
Group II	31.7	27.8	34.8	4.2	1.4	100	87
Group III	54.3	11.1	28.4	2.1	4.1	100	61
Total							
Group I	23.7	24.7	45.5	3.7	2.3	100	367
Group II	25.9	26.5	41.2	4.3	2.1	100	304
Group III	53.0	10.1	29.6	3.9	3.5	100	134

Table B-4. *Desired Allocation of Time to Various Activities, 1960-61: Assistant Professors*

Field and Institution Group	Teaching and Preparation		Mean Time (percent)			Total	Number
	Under-graduate (1)	Graduate (2)	Research (3)	Adminis-tration (4)	Other Academic Activity (5)		
Sciences							
Group I	19.7 %	23.1 %	54.0 %	1.7 %	1.5 %	100 %	197
Group II	18.5	23.2	53.8	2.4	2.2	100	106
Group III	52.3	9.3	34.1	1.9	2.5	100	59
Social Sciences							
Group I	19.6	25.1	49.4	2.8	3.0	100	114
Group II	23.2	27.7	41.2	2.5	5.3	100	89
Group III	41.8	16.9	32.8	2.1	6.4	100	35
Humanities							
Group I	31.5	25.3	37.2	3.9	2.1	100	124
Group II	39.9	23.5	30.5	3.0	3.1	100	100
Group III	57.2	9.3	29.4	1.0	3.0	100	55
Total							
Group I	23.0	24.3	48.0	2.6	2.1	100	435
Group II	27.2	24.6	42.1	2.6	3.4	100	295
Group III	51.6	11.1	32.1	1.6	3.6	100	149

Table B-5. *Desired Allocation of Time to Various Activities, 1960-61: Instructors*

Field and Institution Group	Teaching and Preparation		Research	Administration	Other Academic Activity	Total	Number
	Under-graduate	Graduate					
	(1)	(2)	(3)	(4)	(5)		
Sciences							
Group I	27.0 %	21.1 %	48.2 %	2.7 %	1.0 %	100 %	62
Group II	37.1	21.4	36.6	2.1	2.7	100	27
Group III	52.8	11.9	32.2	.9	2.2	100	16
Social Sciences							
Group I	24.2	25.0	45.3	3.8	1.7	100	44
Group II	32.2	22.7	33.4	6.9	4.7	100	18
Group III	46.9	14.6	30.6	6.4	1.4	100	14
Humanities							
Group I	33.6	26.9	34.6	2.9	2.1	100	79
Group II	43.4	20.4	30.7	2.6	2.9	100	59
Group III	50.8	14.1	29.8	2.2	3.0	100	41
Total							
Group I	29.1	24.5	41.7	3.0	1.6	100	185
Group II	39.8	21.1	32.7	3.2	3.2	100	104
Group III	50.5	13.7	30.5	2.8	2.5	100	71

Mean Time (percent)

Table B-6. *Actual Allocation of Time to Various Activities, 1960-61: All Faculty Ranks**

Field and Institution Group	Teaching and Preparation		Mean Time (percent)				
	Under-graduate	Graduate	Research	Adminis-tration	Other Academic Activity	Total	Number
	(1)	(2)	(3)	(4)	(5)		
Sciences							
Group I	26.4 %	19.5 %	35.5 %	14.4 %	4.2 %	100 %	808
Group II	32.1	22.2	28.7	12.1	4.8	100	437
Group III	76.6	.9	8.7	8.6	5.2	100	173
Social Sciences							
Group I	29.1	23.3	29.2	14.2	4.2	100	483
Group II	37.3	21.4	23.6	12.4	5.4	100	291
Group III	68.6	.5	14.4	10.8	5.7	100	123
Humanities							
Group I	44.5	17.8	18.8	15.3	3.6	100	504
Group II	54.1	16.4	15.5	10.7	3.4	100	360
Group III	78.1	.7	9.7	6.9	4.7	100	228
Total							
Group I	32.2	20.1	29.1	14.6	4.0	100	1,795
Group II	40.7	20.1	23.0	11.7	4.5	100	1,088
Group III	75.4	.7	10.5	8.4	5.1	100	524

* Including a few respondents of unknown rank. Tables B-6 through B-10 represent the mean response to the question: "How did you <u>actually</u> spend your working time this academic year--September 1960 to date? (Enter percent of time you <u>devoted</u> to each activity. Rough approximations will do but totals should come to 100%.)"

Table B-7. *Actual Allocation of Time to Various Activities, 1960-61: Professors*

Field and Institution Group	Mean Time (percent)						Number
	Teaching and Preparation		Research	Administration	Other Academic Activity	Total	
	Undergraduate (1)	Graduate (2)	(3)	(4)	(5)		
Sciences							
Group I	20.6 %	22.6 %	30.8 %	21.2 %	4.8 %	100 %	364
Group II	26.8	23.2	25.6	18.9	5.5	100	168
Group III	68.3	2.0	8.1	13.9	7.7	100	56
Social Sciences							
Group I	21.8	27.1	27.0	20.1	4.1	100	210
Group II	29.0	22.7	22.7	21.4	4.3	100	99
Group III	64.3	.5	14.5	17.4	3.4	100	40
Humanities							
Group I	30.6	25.9	19.2	20.6	3.8	100	192
Group II	37.6	26.9	16.8	14.2	4.5	100	108
Group III	71.6	.6	11.4	11.0	5.4	100	72
Total							
Group I	23.4	24.6	26.8	20.7	4.3	100	766
Group II	30.5	24.1	22.3	18.2	4.9	100	375
Group III	68.8	1.0	11.0	13.5	5.7	100	168

Table B-8.   *Actual Allocation of Time to Various Activities, 1960-61: Associate Professors*

Field and Institution Group	Teaching and Preparation		Mean Time (percent)			Total	Number
	Under-graduate	Graduate	Research	Adminis-tration	Other Academic Activity		
	(1)	(2)	(3)	(4)	(5)		
Sciences							
Group I	25.8 %	21.5 %	37.7 %	10.5 %	4.5 %	100 %	166
Group II	31.8	25.0	28.6	9.3	5.3	100	134
Group III	74.4	.6	8.3	11.6	5.1	100	41
Social Sciences							
Group I	27.1	24.9	28.9	14.0	5.0	100	107
Group II	37.6	23.2	25.1	10.0	4.1	100	84
Group III	70.0	.8	12.6	11.0	5.5	100	33
Humanities							
Group I	43.9	16.7	17.5	17.1	4.9	100	107
Group II	52.0	16.4	15.5	13.3	2.8	100	89
Group III	77.3	.5	9.1	7.6	5.4	100	61
Total							
Group I	31.3	21.1	29.5	13.3	4.8	100	380
Group II	39.2	22.0	23.8	10.7	4.2	100	307
Group III	74.7	.6	9.7	9.7	5.3	100	135

Table B-9. Actual Allocation of Time to Various Activities, 1960-61: Assistant Professors

Field and Institution Group	Teaching and Preparation		Research	Administration	Other Academic Activity	Total	Number
	Under-graduate	Graduate					
	(1)	(2)	(3)	(4)	(5)		
Sciences							
Group I	31.8 %	17.1 %	39.5 %	8.3 %	3.3 %	100 %	203
Group II	32.2	21.2	36.1	7.3	3.3	100	107
Group III	82.9	.2	10.0	3.3	3.6	100	60
Social Sciences							
Group I	37.1	20.0	31.5	7.1	4.3	100	118
Group II	44.1	20.9	21.5	5.1	8.5	100	89
Group III	70.1	.0	17.0	4.0	8.9	100	36
Humanities							
Group I	52.5	14.0	19.7	11.2	2.7	100	123
Group II	62.6	12.2	13.5	8.5	3.2	100	99
Group III	85.0	.3	8.5	2.2	4.1	100	55
Total							
Group I	38.9	17.0	31.9	8.8	3.4	100	444
Group II	46.0	18.1	24.1	7.0	4.8	100	295
Group III	80.6	.2	11.1	3.1	5.0	100	151

Mean Time (percent)

Table B-10. *Actual Allocation of Time to Various Activities, 1960-61: Instructors*

	Teaching and Preparation		Mean Time (percent)				
	Under-graduate	Graduate	Research	Adminis-tration	Other Academic Activity	Total	Number
Field and Institution Group	(1)	(2)	(3)	(4)	(5)		
Sciences							
Group I	46.9 %	7.9 %	42.1 %	2.1 %	.9 %	100 %	63
Group II	66.4	6.6	19.3	2.7	5.0	100	27
Group III	87.7	.0	7.2	1.9	3.3	100	16
Social Sciences							
Group I	49.3	11.8	30.4	6.7	1.9	100	45
Group II	50.6	10.2	27.1	10.2	1.9	100	18
Group III	74.2	1.0	11.6	8.9	4.4	100	14
Humanities							
Group I	68.3	6.4	17.5	5.2	2.7	100	79
Group II	75.6	5.4	13.8	2.8	2.5	100	60
Group III	83.7	1.5	7.4	4.3	3.1	100	39
Total							
Group I	56.5	8.2	28.9	4.5	1.9	100	187
Group II	68.9	6.5	17.5	4.1	3.0	100	105
Group III	82.7	1.1	8.2	4.7	3.4	100	69

325

Table B-11. *Allocation of Time to Various Activities: Faculty Spending 25 Percent or More of Their Time on Research, 1960-61**

Field and Institution Group	Teaching and Preparation		Research	Adminis-tration	Other Academic Activity	Total	Number
	Under-graduate (1)	Graduate (2)	(3)	(4)	(5)		
Sciences							
Group I	21.3 %	19.2 %	47.0 %	9.8 %	2.7 %	100 %	542
Group II	22.1	21.4	45.2	8.6	2.7	100	237
Group III	57.8	.7	34.4	4.2	2.8	100	18
Social Sciences							
Group I	22.6	23.3	41.9	10.1	2.0	100	272
Group II	28.6	21.0	40.8	7.1	2.5	100	125
Group III	50.1	.8	38.9	5.9	4.3	100	29
Humanities							
Group I	36.2	17.7	36.8	7.0	2.4	100	170
Group II	38.2	18.7	35.5	4.4	3.2	100	86
Group III	51.7	.0	41.0	4.0	3.4	100	24
Total							
Group I	24.2	20.1	43.8	9.4	2.5	100	984
Group II	27.0	20.8	42.1	7.4	2.7	100	448
Group III	52.6	.5	38.5	4.8	3.6	100	71

* Representing the mean response to the question: "How did you actually spend your working time this academic year--September 1960 to date? (Enter percent of time you devoted to each activity. Rough approximations will do but totals should come to 100%.)"

Table B-12. *Allocation of Time to Various Activities: Faculty Spending 24 Percent or Less of Their Time on Research, 1960-61**

Field and Institution Group	Teaching and Preparation		Mean Time (percent) Research	Administration	Other Academic Activity	Total	Number
	Undergraduate (1)	Graduate (2)	(3)	(4)	(5)		
Sciences							
Group I	38.0 %	20.9 %	11.0 %	23.3 %	6.8 %	100 %	257
Group II	43.9	23.2	9.2	16.3	7.4	100	200
Group III	78.8	.9	5.7	9.1	5.5	100	155
Social Sciences							
Group I	38.1	23.6	11.7	19.8	6.9	100	208
Group II	44.2	21.9	10.0	16.4	7.5	100	165
Group III	74.4	.4	6.8	12.3	6.1	100	94
Humanities							
Group I	48.9	18.0	9.4	19.6	4.2	100	333
Group II	59.7	15.9	8.6	12.4	3.5	100	271
Group III	81.6	.7	5.6	7.1	4.8	100	203
Total							
Group I	42.6	20.4	10.5	20.8	5.7	100	798
Group II	50.7	19.8	9.1	14.7	5.7	100	636
Group III	79.2	.7	5.9	8.9	5.3	100	452

* Representing the mean response to the question: "How did you actually spend your working time this academic year--September 1960 to date? (Enter percent of time you devoted to each activity. Rough approximations will do but totals should come to 100%.)"

APPENDIX C

Survey Method and Questionnaire

Survey Method

GIVEN THIRTY-SIX INSTITUTIONS participating in the study and given a focus of interest on the "core fields" of the liberal arts curriculum, the population to be canvassed in our survey virtually picked itself. It should be stressed that this population was *not* chosen to represent either all university and college faculty or all faculty in designated fields, but simply the faculty in certain important liberal arts fields at our twenty-four universities and twelve colleges.

The rationale underlying the choice of institutions has already been explained (see Introduction). It is obvious on the face of it that the twelve institutions in Group I well represent the twenty-five in the class from which they were drawn—those receiving $4 million or more from the federal government in 1957-58; even if they did not, they would be important in their own right, as they received 44 percent of all federal income reported that year by 1,940 institutions of higher education. The twelve institutions in Group II may be somewhat stronger, educationally, than the average of the fifty-four institutions in the class from which they were chosen—those receiving $0.5-$1.9 million in federal funds in 1957-58; and the twelve colleges in Group III are unquestionably much stronger than the average four-year liberal arts college.

Several factors governed the choice of fields for study. Professional schools (agriculture, business, education, engineering, medicine, etc.) were excluded by the original terms of reference. The desirability of maintaining comparability between the faculty at universities and colleges further restricted the range of departments from which the survey population could be drawn. For example, geology was considered for inclusion in the sciences, but excluded because it was not established as a department at many institutions, particularly in Groups II and III; for the same reason, area study programs, astronomy, geography, international relations, public administration, and Slavic languages were also excluded. The further exclusion of the fine arts and music led to the following list of basic "academic" departments in which instruction is commonly available at both the undergraduate level and at graduate levels through the doctorate:

Sciences: chemistry, mathematics, physics, and the biological fields, biology, zoology, botany, biochemistry, bacteriology, biophysics, the last three fields often being located at medical schools.

Social Sciences: economics, political science and government, psychology, sociology, and anthropology.

Humanities: classics (including Latin and Greek), English (including both composition and literature, but not separate departments of speech and journalism), history, modern foreign languages (restricted to Romance and Germanic languages), and philosophy.

The foregoing classification of major fields' generally conforms to common usage, although many studies put psychology with the sciences and history with the social sciences. The former classification is justified for the physiological and comparative psychologists who still constitute a decided minority of the profession, but not, we believe, for clinical, experimental and social psychologists and those interested in operations research. Why history is so often classified as a social science it is difficult to comprehend on any other ground than thoughtless repetitiveness, or, perhaps, that some people oddly regard the social sciences as more honorific or, less oddly, as more prosperous.

An attempt was made to eliminate faculty teaching excluded subjects within included departments (for example, Russian within departments of modern languages; or business methods and accountancy within departments of economics) but undoubtedly a good many slipped through. The preparation of a "pure" list of faculty in designated disciplines is an extraordinarily difficult and probably impossible task, since lists can be no purer than men. Without claiming any such specious purity for the list of faculty to whom our questionnaire was addressed, we can say that the list was compiled with some care and the task was not delegated.

Faculty names were obtained from current catalogues or more current faculty lists and directories. Only for three schools (one in each group) was it necessary to rely upon a catalogue older than the current (1960-61) academic year.

Had this inquiry been restricted solely to a questionnaire survey of faculty experience with and attitudes toward various federal programs, it would obviously have been desirable to obtain relatively equal and representative numbers of respondents for each of the nine basic cells to be utilized in the final analysis—faculty in (a) the sciences, (b) social sciences, and (c) humanities, at (1) universities with large sums from the federal government, (2) universities with smaller sums, and (3) liberal arts colleges. The best way to do this would clearly have been to increase the number of institutions sampled, especially in groups 2 and 3.

However, this inquiry was not designed primarily as a questionnaire survey, and information obtained from campus visits, interviews, and the analysis of other data on the institutions examined were to be weighted just as heavily as the survey data collected from faculty at the same institutions. Practical reasons therefore dictated that the number of institutions to be surveyed be kept quite small, since time and budgetary limitations restricted the number which could be visited and the number about which considerable and varied statistics could be collected. The resulting survey design, accordingly, represented a compromise between the requirements of the study and those of an ideal survey. As a matter of fact, the initial intent was to make the survey much more modest and, in keeping with our essentially *case study* approach, limit the number of schools to perhaps twenty-four (eight in each Group). This was expanded to thirty-six (twelve in each Group) only as a safeguard should significant data not be available for certain institutions, and should some schools, which have been notoriously overburdened with studies piled upon studies, subsequently weary of the work. The former fear was, in part, confirmed by the unavailability of some Scholastic Aptitude Test scores and other bits of data; but happily, all institutions participating in the study bore with us until the end.

A man with wide survey experience has remarked that somehow most faculty surveys are mailed out at the worst possible time—examination periods and the end of term. This was certainly true of our questionnaires, which were mailed

TABLE C-1. *Faculty Mailing and Response, by Field and Institution Group*

Field	Number of Faculty by Institution Group							
	Questionnaires Mailed				Questionnaires Used*			
	I	II	III	Total	I	II	III	Total
Total	3,656	2,097	756	6,509	1,861	1,123	538	3,522
Sciences	1,480	778	221	2,479	828	451	175	1,454
Biological Sciences	386	270	62	718	245	169	51	465
Chemistry	302	179	54	535	186	112	47	345
Mathematics	407	185	61	653	181	81	41	303
Physics	385	144	44	573	195	79	36	310
Unclassified	—	—	—	—	21	10	—	31
Social Sciences	925	493	170	1,588	501	300	125	929
Economics	244	124	50	418	134	70	37	241
Political Science, Government	204	88	42	334	91	50	28	169
Psychology	245	168	53	466	144	109	38	291
Sociology, Anthropology	232	113	25	370	128	70	22	220
Unclassified	—	—	—	—	4	1	—	5
Humanities	1,251	826	365	2,442	532	372	238	1,142
Classics	73	57	22	152	33	19	15	67
English	435	346	122	903	183	144	76	403
History	253	147	68	468	91	83	49	223
Modern Languages	375	187	112	674	160	84	68	312
Philosophy	115	89	41	245	49	41	29	119
Unclassified	—	—	—	—	16	1	1	18

* For percent, See Table C-2.

in the middle of May 1961. Pressure of time prevented adequate pretesting (which was limited to some eighteen faculty at eight institutions), and required that most questions be precoded.

Our first potential mailing list, restricted to full-time regular faculty at the rank of instructor or above, is indicated in Table C-1. Examining these figures, we lamented again that circumstances precluded an increase in the number of colleges in Group III and that (for reasons given above) there *were* no other significant departments that could be added in the sciences and social sciences. Indeed, the only significant adjustment possible at this stage to balance out our initial population was to halve the number of Group II faculty and quarter that of Group I. This alternative was dismissed, however, because: (1) the response rate during the end-of-term maelstrom was uncertain, and (2) the importance of Group I scientists as those faculty with the greatest experience of federal programs suggested the advisability of maximizing that population for possible special analyses. Therefore we resolved to mail to the entire group, and our initial list became our final list of addresses.

This resulted in a large mailing—6,509 questionnaires to 3,656 faculty at Group I universities, 2,097 at Group II universities, and 756 at Group III colleges. (The questionnaire is reproduced at the end of this section.)

Considering the time of year, we would rate our response as good: excellent from the colleges in all fields (65-79 percent), good from university scientists and social scientists (54-61 percent), and not as good as we would have liked from university humanists (43-45 percent). Full details on the response of faculty in each field and institution group are reported in Tables C-1 and C-2. Judging from the situation at two institutions, some 10 percent of those addressed did not receive the questionnaire in time to respond, due to errors in addressing or delivery, or because they were away from campus.

The response was, of course, a function of the interest of faculty in federal programs. It was increased by the help of the representative appointed by the president of each institution (usually a vice president, dean, or research officer) who undertook the mail distribution on most campuses and, in several cases, attached to the questionnaire a note indicating that the institution was cooperating with the study and encouraging faculty to respond. The questionnaire itself was relatively simple to answer, and was printed in a self-contained, postage-prepaid form to facilitate mailing.

TABLE C-2. *Percent of Questionnaires Used, By Field and Institution Group**

Field	Institution Group			
	I	II	III	Total
Total	51%	54%	71%	54%
Sciences**	56	58	79	59
Biological Sciences	63	63	82	65
Chemistry	62	63	87	64
Mathematics	44	44	67	46
Physics	51	55	82	54
Social Sciences**	54	61	74	58
Economics	55	56	74	58
Political Science, Government	45	57	67	51
Psychology	59	65	72	62
Sociology, Anthropology	55	62	88	59
Humanities**	43	45	65	47
Classics	45	33	68	44
English	42	42	62	45
History	36	56	72	48
Modern Languages	43	45	61	46
Philosophy	43	46	71	49

* See Table C-1 for number of questionnaires mailed and used.
** Including a few respondents in fields not classifiable below.

The poorer response of humanists can be explained by their lack of experience with federal programs: but what, then, are we to make of the high response of college faculty, when the same reasoning had led us to expect a lower response from them than from university faculty?

We credit the exceptional response of college faculty—100 percent of the faculty at one college replied—to ·two factors. (1) This was a highly selected group of colleges which, with the expanding scope of many federal programs, are just the sort likely to be included in a new venture of the National Science Foundation, the National Institutes of Health, or the Office of Education; in short, our interest in federal programs, and theirs, happened to coincide. (2) On a small campus, a word from the dean encouraging response reached relatively more faculty and was relatively more effective than on a large campus. During our visits, which preceded and coincided with the arrival of questionnaires, we met relatively more faculty on small campuses than on large ones and, to that extent, relatively more were already acquainted with the inquiry.

TABLE C-3. *Response of Faculty by Rank and Institution Group*

| | Number of Questionnaires | | | | | | Percent | | |
| | Mailed to Institution Group | | | Used by Institution Group | | | Institution Group | | |
Rank	I	II	III	I	II	III	I	II	III
Professor	1,473	655	247	807	390	179	55	60	72
Associate Professor	809	469	171	397	319	136	49	68	80
Assistant Professor	864	529	186	455	303	152	53	57	82
Instructor	556	381	169	196	109	71	35	29	42
Unknown	—	—	—	6	2	—	—	—	—
Total	3,702	2,034	773	1,861	1,123	538	50	55	70

There was no pronounced tendency for any particular rank from assistant professor on up to respond more frequently than other ranks; but a poor response was received from instructors (Table C-3). This we put down to the difficulty of obtaining a complete and up-to-date list of members of this highly mobile and short-term group.

We will close by emphasizing one point that should be evident from the foregoing discussion: the design of this survey renders meaningful only comparisons between faculty in the nine basic cells of our survey population—

| Field | | Institution Group | | |
		I	II	III
A.	Sciences	X	X	X
B.	Social Sciences	X	X	X
C.	Humanities	X	X	X

but *not* between totals by field or, strictly speaking, Institution Group. It is meaningless to add the totals of all scientists in Groups I, II, and III (line A) and compare that with all social scientists (line B) or all humanists (line C), and no such totals have been presented in the text. A comparison of the total faculty within an Institution Group (Column I, II, and III) has, for convenience, been reported in most text tables, but it has only a limited utility, as the number and proportion of faculty in the component fields varies considerably. We repeat: *the significant analysis of data in our faculty survey must be restricted to comparisons between the nine discrete, basic cells.*

(For the survey questionnaire, see page 337)

The Brookings Institution

1775 MASSACHUSETTS AVENUE. N.W.

Washington 6, D. C.

ROBERT D. CALKINS
PRESIDENT
ROBERT W. HARTLEY
VICE PRESIDENT

GOVERNMENTAL STUDIES
GEORGE A. GRAHAM
DIRECTOR
CHARLES L. CLAPP
MILTON C. CUMMINGS, JR.
JAMESON W. DOIG
LUTHER H. EVANS
LAURIN L. HENRY
M. KENT JENNINGS
F. P. KILPATRICK
DEAN E. MANN
LIONEL V. MURPHY
HAROLD ORLANS
FRANCES M. SHATTUCK

May 11, 1961

To Faculty Members:

This questionnaire constitutes one part of a study of the effect of federal programs on higher education which the Brookings Institution is conducting. (For a brief description of the Brookings Institution, see the inside back cover.)

In this study we are examining three types of institutions: some now receiving relatively large sums from the federal government, some with a smaller amount of federal funds, and a group of independent liberal arts colleges. Your institution has agreed to cooperate in our study, but no school and no individual respondent will be identified in the final report.

We are sending this questionnaire to selected faculty in departments of science, social science, and the humanities, and we are equally interested in the replies of faculty who are and those who are not involved in the federal programs. Our inquiry revolves around three issues: 1. What has been the effect (direct or indirect) of federal programs on the quality of education? 2. Is a broader institutional dispersion of federal funds desirable? 3. What has been your experience with the administration of current federal programs? While the questions which follow can be answered, in most cases, by a simple check mark, we would be very glad to receive any further comments you may wish to offer on the foregoing issues.

We know that end-of-term is a very busy time for you, and have done our best to keep this form brief. It should take only 15 minutes to complete, and may be mailed by folding over the back page and moistening the gummed edge. Your cooperation will serve to advance public knowledge (and, hopefully, public policy) in an area important to higher education and to the nation.

Sincerely,

Harold Orlans

Harold Orlans

A STUDY OF THE EFFECT OF FEDERAL
PROGRAMS ON HIGHER EDUCATION

1. *Please complete and mail by May 31.* It should take only 15 minutes to complete this form.

2. To mail: follow instructions under flap of back cover. No envelope or postage is needed.

3. Disregard the small numbers next to the answer boxes. These are simply to help in coding and tabulating.

4. *All replies will be held in confidence. No individual or institution will be identified in the report of this study.*

5. Thank you for your help.

I. BACKGROUND INFORMATION

Institution _____   Department _____

1. Your age _____   Sex: M ☐   F ☐

2. Were you in this institution 5 or 6 years ago—in 1956 or '55?   Yes ☐   No ☐

3. Your present rank (if lecturer or other title, check equivalent in conventional rank):

   1 ☐ Full professor   4 ☐ Instructor
   2 ☐ Associate professor   5 ☐ Below instructor
   3 ☐ Assistant professor

   a. Is this a full-time appointment?   Yes ☐   No ☐

4. When did you first hold this rank (at any institution)? _____ (year)

5. *For those above the rank of instructor:*

   _____ Year you first held the rank of instructor (or equivalent) at any institution.

   ☐ I never held the rank of instructor. My first appointment was as (or equivalent to):

   ☐ Full professor
   ☐ Associate professor
   ☐ Assistant professor

   This was in _____ (year).

6. Are you now chairman or head of this department?   Yes ☐   No ☐

   a. If *no,* have you ever been chairman or head of this department?
      Yes ☐   No ☐

- 1 -

II. EXPERIENCE WITH FEDERAL AGENCIES

7. Have you ever submitted an application to a federal agency for a research grant or contract?

Yes ☐   No ☐   (If *no*, go on to question 9.)

a. If *yes*, how many applications have you made? (If the same proposal went to two agencies, count it as two applications.)

☐ 1   ☐ 6-10
☐ 2   ☐ More than 10
☐ 3-5

b. How many have resulted in the award of funds?

☐ None   ☐ 3-5
☐ 1   ☐ 6-10
☐ 2   ☐ More than 10

c. Which agencies have you applied to?

(Check as many as applicable)

c. Have applied to	Agency
1 ☐	Air Force
2 ☐	Army
3 ☐	Navy
4 ☐	Other Department of Defense
5 ☐	Atomic Energy Commission
6 ☐	International Cooperation Administration
7 ☐	National Aeronautics and Space Administration (or NACA)
8 ☐	National Science Foundation
9 ☐	Office of Education
0 ☐	Public Health Service (including National Institutes of Health)
x ☐	State Department
y ☐	Other agency (specify)_____
r ☐	_____

8. Reviewing your experience with the agencies with which you have dealt in connection with research proposals, do you feel that you have been treated--

a. Fairly and equitably?

b. Efficiently, without undue delay or red tape?

(Check as many as applicable)

a. Fairly		b. Efficiently		
Yes	No	Yes	No	Agency
1 ☐	☐	1 ☐	☐	Air Force
2 ☐	☐	2 ☐	☐	Army
3 ☐	☐	3 ☐	☐	Navy
4 ☐	☐	4 ☐	☐	Other Department of Defense
5 ☐	☐	5 ☐	☐	Atomic Energy Commission
6 ☐	☐	6 ☐	☐	International Cooperation Administration
7 ☐	☐	7 ☐	☐	National Aeronautics and Space Administration
8 ☐	☐	8 ☐	☐	National Science Foundation
9 ☐	☐	9 ☐	☐	Office of Education
0 ☐	☐	0 ☐	☐	Public Health Service (including NIH)
x ☐	☐	x ☐	☐	State Department
y ☐	☐	y ☐	☐	Other agency (specify)_____
r ☐	☐	r ☐	☐	_____

☐ No contacts with any federal agency

9. Do you feel adequately informed about the current research programs and policies of federal agencies in areas of professional interest to you?

1 ☐ Yes, all agencies
2 ☐ Yes, some agencies, but not others
3 ☐ No, no agencies
4 ☐ I have no serious interest in research

a. At which agency(s) do you know a staff member well enough to ring him up and get his informal advice on an idea you have?

b. Which agency's research programs or policies would you like to know more about?

(Check as many as applicable)

a. Can get advice from staff member	b. Want to know more about program or policy	Agency
1 ☐	1 ☐	Air Force
2 ☐	2 ☐	Army
3 ☐	3 ☐	Navy
4 ☐	4 ☐	Other Department of Defense
5 ☐	5 ☐	Atomic Energy Commission
6 ☐	6 ☐	International Cooperation Administration
7 ☐	7 ☐	National Aeronautics and Space Administration
8 ☐	8 ☐	National Science Foundation
9 ☐	9 ☐	Office of Education
0 ☐	0 ☐	Public Health Service (including NIH)
x ☐	x ☐	State Department
y ☐	y ☐	Other agency (specify)_____
r ☐	r ☐	_____
m ☐	m ☐	All of these agencies

☐ Don't know which agency, if any, is concerned with my field.

10. Since *and including* last summer, has any of your research, teaching, study or consulting been financed by the federal government? (Do *not* include this coming summer.)

Yes ☐ No ☐ (If *no*, go on to question 11.)

a. If *yes*, which agency(s) financed this?

(Check as many as applicable)

Research	Teaching	Study	Consulting	Agency
1 ☐	☐	☐	☐	Air Force
2 ☐	☐	☐	☐	Army
3 ☐	☐	☐	☐	Navy
4 ☐	☐	☐	☐	Other Department of Defense
5 ☐	☐	☐	☐	Atomic Energy Commission
6 ☐	☐	☐	☐	International Cooperation Administration
7 ☐	☐	☐	☐	National Aeronautics and Space Administration
8 ☐	☐	☐	☐	National Science Foundation
9 ☐	☐	☐	☐	Office of Education
0 ☐	☐	☐	☐	Public Health Service (including NIH)
x ☐	☐	☐	☐	State Department
y ☐	☐	☐	☐	Other agency (specify)_____
r ☐	☐	☐	☐	_____

b. Was this last summer or during the regular academic year?

1 ☐ Last summer
2 ☐ During the academic year
3 ☐ Both last summer and during the academic year

c. Was any of your regular salary *during the academic year* drawn from federal funds?

1 ☐ No
2 ☐ Yes, some of my salary, but less than half
3 ☐ Yes, 50% or more of my salary
4 ☐ Don't know

III. RECENT SHIFTS IN QUALITY

11. Comparing the present picture in this department with that a few years ago—about 1955-56—I would say that:

    a. The average quality of our undergraduate majors has

       1 ☐ improved markedly
       2 ☐ improved slightly
       3 ☐ stayed about the same
       4 ☐ declined slightly
       5 ☐ declined markedly
       6 ☐ no undergraduate majors in department
       7 ☐ can't say

    b. The average quality of other undergraduates taking courses in the department has

       1 ☐ improved markedly
       2 ☐ improved slightly
       3 ☐ stayed about the same
       4 ☐ declined slightly
       5 ☐ declined markedly
       6 ☐ no undergraduates in department
       7 ☐ can't say

    c. The average quality of the department's graduate students has

       1 ☐ improved markedly
       2 ☐ improved slightly
       3 ☐ stayed about the same
       4 ☐ declined slightly
       5 ☐ declined markedly
       6 ☐ no graduate students in department
       7 ☐ can't say

    d. The average quality of the staff in the department has

       1 ☐ improved markedly
       2 ☐ improved slightly
       3 ☐ stayed about the same
       4 ☐ declined slightly
       5 ☐ declined markedly
       6 ☐ can't say

    e. The over-all quality of the education this department is giving has

       1 ☐ improved markedly
       2 ☐ improved slightly
       3 ☐ stayed about the same
       4 ☐ declined slightly
       5 ☐ declined markedly
       6 ☐ can't say

12. Your explanation of any shifts in quality noted above would be welcome—particularly any attributable to federal programs.

13. (This question refers to *all* federal programs at your institution, including student loans and fellowships, and funds for facilities, teaching institutes, and research. However, we are concerned here with their effect *only on your department.*)

    a. What has been the over-all effect of federal programs on the ability of your department to retain and attract the best *undergraduate* students?

       Federal programs have:

       1 ☐ helped us very much
       2 ☐ helped us somewhat
       3 ☐ had no visible effect
       4 ☐ handicapped us somewhat
       5 ☐ handicapped us very much
       6 ☐ don't know

    b. What has been the over-all effect of federal programs on the ability of your department to attract and hold the best *graduate* students?

       Federal programs have:

       1 ☐ helped us very much
       2 ☐ helped us somewhat
       3 ☐ had no visible effect
       4 ☐ handicapped us somewhat
       5 ☐ handicapped us very much
       6 ☐ don't know
       7 ☐ no graduate students here

    c. And their effect on the ability of your department to attract and hold the best faculty?

       Federal programs have:

       1 ☐ helped us very much
       2 ☐ helped us somewhat
       3 ☐ had no visible effect
       4 ☐ handicapped us somewhat
       5 ☐ handicapped us very much
       6 ☐ don't know

14. Assume that there are two men in your department of equal professional standing and teaching ability. Both are, also, equally able and productive when it comes to research. However, *Alpha* is active in an area sponsored by the government and has obtained a number of grants and contracts for his research work, including funds for the support of student assistants and the purchase of special equipment; *Beta* is in a field of research with no financial sponsorship from government or other sources. What is likely to be their relative standing in the eyes of:

a. undergraduate majors in elective courses?

    1 ☐ Alpha is apt to attract more undergraduates.
    2 ☐ Beta is apt to attract more undergraduates.
    3 ☐ Both are apt to attract the same number of undergraduates.

b. graduate students?

    1 ☐ Alpha is apt to attract more graduate students.
    2 ☐ Beta is apt to attract more graduate students.
    3 ☐ Both are apt to attract the same number of graduate students.
    4 ☐ No graduate students in this department.

c. colleagues in the department?

    1 ☐ Alpha will probably be held in somewhat higher esteem.
    2 ☐ Beta will probably be held in somewhat higher esteem.
    3 ☐ Both will probably be held in equal esteem.

d. the central administration--deans and members of the president's office (as indicated by relative salary, promotion, and prestige)?

    1 ☐ Alpha is apt to come off better.
    2 ☐ Beta is apt to come off better.
    3 ☐ Both are apt to receive equal treatment.

IV. THE BALANCE OF FEDERAL PROGRAMS

15. The current pattern of federal financing of research and training in the sciences tends to concentrate funds at a few well-known universities. Do you think that this distribution is fundamentally:

a. a reflection of the present institutional
distribution of

(Answer each question)	Yes	No	Don't know
i. faculty talent?	1 ☐	·2 ☐	3 ☐
ii. research equipment?	1 ☐	2 ☐	3 ☐
iii. graduate students?	1 ☐	2 ☐	3 ☐
iv. advisory panels of scientists?	1 ☐	2 ☐	3 ☐
v. prestige?	1 ☐	2 ☐	3 ☐
b. in the present national interest?	1 ☐	2 ☐	3 ☐
c. in the long-run national interest?	1 ☐	2 ☐	3 ☐

16. What about the present concentration of federal funds in the natural sciences and relative neglect of the humanities? Do you regard this as:

	Yes	No	Don't know
a. in the present national interest?	1 ☐	2 ☐	3 ☐
b. in the long-run national interest?	1 ☐	2 ☐	3 ☐
c. in the best interest of your institution?	1 ☐	2 ☐	3 ☐

d. If you could redistribute the federal funds presently available, what would you do?

1 ☐ Retain the present relative distribution between sciences and humanities.

2 ☐ Give the sciences still more and the humanities less.

3 ☐ Give the humanities somewhat more and the sciences somewhat less, but still the major portion.

4 ☐ Give the humanities a great deal more and the sciences a great deal less.

17. And what is your opinion about the present concentration of federal funds on research rather than teaching?

1 ☐ The present concentration on research should continue.

2 ☐ Federal funds should be more evenly balanced between research and teaching.

3 ☐ Federal funds should concentrate on teaching rather than research.

18. Finally, what is your view on the over-all issue of the role of the federal government in higher education?

   1 ☐ Federal programs are unnecessary and should be discontinued.

   2 ☐ Federal programs are unfortunately necessary, but it would be best for the nation if colleges and universities could do without them.

   3 ☐ Federal programs are necessary and desirable in the national interest, regardless of the financial condition of colleges and universities.

V. CLASS SIZE AND STUDENT CONTACTS

19. Does this department offer courses for

	Yes	No
freshmen or sophomores	1 ☐	☐
juniors or seniors	2 ☐	☐
graduate students	3 ☐	☐

  a. Does it offer the doctorate? 4 ☐   ☐

20. What has happened to the average size of classes in your department in recent years—since 1955 or 1956?

  a. Freshman and sophomore classes

    1 ☐ average size has increased
    2 ☐ average size has remained the same
    3 ☐ average size has decreased
    4 ☐ don't know
    5 ☐ no freshman or sophomore class in department

  b. Junior and senior classes

    1 ☐ average size has increased
    2 ☐ average size has remained the same
    3 ☐ average size has decreased
    4 ☐ don't know
    5 ☐ no junior or senior class in department

  c. Graduate classes

    1 ☐ average size has increased
    2 ☐ average size has remained the same
    3 ☐ average size has decreased
    4 ☐ don't know
    5 ☐ no graduate classes in department

21. What is the size of the largest single class (lecture or section) in any undergraduate course in the department?

    1 ☐ 1-19 students   6 ☐ 100-199 students
    2 ☐ 20-39   7 ☐ 200 or larger
    3 ☐ 40-59   8 ☐ don't know
    4 ☐ 60-79   9 ☐ no undergraduate course in
    5 ☐ 80-99   department

22. And the largest graduate class?

1 ☐ 1-19 students   6 ☐ 100-199 students
2 ☐ 20-39   7 ☐ 200 or larger
3 ☐ 40-59   8 ☐ don't know
4 ☐ 60-79   9 ☐ no graduate course in
5 ☐ 80-99   department

23. Do students come to your office to discuss matters of concern to them?

a. Lower classmen	b. Upper classmen	c. Graduate students
1 ☐ constantly	1 ☐ constantly	1 ☐ constantly
2 ☐ often	2 ☐ often	2 ☐ often
3 ☐ occasionally	3 ☐ occasionally	3 ☐ occasionally
4 ☐ seldom	4 ☐ seldom	4 ☐ seldom
5 ☐ never	5 ☐ never	5 ☐ never
6 ☐ none in department	6 ☐ none in department	6 ☐ none in department

24. Do you ever have any students in your home, either in connection with their work or for a social occasion?

a. Lower classmen	b. Upper classmen	c. Graduate students
1 ☐ frequently	1 ☐ frequently	1 ☐ frequently
2 ☐ occasionally	2 ☐ occasionally	2 ☐ occasionally
3 ☐ seldom	3 ☐ seldom	3 ☐ seldom
4 ☐ never	4 ☐ never	4 ☐ never
		5 ☐ no graduate students here

25. Do you live on, or near to, the campus?

1 ☐ on campus   2 ☐ near to campus   3 ☐ away from campus

26. Roughly how many senior majors are there in your department?

1 ☐ None   2 ☐ 1-9   3 ☐ 10-19
4 ☐ 20-29   5 ☐ 30-49   6 ☐ 50-99
     7 ☐ 100 or more   8 ☐ Don't know

a. How many can you greet by name?

1 ☐ All   2 ☐ Most   3 ☐ About half
4 ☐ Less than half   5 ☐ A few   6 ☐ None

27. And full-time graduate students beyond their first year— how many are there in the department?

1 ☐ None   2 ☐ 1-9   3 ☐ 10-19
4 ☐ 20-29   5 ☐ 30-49   6 ☐ 50-99
     7 ☐ 100 or more   8 ☐ Don't know

a. And how many can you greet by name?

1 ☐ All   2 ☐ Most   3 ☐ About half
4 ☐ Less than half   5 ☐ A few   6 ☐ None

VI. TEACHING ASSISTANTS

28. Does your department make use of student teaching assistants?

    Yes ☐ No ☐ (If *no*, go on to question 29.)

    a. If yes, are they

        1 ☐ undergraduates
        2 ☐ graduate students
        3 ☐ both undergraduate and graduate students

    b. Has the number of student teaching assistants in the department increased in recent years (since 1955 or '56) *relative to the number of faculty?*

        1 ☐ Markedly
        2 ☐ Slightly
        3 ☐ No, it has stayed the same
        4 ☐ No, it has decreased
        5 ☐ Don't know

    c. What are they used for? *(Check as many as necessary)*

        1 ☐ Grading papers
        2 ☐ Discussion sections in undergraduate classes
        3 ☐ Lecturing in undergraduate classes
        4 ☐ Discussion sections in graduate classes
        5 ☐ Lecturing in graduate classes
        6 ☐ Undergraduate laboratory sections
        7 ☐ Graduate laboratory sections
        8 ☐ Other *(specify)*_____

    d. Particularly in their first year, the best graduate students are said to be on fellowships, and therefore, the graduate students who serve as teaching assistants are not on the whole the best in the department. Is this true in your department?

        1 ☐ Don't know
        2 ☐ No graduate students   If *no:* Do any of your first year graduate students hold fellow-
        3 ☐ Yes   ships which pay as well as teaching assistantships?
        4 ☐ No   1 Yes ☐ 2 No ☐ 3 Don't know ☐

    e. *For those in departments using student teaching assistants in laboratory sections:*

        It is said that the use of student assistants to monitor laboratory work has led to a decline in the quality of laboratory instruction. Has this happened in your department?

        1 ☐ Yes
        2 ☐ No
        3 ☐ Don't know

VII. ON TEACHING AND RESEARCH

29. If you were free to choose, how would you like to spend your working time?

    (Enter percent of time you would like to devote to each activity.
    Please see that percentages total 100!)

    ____% teaching undergraduates (including preparation)
    ____% teaching graduate students (including preparation)
    ____% research
    ____% administration
    ____% other academic activity *(specify)* _____

    _____

30. How did you *actually* spend your working time this academic year—September 1960 to date?

    (Enter percent of time you devoted to each activity. Rough approximations
    will do but totals should come to 100%.)

    ____% teaching undergraduates (including preparation)
    ____% teaching graduate students (including preparation)
    ____% research
    ____% administration
    ____% other academic activity *(specify)* _____

    _____

31. The man who teaches undergraduates exclusively may be held in less esteem than the man who teaches graduate students. Is this true:

    a. at your institution?

        1 ☐ yes
        2 ☐ no
        3 ☐ no one here teaches only undergraduates

    b. in your department?

        1 ☐ yes
        2 ☐ no
        3 ☐ no one in department teaches only undergraduates

32. *For faculty at universities and technical institutes:*

Have you ever taught at an independent, four-year, liberal arts college (i.e., one that is not part of a university)?

Yes ☐   No ☐   (If *no*, go on to question 33.)

a. If *yes*, when did you last teach there?

   1 ☐ January 1956 or after.
   2 ☐ December 1955 or earlier.

b. Was it a college with a national reputation, which draws students from all over the country, or one with a more local reputation and student body?

   1 ☐ 1. Nationally known
   2 ☐ 2. More of a local reputation
   3 ☐ 3. Somewhere in between 1 and 2

   Name of college _____ State _____

c. If the pay, auxiliary benefits, teaching load, and prospects of promotion were as good there as at your present institution, where would you rather be?

   1 ☐ The college
   2 ☐ My present institution
   3 ☐ Either place—no particular preference

33. In your experience, does research and scholarly work in your field tend to reduce the time a man will put into preparing for his classes?

   1 ☐ Yes, markedly
   2 ☐ Yes, slightly
   3 ☐ No, it does not
   4 ☐ Quite the contrary—it tends to increase the time put into class preparation
   5 ☐ I can't meaningfully separate research and teaching
   6 ☐ Can't say

34. What about contact with students (particularly the more informal kinds of contact)—does active involvement in research tend to reduce this?

   1 ☐ Yes, reduces both frequency and depth of contact
   2 ☐ Yes, reduces frequency but increases depth of contact
   3 ☐ No, it does not affect frequency or depth of contact
   4 ☐ Quite the contrary—it tends to increase the frequency of contact
   5 ☐ Can't say

35. What is the average full teaching load (classroom hours) in your department today? (Exclude hours spent on thesis supervision and independent study courses.)

_____ hours per week. Ranges from _____ to _____ hours.

a. What was it half a dozen years ago (1954-55)?

1 ☐ the same
2 ☐ more
3 ☐ less
4 ☐ don't know

36. How many classroom hours per week do *you* teach, on the average? _____

a. How many of these are in undergraduate courses? _____

37. How do you feel about your present

	It's fine	It's satisfactory	It's not so good	It's terrible
a. office?	1 ☐	2 ☐	3 ☐	4 ☐
b. secretarial help?	1 ☐	2 ☐	3 ☐	4 ☐
c. salary?	1 ☐	2 ☐	3 ☐	4 ☐
d. teaching load?	1 ☐	2 ☐	3 ☐	4 ☐
e. general academic status	1 ☐	2 ☐	3 ☐	4 ☐

That does it, and thank you for having come this far. As we said in the introductory note, we would be glad to have any additional comments you may wish to make below on the effect of federal programs at your institution.

Index

Abbott, Frank C., 90n
Adams, Walter, 285n
Administration:
  Faculty time spent on, 62-64, 288, 321-27
  Federal research, 189-94, 218, 227, 244, 263-64, 264n, 268-71, 288-89
  Institutional, 65n
  Institutional research, 12, 86, 194-203
Advanced Research Projects Agency, 276, 287
Agriculture, Department of, 25
Air Force, Department of the (*see also* Defense, Department of; Office of Scientific Research):
  Faculty: acquaintance with staff of, 238, 239, 244; applying to, 192; interest in, 242-44 *passim;* opinion of, 193, 194, 244
  "Hardware" approach, 227
  Overhead policy, 266
Allen, Ernest, 222n
Allen, Hollis P., 269n
American Assembly, 2n
American Association of Junior Colleges, 283n
American Association of School Administrators, 283n
American Association of University Professors, 124n, 182-83, 183n, 215-16
American Civil Liberties Union, 292n
American College Testing Program, 147n
American Council of Learned Societies, awards won by faculty, 156, 158
American Council on Education, 136n, 140n, 174n, 247-48, 251n, 283n
American Men of Science:
  Alumni in, 149, 151, 154
  Faculty in, 156, 158
American Philosophical Society:
  Grant policies, 223-24
  Grants to faculty, 156
  Members on faculty, 17, 18, 156, 158

American Sociological Association, 91
American Vocational Association, 283n
Amherst College, 31n, 48n
Anderson, Oscar E., Jr., 253n
Anthropology, federal funds for, 96-99 *passim,* 240-41
Applicants, selection of college, 30-31, 34-35
Archimedes, 250-51
Argonne National Laboratory, 127
Armed Services Committee, House, 131
Armed Services Procurement Regulation (*see also* Defense, Department of), 217, 226
Army, Department of the (*see also* Defense, Department of; Office of Ordnance Research):
  Faculty: acquaintance with staff of, 238, 239, 244; applying to, 192; interest in, 242-44 *passim;* opinion of, 194, 244
  "Hardware" approach, 227
  Overhead policy, 266
Association of American Colleges, 281-82, 282n, 283n
Association of American Universities, 4, 5, 55, 84
Association of State Universities and Land-Grant Colleges, 140n, 168n, 281, 281n, 283n
Astin, Alexander W., 164, 311
Atomic Energy Commission (*see also* individual laboratories — Argonne, Brookhaven, etc.):
  College grants, 177, 243
  Concentration of research, 142, 143, 166-67, 178, 179
  Faculty: acquaintance with staff of, 238; applying to, 192; interest in, 242-44 *passim*
  Fellowships, 304
  Research policies, 126, 207, 233-34, 265

353

Auditing of institutions, federal, 217-18, 224-27 *passim*
Axelrod, Joseph, 52*n*
Axt, Richard G., 287-88, 288*n*

Babbidge, Homer D., Jr., 2*n*, 281*n*, 286*n*
Bachelor degrees, 36-37, 301
  At institutions studied, 150
"Balance" of federal research programs:
  Between fields, 101-08, 230-31
  Within fields, 89-101
Baumol, William J., 183*n*
Berelson, Bernard, 14, 84*n*, 90, 152*n*, 158*n*, 159, 160
Berson, Robert C., 53, 53*n*
Birney Robert C., 48*n*
Bloomgarden, Lawrence, 31*n*
"Blue book." *See* "Mills formula"
Booker, Edna D., 6*n*
Bosley, Howard E., 45*n*
Bowman Committee, 140
Brookhaven National Laboratory, 127, 174
Brown University, decreasing stress on SAT scores, 34*n*
Bryce, James, 136
Bundy, McGeorge, 284*n*
Burchard, John, 170, 231*n*
Bureau of Applied Social Science Research, 158*n*
Bureau of the Budget, 195, 273
  Overhead policy, 225*n*, 226, 228-29, 234*n*, 266
Burlo, Comegys R. de, Jr. *See* de Burlo
Bush, Vannevar, 140, 269

Cagle, Fred R., 260*n*, 209*n*, 251*n*
California, University of, 139, 142, 170, 173, 275
  Faculty-student contact at, 46, 52*n*, 53
  Faculty view of research policies, 200-01
  Summer salary policy, 126-27, 127*n*
California Institute of Technology, 142, 166
Carnegie Foundation, 248
Carnegie Foundation for the Advancement of Teaching, 2*n*, 33*n*
Center for Advanced Study in the Behavioral Sciences, 257-58
Central Intelligence Agency, 99
Chicago, University of, 139, 142, 166, 173

Children's Bureau, U.S., 234
Church and state issue, 282-83, 282*n*
Clark, Kenneth E., 65*n*
Classified research, 120, 120*n*, 179
Class size, 16, 44-46, 52*n*, 65, 65*n*, 303
Coggeshall, Lowell T., 275
College Entrance Examination Board, 4, 5, 5*n*, 29, 32-33, 33*n*
College Housing Loan Program, 31, 281-82, 281*n*, 282*n*
College Scholarship Service, 5*n*
Columbia University, 52*n*, 275
Commissioner of Education, U.S., 1, 1*n*
Commission on Civil Rights, U.S., 283
Commission on Financing Higher Education, 287-88, 288*n*
Committee on the University and World Affairs, 284*n*
Comptroller General. *See* General Accounting Office
Condon, Edward U., 231*n*
Conference of Biological Editors, 254*n*
Conflict of interest, 131, 260-61
Congress (*see also* General Accounting Office; Government Operations Committee; separate agencies and departments), 8, 121, 140, 144, 185, 195, 231, 248*n*, 249, 262, 291-92
  And overhead policy, 234, 265-66
  Pressure to control agency funds, 265, 268
Connally, John, Secretary of the Navy, 248*n*
Consultants, faculty (*see also* Panels, advisory), 129-30, 213-34
Contracts, research (*see also* Grants *vs.* contracts), 264-69
Cost-sharing in research, federal-institutional, 207, 210, 221-35 *passim*
Council of Chief State School Officers, 283*n*
Council of Graduate Schools in the U.S., 248
Cowley, W. H., 55*n*
Curricula, effect of federal programs on, 89-91

D'Amico, Louis, 123*n*
de Burlo, Comegys R., Jr., 216, 216*n*, 251*n*, 267, 267*n*
Defense, Department of (*see also* Air Force, Army, Navy):
  Concentration of research, 142, 143, 166, 178-79, 184, 184*n*
  Faculty: applying to, 192; opinion of, 193

Faculty: acquaintance with staff of, 238, 244; applying to, 192, 193; interest in, 242-44 *passim;* opinion of, 97, 193, 244, 247
Studies needed, 70, 138-39, 182
Survey of Federal Programs in Higher Education, 2*n*, 5
Office of Naval Research (*see also* Navy, Department of the), 143, 192, 225*n*, 228, 266
Office of Ordnance Research (*see also* Army, Department of the), 228
Office of Science and Technology, 196, 196*n*
Office of Scientific Research (*see also* Air Force, Department of the), 228
Office of Scientific Research and Development, 139-40, 269
Ohio State University, 167
Operations Research Office, 175
Overhead, 196, 205, 213*n*, 214, 221-35, 265-66

Panels, advisory (*see also* Consultants), 193, 209, 252-53
Bias charged, 101, 170-71, 258-61
Composition of, 259-60, 259*n*
Pennsylvania, University of, 166
Perkins, John A., 56*n*
Ph.D's:
Employment of, 20-22, 22*n*: regional, 183-84
Faculty with, 311: new faculty, 13-16, 296; not a satisfactory index of quality, 16-17
Number, 37: at institutions studied, 154
Proportion, 301
Years to earn, 117, 152*n*
President's Committee on Government Contracting for Research and Development, 265, 265*n*
President's Science Advisory Committee:
Composition of, 259*n*
Conflict of interest, 131
Recommendation on: federal aid, 277; federal salary payments, 119, 206; increasing number of strong universities, 136, 184; promoting originality, 255; social science expenditures, 95; union of research and education, 85
President's Scientific Research Board, 251*n*

Price, Don K., 223*n*, 251*n*
Princeton University, 31*n*, 53
Professional schools (*see also* Engineering departments; Medical schools), 3*n*, 25, 118, 124
Excluded from study, 3-4, 330
Project system, 197, 250-79
Proposals, research, 189-94, 240, 245-47, 270, 312
Psychology, federal funds for, 95-98 *passim*
Publication, agency policy on, 223, 224, 232, 253-54, 254*n*
Publications, faculty, 21, 22*n*, 158, 158*n*, 159, 253
Public Health Service, U.S. (*see also* National Institutes of Health), 94*n*, 129, 143, 263
Faculty: acquaintance with staff of, 238, 239; applying to, 192, 193; interest in, 242-44 *passim;* opinion of, 193, 194
Institutional grants, 273-75
Stipends, 304
"Purchased" research. *See* Research, "purchased"
Purdue University, 166
Pusey, Nathan, 236-37

Quattlebaum, Charles A., 5, 6*n*

Rabi, Isidor, 24
Rand, 175
Rennselaer Polytechnic Institute, 166, 179
Research (*see also* Administration, research; Proposals, research):
Awards, 189-93, 312, 313
Benefits of, 177
Early status low, 55
Effect on curriculum, 89-91
Factors promoting, 164-71, 176, 178, 178*n*, 190
Faculty time devoted to, 59, 61-64, 85*n*, 321-27
Quality of federally-supported, 143-44, 180-81, 181*n*, 262-63
"Purchased" *vs.* "supported," 228, 232-33, 232*n*
Reduces contact with undergraduates, 57-64
Summer, 61, 124-28, 307
Research and Development Board, Department of Defense, 251*n*